Sermons
ON SEVERAL OCCASIONS

VOLUME 3
Sermons 29–44

BY THE REV. JOHN WESLEY, A.M.

Sometime Fellow of Lincoln College,
with Commentary by
William J. Abraham, Editor

Volume III
Sermons on Several Occasions: Sermons 29–44

The General Board of Higher Education and Ministry leads and serves The United Methodist Church in the recruitment, preparation, nurture, education, and support of Christian leaders—lay and clergy—for the work of making disciples of Jesus Christ for the transformation of the world. Its vision is that a new generation of Christian leaders will commit boldly to Jesus Christ and be characterized by intellectual excellence, moral integrity, spiritual courage, and holiness of heart and life. The General Board of Higher Education and Ministry of The United Methodist Church serves as an advocate for the intellectual life of the church. The Board's mission embodies the Wesleyan tradition of commitment to the education of laypersons and ordained persons by providing access to higher education for all persons.

Wesley's Foundery Books is named for the abandoned foundery that early followers of John Wesley transformed, which later became the cradle of London's Methodist movement.

Copyright © 2021 by Wesley's Foundery Books

Wesley's Foundery Books is an imprint of the General Board of Higher Education and Ministry, The United Methodist Church. All rights reserved.

Volume III
Sermons on Several Occasions: Sermons 29–44

No part of this book may be reproduced in any form whatsoever, print or electronic, without written permission, except in the case of brief quotations embodied in critical articles or reviews. For information regarding rights and permissions, contact the Publisher, General Board of Higher Education and Ministry, PO Box 340007, Nashville, TN 37203-0007; phone 615-340-7393; fax 615-340-7048. Visit our website at www.gbhem.org.

All web addresses were correct and operational at the time of publication.

ISBN 978-1-945935-85-5

GBHEM Publishing is an affiliate member of the Association of University Presses.

Contents

Acknowledgments vii

Editor's Introduction to Volume III: How to Remain a Christian
    William J. Abraham 1

John Wesley Sermons

Editor's Introduction to Sermons 29–31 3
29. The Original, Nature, Property, and Use of the Law 5
30. The Law Established through Faith: Discourse One 21
31. The Law Established through Faith: Discourse Two 35

Editor's Introduction to Sermon 32 47
32. The Nature of Enthusiasm 49

Editor's Introduction to Sermons 33–34 63
33. A Caution against Bigotry 65
34. Catholic Spirit 81

Editor's Introduction to Sermons 35–37 97
35. Christian Perfection 99
36. Wandering Thoughts 123
37. Satan's Devices 135

Editor's Introduction to Sermon 38 149
38. Original Sin 151

Editor's Introduction to Sermon 39 165
39. The New Birth 167

Editor's Introduction to Sermons 40–41 181
40. The Wilderness State 183
41. Heaviness through Manifold Temptations 201

Editor's Introduction to Sermons 42–44 215
42. Self-Denial 217
43. The Cure of Evil-Speaking 229
44. The Use of Money 241

Acknowledgments

The originals from which these sermons were initially provided are used with kind permission by the "Wesley Center Online," a service of the Wesley Center for Servant Leadership at Northwest Nazarene University, 623 S. University Boulevard, Nampa, ID 83686, and available at http://wesley.nnu.edu.

I want to pay special thanks to Laura Beagles and to members of my study groups at Highland Park United Methodist Church, Dallas, Texas, who have given me much encouragement in the work, not least when I found the challenge way beyond my talents and energy. I also want to thank Dr. Heather Oglevie, who provided invaluable help in an earlier iteration of this material.

Special thanks go to Dr. Kathy Armistead, who has been an ideal person to work with at GBHEM Publishing. Her patience and non-anxious presence is a great gift in the undertaking of a project of this magnitude.

Editor's Introduction to Volume III: *How to Remain a Christian*

William J. Abraham

John Wesley and the early Methodists developed their own unique appropriation of the Christian faith that had survived from the days of Christ. We can identify various streams of the earlier tradition that fed into this experiment, but the synthesis was new and has borne significant fruit across the centuries. Wesley expressed his position crisply when he noted at the end of Sermon 28 that true religion was the religion of the heart. As we have seen again and again, the goal of Christianity is to bring about holiness here and now.

There are, of course, no problem-free situations in life. And there are no problem-free situations when it comes to articulating and implementing any vision of Christianity. Each of the great interpretations of the Christian faith has to deal with its own characteristic temptations and potential problems. Different groups of Christians sin differently. The Irish have been religious, and it has been impossible to make them moral. The English have been moral, and it has been impossible to make them religious. The wise will take steps to identify the relevant temptations and seek to provide an effective antidote. Wesley was certainly wise in this respect.

We can see this wisdom at work in the third network of sermons that make up the forty-four that became standard for his people and that were handed over and studied until they fell out of favor for various reasons. Any treatment of Wesley's life and work must surely look again at what he proposed for his earliest converts and that he intended to be essential to his legacy across the generations.

The problems that he identified do not, of course, cover all the problems that even his earliest disciples encountered. However, they do identify where things can go wrong. Moreover, once we detect the strategy at work, we can readily extend it to old problems he may have missed and to new ones that were beyond his anticipation. There is no need to see this network of sermons as the last word on the subject. However, they are an extremely illuminating first word that deserves close attention.

We can begin to catalogue the issues that caught his attention. The batch of sermons in volume 3 begins with three sermons on the problem of antinomianism (the rejection of law) and ends with the problem of how to handle money. In between we have sermons on such topics as spiritual delusion, bigotry, and the problem of how to relate to other Christians who do not share our deepest convictions. As we should expect, Wesley handles worries about his vision of radical transformation (perfection), doubts about teaching on sin, deeper queries about new birth, the challenge of backsliding, queries about various forms of spiritual depression, and issues related to self-denial, including the challenge of speaking evil of others and the temptations that come from making money.

There is surely much wisdom to be gleaned from walking through this catalogue of challenges. We can then build on this as we make our own journey to the promised land. We now turn to the challenge of how to survive as Christians.

How to Use This Book

At the end of each sermon, I have added a section called "For Readers." In it you will find some questions and helpful information about the sermon to help guide and strengthen Christian faith and understanding.

Editor's Introduction to Sermons 29–31

It is no accident that Wesley begins his treatment of relevant challenges by taking up the need to ensure that law is taken seriously by the Christian believer. In doing so he is heading off an obvious temptation for those who insist that Christianity is first and foremost a religion of the heart. In fact, two obvious temptations often occur in tandem.

The first temptation is that those who take Wesley seriously will think it is enough to follow one's feelings as the way to secure appropriate guidance about God's will. It is common in this case to rely entirely on our emotions to discern what the will of God is. Equally, it is very tempting to think that those who grasp the crucial emphasis on love as the heart of the life of faith will become so confident that they will set aside the law of God. Thus, it is common in the latter case to treat emphasis on divine law as a form of legalism from which Christ has delivered them.

However, while these temptations are obvious to those who came to faith under his care, Wesley tackles them first and foremost as a network of theological problems that take him into very deep waters. Thus, in the first sermon he sets the table by working out what Paul means by "law" when he speaks of the law being holy and just and good. In pursuing this line, Wesley develops a fascinating vision of the moral law and its relation to the very being of God. This is not bedtime reading. He expects his converts by this stage to follow him into very deep waters. In the two sermons that follow, he provides a much simpler analysis that shows how faith, far from undermining the place of law in our lives, gives us a whole new perspective on the proper place of law in the life of faith. In all this he is combating those who want to make a disjunction between faith and law. So, we effectively have an additional excuse for setting aside law: law is ruled out by faith.

Wesley will have none of this. He sees the problem as so acute that he devotes no less than three sermons to the challenge. His advice and admonitions are as pertinent today as they were in the eighteenth century. Back of Wesley's response to these temptations is a sophisticated vision of divine revelation in which God reveals his will initially in conscience; however, this can be readily clouded or corrupted by sin. Hence God sends a clearer vision of what he requires of us in the teaching of Moses and the prophets. Beyond this, God fully and finally reveals his will for us in the teaching of his Son. Given the role assigned to divine revelation, it is then a serious mistake either to rely merely on our feelings or to set aside the law of God as revealed over time and brought to a fitting climax in the life and teaching of Christ.

Wesley, of course, is also seeking to resolve a long-standing debate that has been in play since the days of Paul and James. However, his primary concern here is to make sure that Christian converts heed what God requires of us across space and time.

SERMON 29

The Original, Nature, Property, and Use of the Law

"For this reason the law is holy, and the commandment holy, and just, and good" (Rom. 7:12).

1. Perhaps there are few subjects within the whole compass of religion so little understood as this. The reader of this Epistle is usually told that by the law St. Paul means the Jewish law; and so, apprehending himself to have no concern with it, passes on without further thought about it. Indeed some are not satisfied with this account; but, observing the Epistle is directed to the Romans, infer from this that the Apostle in the beginning of this chapter alludes to the old Roman law. But as they have no more concern with this than with the ceremonial law of Moses, they spend not much thought on what they suppose is occasionally mentioned merely to illustrate another thing.

2. But a careful observer of the Apostle's discourse will not be content with these light explications of it. And the more he weighs the words, the more convinced he will be that St. Paul, by the law mentioned in this chapter, does not mean either the ancient law of Rome or the ceremonial law of Moses. This will clearly appear to all who attentively consider the tone of his discourse. He begins the chapter, "Do you not know, brethren (for I speak to those that know the law)," to those who have been instructed in it from their youth, "that the law has dominion over a man as long as he lives?" (What! the law of Rome only, or the ceremonial law? Neither, surely; but the moral law.) "For," to give a clear example, "the woman who has a husband is bound by the" moral "law to her husband so long as he lives; but if the husband is dead she is loosed from the law of her husband. So then if, while her husband lives, she marries another man, she shall be called an adulteress: but if her husband is dead she is free from that law: so that she is not an adulteress even though she marries another man." From this particular instance the Apostle proceeds to draw that general conclusion: "In this way, my brethren," by a plain parity of reason, "you also have become dead to the law," the whole Mosaic institution, "by the body of Christ,"

offered for you, and bringing you under a new dispensation: "that you should" without any blame "be married to another, even to him who is raised from the dead"; and has thus given proof of his authority to make the change; "that we should bring forth fruit unto God." And this we can do now, whereas before we could not: "for when we were in the flesh"—under the power of the flesh, that is, of the corrupt nature, which was necessarily the case before we knew the power of Christ's resurrection, "the motions of sins, which were by the law"—which were shown and inflamed by the Mosaic law, not conquered, "worked in our members"—broke out various ways, "to bring forth fruit unto death." "But now we are delivered from the law"; from that whole moral as well as ceremonial economy; "that being dead by which we were held"—that entire institution being now as it were dead and having no more authority over us than a husband, when dead, has over his wife: "so that we should serve him," who died for us and rose again, "in newness of spirit"—in a new spiritual dispensation—"and not in the oldness of the letter"—with a bare outward service, according to the letter of the Mosaic institution (Rom. 7:1–6).

3. The Apostle, having gone thus far in proving that the Christian had set aside the Jewish dispensation and that the moral law itself, though it could never pass away, nevertheless stood on a different foundation from what it did before, now stops to propose and answer an objection: "What shall we say then? Is the law sin?" as some might infer from a misapprehension of those words, "the motions of sins, which were by the law." "God forbid!" says the Apostle, that we should say so. No, the law is an irreconcilable enemy to sin; by the law: "for I had not known lust," evil desire, to be sin, "except the law had said, 'You shall not covet'" (Rom. 7:7). After opening this farther, in the four following verses, he appends this general conclusion, with regard more especially to the moral law, from which the preceding instance was taken: "For this reason the law is holy, and the commandment holy, and just, and good."

4. In order to explain and enforce these deep words, so little regarded because so little understood, I shall endeavour to show, first, the original of this law; secondly, the nature of it; thirdly, the properties; that it is holy, and just, and good; and, fourthly, the uses of it.

THE ORIGINAL, NATURE, PROPERTY, AND USE OF THE LAW

I. 1. I shall, first, endeavour to show the original of the moral law, often called "the law," by way of eminence. Now this is not, as some may have possibly imagined, of so late an institution as the time of Moses. Noah declared it to men long before that time, and Enoch before him. But we may trace its origin higher still, even beyond the foundation of the world: to that period, unknown indeed to men but doubtless recorded in the annals of eternity, when "the morning stars" first "sang together," being newly called into existence. It pleased the great Creator to make these, his first-born sons, intelligent beings, that they might know him who created them. For this end he endued them with understanding, to discern truth from falsehood, good from evil and, as a necessary result of this, with liberty—a capacity of choosing the one and refusing the other. By this they were, likewise, made able to offer him a free and willing service; a service commendable in itself as well as most acceptable to their gracious Master.

2. To employ all the faculties which he had given them, particularly their understanding and liberty, he gave the law, a complete model of all truth so far as is intelligible to a finite being; and of all good so far as angelic minds were capable of embracing it. It was also the design of their beneficent Governor by this to provide for a continual increase of their happiness; seeing every instance of obedience to that law would both add to the perfection of their nature and entitle them to a higher reward, which the righteous Judge would give in its season.

3. In like manner, when God, in his appointed time, had created a new order of intelligent beings, when he had raised man from the dust of the earth, breathed into him the breath of life, and caused him to become a living soul, endued with power to choose good or evil; he gave to this free, intelligent creature the same law as to his first-born children—not written, indeed, upon tables of stone, or any corruptible substance, but engraved on his heart by the finger of God; written on the inmost spirit both of men and of angels; with the intent it might never be far off, never be hard to understand, but always available and always shining with clear light, even as the sun in the midst of heaven.

4. Such was the original of the law of God. With regard to man, it was proportionate to his nature; but with regard to the elder sons of God it shone in its full splendour "or ever the mountains were brought forth, or the earth and the round world were made." But it was not long before man rebelled against God, and, by breaking this glorious law, nearly erased it from his heart; the eyes of his understanding being darkened in the same measure as his soul was "alienated from the life of God." And yet God did not despise the work of his own hands; but, being reconciled to man through the Son of his love, he, in some measure, re-inscribed the law on the heart of his dark, sinful creature. "He" again "showed you, O man, what is good," although not as in the beginning; "to do justly, and to love mercy, and to walk humbly with your God."

5. And this he showed, not only to our first parents but likewise to all their posterity, by "that true light which gives light to every man who comes into the world." But, notwithstanding this light, all flesh had, in the course of time, "corrupted their way before him"; till he chose out of mankind a certain people, to whom he gave a more perfect knowledge of his law; and the principles of this, because they were slow of understanding, he wrote on two tablets of stone, which he commanded the fathers to teach their children, through all succeeding generations.

6. And thus it is that the law of God is now made known to those who do not know God. They hear, with the hearing of the ear, the things that were written before now for our instruction. But this does not suffice: they cannot, by this means, comprehend the height, and depth, and length, and breadth of it. God alone can reveal this by his Spirit. And so he does for all who truly believe, because of that gracious promise made to all the Israel of God: "'Behold, the days are coming,' says the Lord, 'when I will make a new covenant with the house of Israel. And this shall be the covenant that I will make: I will put My law in their innermost being and write it on their hearts; and I will be their God, and they shall be My people'" (Jer. 31:31ff).

II. 1. The nature of that law which was originally given to angels in heaven and man in paradise, and which God has so mercifully promised to write afresh in the hearts of all true believers, was the second thing I proposed to show. Therefore, I would first observe that although the "law" and the "commandment" are sometimes differently interpreted (the commandment meaning but a part of the law) yet, in the text they are used as equivalent terms, implying one and the same thing. But we cannot understand here, either by one or the other, the ceremonial law. It is not the ceremonial law of which the Apostle says, in the words above recited, "I had not known sin but by the law": this is too plain to need a proof. Neither is it the ceremonial law which says, in the words immediately subjoined, "You shall not covet." Therefore the ceremonial law has no place in the present question.

2. Neither can we understand by the law mentioned in the text the Mosaic dispensation. It is true, the word is sometimes so understood; as when the Apostle says, speaking to the Galatians (Gal. 3:17), "The covenant that was confirmed before"; namely, with Abraham, the father of the faithful, "cannot annul the law," that is, the Mosaic dispensation, "which was four hundred and thirty years after." But it cannot be so understood in this text; for the Apostle never bestows such a high commendation upon that imperfect and shadowy dispensation. He nowhere affirms the Mosaic to be a spiritual law; or, that it is holy, and just, and good. Neither is it true that God will write that law in the hearts of those whose iniquities he remembers no more. It remains, that "the law," eminently so termed, is nothing but the moral law.

3. Now, this law is an incorruptible picture of the High and Holy One who dwells in eternity. It is he whom, in his essence, no man has seen or can see, made visible to men and angels. It is the face of God unveiled; God manifested to his creatures as they are able to bear it; manifested to give, and not to destroy, life—that they may see God and live. It is the heart of God disclosed to man. Yes, in some sense, we may even apply to this law what the Apostle says of his Son: it is "the radiance of his glory, the exact representation of his person."

4. "If virtue," said the ancient Heathen, "could assume such a shape as that we could behold her with our eyes, what wonderful love would she excite in us!" If virtue could do this! It is done already. The law of God is all virtues in one, in such a shape as to be beheld

with open face by all those whose eyes God has enlightened. What is the law but divine virtue and wisdom assuming a visible form? What is it but the original ideas of truth and good, which were lodged in the uncreated mind from eternity, now drawn forth and clothed with such a vehicle as to appear even to human understanding?

5. If we survey the law of God from another point of view, it is supreme, unchangeable reason; it is unalterable rectitude, it is the everlasting fitness of all things that are or ever were created. I am aware of how lacking, and even inappropriate, are these and all other human expressions when we endeavour by these poor images to sketch out the deep things of God. Nevertheless we have no better, indeed no other, way, during this infant state of our existence. As we now "know" but "in part," so we are also constrained to "prophesy," that is, to speak of the things of God, "in part." "We cannot order our speech because of the darkness," while we are in this house of clay. While I am "a child," I must "speak as a child": but I shall soon "put away childish things": for "when that which is perfect has come, that which is partial shall pass away."

6. But to return, the law of God (speaking according to the manner of men) is a copy of the eternal mind, a transcript of the divine nature. Indeed, it is the fairest offspring of the everlasting Father, the brightest issue of his essential wisdom, the visible beauty of the Most High. It is the delight and wonder of cherubim and seraphim and all the company of heaven, and the glory and joy of every wise believer, every well-instructed child of God upon earth.

III. 1. Such is the nature of the ever-blessed law of God. I am, in the third place, to show the properties of it—not all; for that would exceed the wisdom of an angel, but only those which are mentioned in the text. These are three: it is holy, just, and good.

And, first, the law is holy.

2. In this expression the Apostle does not appear to speak of its effects but rather of its nature: As St. James, speaking of the same thing under another name, says, "The wisdom from above" (which is none other than this law, written in our hearts) "is first pure"

(Jas. 3:17); ἁγνή—"chaste, spotless"; eternally and essentially holy. And consequently, when it is transcribed into the life, as well as the soul, it is (as the same Apostle terms it, Jas. 1:27) θρησκεία καθαρὰ καὶ ἀμίαντος—"pure religion and undefiled"; the pure, clean, unpolluted worship of God.

3. It is indeed, in the highest degree, pure, chaste, clean, holy. Otherwise it could not be the immediate offspring, and much less the exact representation, of God, who is essential holiness. It is pure from all sin, clean and unspotted from any touch of evil. It is a chaste virgin, incapable of any defilement, of any mixture with that which is unclean or unholy. It has no fellowship with sin of any kind. For "what communion has light with darkness?" As sin is, in its very nature, enmity to God, so his law is enmity to sin.

4. Therefore it is that the Apostle rejects with such abhorrence that blasphemous supposition that the law of God is either sin itself, or the cause of sin. God forbid that we should suppose it is the cause of sin because it is the revealer of it; because it detects the hidden things of darkness and drags them out into the light. It is true, by this means (as the Apostle observes, Rom. 7:13), "sin appears to be sin." All its disguises are torn away and it appears in its native deformity. It is true likewise, that "sin, by the commandment, becomes even more sinful." Being now committed against light and knowledge, being stripped even of the poor plea of ignorance, it loses its excuse as well as its disguise, and becomes far more repulsive to both God and man. Yes, it is even true that "sin causes death through that which is good"; which in itself is pure and holy. When it is dragged out into the light, it rages all the more; when it is restrained, it bursts out with greater violence. Thus the Apostle (speaking like one who was convinced of sin but not yet delivered from it), "Sin, taking occasion by the commandment" detecting and endeavouring to restrain it, disdained the restraint, and so much the more "created in me all manner of concupiscence" (Rom. 7:8); all manner of foolish and hurtful desire, which that commandment sought to restrain. Thus, "when the commandment came, sin revived" (Rom. 7:9); it fretted and raged the more. But this is no knock on the commandment. Though it is abused, it cannot be defiled. This only proves that

"the heart of man is desperately wicked." But "the law" of God "is holy" still.

5. And it is, secondly, just. It renders to everyone his due. It prescribes exactly what is right, precisely what ought to be done, said, or thought, both with regard to the Author of our being, with regard to ourselves, and with regard to every creature which he has made. It is adapted, in all respects, to the nature of things, of the whole universe, and every individual. It is suited to all the circumstances of each, and to all their mutual relations, whether those which have existed from the beginning or have begun in any later period. It is exactly agreeable to the properties of things, whether profound or superficial. It clashes with none of these in any degree; nor is ever unconnected with them. If the word is understood in that sense, there is nothing arbitrary in the law of God. Yet the whole and every part of it is still totally dependent upon his will, so that, "Your will be done" is the supreme, universal law both in earth and heaven.

6. "But is the will of God the cause of his law? Is his will the origin of right and wrong? Is a thing therefore right, because God wills it, or does he will it because it is right?" I fear this celebrated question is more curious than useful. And perhaps in the manner it is usually discussed, it is not very consistent with the regard that is due from a creature to the Creator and Governor of all things. It is hardly decent for man to call the supreme God to give him an account. Nevertheless, with awe and reverence we may speak a little. The Lord pardon us if we speak amiss!

7. It seems that the whole difficulty arises from considering God's will as distinct from God: otherwise it vanishes away. For none can doubt but that God is the cause of the law of God. But the will of God is God himself. It is God considered as willing this or that. Consequently, to say that the will of God, or that God himself, is the cause of the law, is one and the same thing.

8. Again: if the law, the immutable rule of right and wrong, depends upon the nature and propriety of things and on their basic relations to each other (I do not say their eternal relations; because the eternal relation of things existing in time is little less than a

contradiction in terms); if, I say, this depends on the nature and relations of things, then it must depend on God, or the will of God; because those things themselves, with all their relations, are the works of his hands. By his will, "for his pleasure" alone, they all "are and were created."

9. And yet it may be granted (which is probably all that a considerate person would contend for), that in every particular case, God wills this or this (for example, that men should honour their parents), because it is right, agreeable to the proper order of things, to the relations in which they stand.

10. The law, then, is right and just concerning all things. And it is good as well as just. This we may easily infer from the fountain from which it flowed. For what was this but the goodness of God? What but goodness alone inclined him to impart that divine copy of himself to the holy angels? To what else can we impute his bestowing upon man the same transcript of his own nature? And what but tender love constrained him to manifest his will once more to fallen man—either to Adam or any of his descendants, who like him had "fallen short of the glory of God"? Was it not love alone that moved him to publish his law after the understandings of men were darkened, and to send his prophets to declare that law to the blind, thoughtless children of men? Doubtless it was his goodness which raised up Enoch and Noah to be preachers of righteousness; which caused Abraham, his friend, and Isaac, and Jacob, to bear witness to his truth. It was his goodness alone which, when "darkness had covered the earth, and thick darkness the people," gave a written law to Moses, and, through him, to the nation whom he had chosen. It was love which explained these living oracles by David and all the prophets that followed; until, when the fullness of time had come, he sent his only-begotten Son, "not to destroy the law, but to fulfill," confirm its every last detail; until, having written it upon the hearts of all his children, and put all his enemies under his feet, "He shall deliver up" his mediatorial "kingdom to the Father, that God may be all in all" (1 Cor. 15:28).

11. And this law, which the goodness of God gave at first and has preserved through all ages, is, like the fountain from whence it springs,

SERMON 29

full of goodness and beneficence; it is mild and kind; it is, as the Psalmist expresses it, "sweeter than honey and the honeycomb." It is winning and amiable. It includes "whatever things are lovely or of good repute. If there is anything virtuous, if there is anything praiseworthy" before God and his holy angels, it is all comprised in this; in it are hidden all the treasures of the divine wisdom, and knowledge, and love.

12. And it is good in its effects, as well as in its nature. As the tree is, so is its fruit. The fruit of the law of God written in the heart is "righteousness, and peace, and assurance forever." Or rather, the law itself is righteousness, filling the soul with a peace which passes all understanding, and causing us to rejoice always in the testimony of a clear conscience before God. It is properly a pledge, as "a guarantee of our inheritance," being a part of the purchased possession. It is God made manifest in our flesh and bringing with him eternal life; assuring us by that pure and perfect love that we are "sealed for the day of redemption"; that he will "spare us as a man spares his own son that serves him," "in that day when he gathers up his jewels"; and that there remains for us "a crown of glory which does not fade away."

IV. 1. It remains only to show, in the fourth and last place, the uses of the law. And the first use of it, without question, is to convict the world of sin. This is, indeed, the particular work of the Holy Spirit; who can accomplish it without any means at all, or by whatever means he pleases, however insufficient in themselves, or even improper, to produce such an effect. And accordingly, there are some whose hearts have been broken in pieces in a moment, either in sickness or in health, without any visible cause or any outward means whatever; and others (one in a million) have been awakened to a sense of the "wrath of God abiding on them by hearing that "God was in Christ, reconciling the world unto himself." But it is the ordinary method of the Spirit of God to convict sinners by the law. It is this which, being set home on the conscience, generally breaks the rock into pieces. It is more especially this part of the word of God which is ζῶν καὶ ἐνεργής—"living and active," full of life and energy, "sharper than any double-edged sword." This, in the hand of God and of those whom he has sent, pierces through all the folds of a deceitful heart, and "separates even the soul and the spirit"; even, as it were, the very "joints and marrow." By this is the sinner revealed to himself. All his fig leaves are torn away, and he sees that he is "wretched, and poor, and miserable, and blind, and naked." The law flashes conviction on every side. He feels himself a naked sinner. He has nothing to pay. His "mouth is stopped," and he stands "guilty before God."

2. To slay the sinner is, then, the first use of the law; to destroy the life and strength in which he trusts and convince him that he is dead while he lives; not only under the sentence of death, but actually dead before God, void of all spiritual life, "dead in trespasses and sins." The second use of it is to bring him to life, to Christ, that he may live. It is true, in performing both these offices, it acts the part of a severe schoolmaster. It drives us by force, rather than draws us by love. And yet love is the spring of all. It is the spirit of love which, by this painful means, tears away our confidence in the flesh, which leaves us no broken reed upon which to lean, and so constrains the sinner, stripped of all, to cry out in the bitterness of his soul, or groan in the depth of his heart,

> I give up every plea beside.
> Lord, I am damn'd; but You have died.

3. The third use of the law is to keep us alive. It is the grand means by which the blessed Spirit prepares the believer for greater portions of the life of God.

    I am afraid this great and important truth is little understood, not only by the world but even by many whom God has taken out of the world, who are real children of God by faith. Many of these lay it down as an unquestioned truth that when we come to Christ, we are finished with the law; and that, in this sense, "Christ is the end of the law to everyone that believes." "The end of the law" so he is, "for righteousness," for justification, "to everyone that believes." In this the law is at an end. It justifies no one but only brings him to Christ; who is also, in another respect, the end or scope of the law—the point at which it continually aims. But when it has brought us to him it has still another office; namely, to keep us with him. For it is continually urging all believers, the more they see of its height, and depth, and length, and breadth, to exhort one another so much the more,

> Closer and closer let us cleave
> To his beloved Embrace;
> Expect his fullness to receive,
> And grace to answer grace.

4. Allowing then, that every believer is finished with the law as it means the Jewish ceremonial law, or the entire Mosaic dispensation (for these Christ has taken out of the way); yes, even allowing we are done with the moral law, as a means of procuring our justification (for we are "justified freely by his grace, through the redemption that is in Jesus"); yet in another sense we have not finished with this law: for it is still of immeasurable use, first, in convicting us of the sin that yet remains both in our hearts and lives, and thus keeping us close to Christ, that his blood may cleanse us every moment; secondly, in drawing strength from our Head into his living members, by which he empowers them to do what his law commands; and, thirdly, in confirming our hope of whatever it commands which we have not yet attained—of receiving grace upon grace until we are in actual possession of the fullness of his promises.

5. How clearly does this accord with the experience of every true believer! While he cries out, "O how I love your law! I study it all the day long." He sees daily, in that divine mirror, more and more of his own sinfulness. He sees more and more clearly that he is still a sinner in all things, that neither his heart nor his ways are right before God; and that every moment sends him to Christ. This shows him the meaning of what is written, "You shall make a plate of pure gold and engrave upon it, 'Holiness to the Lord.' And it shall be upon Aaron's forehead" (the model of our great High Priest), "that Aaron may bear the iniquity of the holy things which the children of Israel shall revere in all their holy gifts" (so far are our prayers or holy things from atoning for the rest of our sins!) "and it shall be always upon his forehead, that they may be accepted before the Lord" (Exod. 28:36, 38).

6. To explain this by a single instance, the law says, "You shall not kill"; and by this (as our Lord teaches), it forbids not only outward

acts but every unkind word or thought. Now, the more I look into this perfect law, the more I feel how far I come short of it; and the more I feel this, the more I feel my need of his blood to atone for all my sin, and of his Spirit to purify my heart, and make me "perfect and entire, lacking nothing."

7. Therefore I cannot live without the law one moment, no more than I can live without Christ; since now I need it as much to keep me to Christ as I ever needed it to bring me to him. Otherwise, this "evil heart of unbelief" would immediately "depart from the living God." Indeed each is continually sending me to the other—the law to Christ and Christ to the law. On the one hand, the height and depth of the law constrain me to fly to the love of God in Christ; on the other, the love of God in Christ endears the law to me "above gold or precious stones"; since I know every part of it is a gracious promise which my Lord will fulfill in its season.

8. Who are you then, O man, who "judges the law and speaks ill of the law," who ranks it alongside sin, Satan, and death and sends them all to hell together? The Apostle James esteemed judging or "speaking evil of the law" so enormous a piece of wickedness that he knew not how to aggravate the guilt of judging our brethren more than by showing it included this. "So now," says he, "you are not a doer of the law, but a judge!" A judge of that which God has ordained to judge you! So you have set up yourself in the judgment-seat of Christ and cast down the rule whereby he will judge the world! O come to know what advantage Satan has gained over you; and from now on, never think or speak lightly of, much less dress up as a scarecrow, this blessed instrument of the grace of God. Indeed, love and value it for the sake of him from whom it came, and of him to whom it leads. Let it be your glory and joy, next to the cross of Christ. Declare its praise and make it honourable before all men.

9. And if you are thoroughly convinced that it is the offspring of God, that it is the copy of all his inimitable perfections, and that it is "holy, and just, and good," especially to those that believe; then, instead of casting it away as a polluted thing, see that you cleave to it more and more. Never let the law of mercy and truth, of love to God and man, of lowliness, meekness, and purity, forsake you.

SERMON 29

"Bind it about your neck; write it on the tablet of your heart." Keep close to the law, if you would keep close to Christ; hold it fast; do not let it go. Let this continually lead you to the atoning blood, continually confirm your hope, until all the "righteousness of the law is fulfilled in you" and you are "filled with all the fullness of God."

10. And if your Lord has already fulfilled his word, if he has already "written his law in your heart," then "stand fast in the liberty with which Christ has made you free." You are not only made free from Jewish ceremonies, from the guilt of sin, and the fear of hell (these are so far from being the whole, that they are the least and lowest part of Christian liberty); but, what is infinitely more, from the power of sin, from serving the Devil, from offending God. O stand fast in this liberty; in comparison to which all the rest is not even worthy to be named! Stand fast in loving God with all your heart and serving him with all your strength! This is perfect freedom; thus to keep his law, and to walk in all his commandments blameless. "Do not be entangled again in the yoke of bondage." I do not mean Jewish bondage; nor even bondage to the fear of hell: these, I trust, are far from you. But beware of being entangled again with the yoke of sin, of any inward or outward transgression of the law. Abhor sin far more than death or hell; abhor sin itself far more than the punishment of it. Beware of the bondage of pride, of desire, of anger; of every evil temper, or word, or work. "Look to Jesus"; and in order to do this, look more and more to the perfect law, "the law of liberty"; and "continue in it"; so shall you daily "grow in grace, and in the knowledge of our Lord Jesus Christ."

For Readers

Questions

1. Why does Wesley jump straight into dealing with the question of the nature of the law? What is he assuming here about the maturity of believers?

2. How do you make sense of the way Wesley ties his account of the law into a story about its origins before creation?

3. Beyond being holy, just, and good, what other terms does Wesley use to describe the moral law?
4. What does it mean to say that the law is just?
5. Identify and explain the three uses of the law that Wesley develops here.

Helpful Information

This is one of the most difficult sermons in the whole of the forty-four canonical sermons. Wesley dives deep into both the story of creation and into a long-standing philosophical problem that shows up in Plato (the Euthyphro problem). He tries his hand at solving this old conundrum: Is something good because God commands it, or does God command something because it is good? What is interesting is that he expects his readers to begin wrestling with this kind of issue. In time his disciples will indeed want to pursue this line of reasoning in its own right.

His primary concern is to make sure we begin to understand what the moral law is as contrasted with the ceremonial law and with the Mosaic dispensation as a whole. The latter takes him into disputes about the relation between Judaism and Christianity, but this is a secondary issue here. He takes us into deep water precisely because he wants to impart a rich vision of the moral law. His deep worry is that this will be set aside through lack of knowledge. The antidote to our problems with respect to the law can only be solved by hard thinking that takes us all the way to the bottom, that is, to the foundations of morality in God's good creation. This is in the end the only way to deal with those today who set law against feeling or law against love.

Wesley is also determined that we begin to see the beauty of the moral law, for minimally it is holy, just, and good. His ultimate goal is for us to grasp not just its origins or its properties, but that it will become written on our hearts. Prior to this development, the uses of the law are clear: it convicts us of sin, drives us to Christ for justification, and then keeps us close to Christ by deepening our vision of what the moral law is and by encouraging us to depend on Christ for its fulfillment. He could have added that the law has a positive role in helping us discern good and evil. This is implicit when he notes that our ability to discern what is good and evil is damaged by sin.

SERMON 30

The Law Established through Faith: Discourse One

"Do we then make void the law through faith? God forbid: truly, we establish the law" (Rom. 3:31).

1. St. Paul, having the beginning of this Epistle laid down his general proposition, namely, that "the gospel of Christ is the power of God for salvation to every one that believes"—the powerful means by which God makes every believer a partaker of present and eternal salvation—goes on to show that there is no other way under heaven by which men can be saved. He speaks particularly of salvation from the guilt of sin, which he commonly terms justification. And that all men stood in need of this, that none could plead their own innocence, he proves at large by various arguments, addressed to the Jews as well as the Heathens. Hence he concludes (in the 19th verse of this chapter), "that every mouth," whether Jew or Heathen, must be "stopped" from excusing or justifying himself, "and all the world become guilty before God." "Therefore," says he, by his own obedience, "by the words of the law, no flesh shall be justified in his sight." "But now the righteousness of God without the law" (without our previous obedience to it) "is manifested," even the righteousness of God, which is by faith in Jesus, "is manifested Christ to all and upon all who believe." "For there is no difference" as to their need of justification or the manner in which they attain it ("for all have sinned and fallen short of the glory of God") "the glorious image of God in which they were created." And all (who attain) "are justified freely by his grace, through the redemption that is in Jesus Christ, whom God has set forth to be a propitiation through faith in his blood; that he might be just, and yet the justifier of him which believes in Jesus—"that without any impeachment to his justice he might show mercy for the sake of that propitiation. "Therefore we conclude" (which was the grand position he had undertaken to establish), "that a man is justified by faith, without the works of the law" (verses 20–28).

2. It was easy to foresee an objection which might be made, and which has in fact been made in all ages; namely, that to say we are justified

without the works of the law is to abolish the law. The Apostle, without entering into a formal dispute, simply denies the charge. "Do we then," says he, "make void the law through faith? God forbid! Truly, we establish the law."

3. The strange imagination of some that St. Paul, when he says, "A man is justified without the works of the law," means only ceremonial law, is abundantly confuted by these very words. For did St. Paul establish the ceremonial law? It is evident he did not. He did make void that law through faith, and openly avowed his doing so. It was the moral law only of which he might truly say, "We do not make this void, but establish it through faith."

4. But not all men are of his mind in this. Many there are who will not agree to it. Many in all ages of the Church, even among those who bore the name of Christian, have contended that "the faith once delivered to the saints" was designed to make void the whole law. They would no more spare the moral than the ceremonial law, but were for "hewing," as it were, both in pieces before the Lord; vehemently maintaining, "If you establish any law, Christ profits you nothing; Christ has become useless to you; you have fallen from grace."

5. But is the zeal of these men according to knowledge? Have they observed the connexion between the law and faith, and that, considering the close connexion between them, to destroy one is indeed to destroy both; that, to abolish the moral law, is, in truth, to abolish faith and the law together, as leaving no proper means either of bringing us to faith, or of stirring up that gift of God in our soul?

6. It therefore behooves all who desire either to come to Christ or to walk in him whom they have received to take heed how they "make void the law through faith." And to secure ourselves effectually against this, let us inquire, first, which are the most usual ways of making "void the law through faith"? And secondly, how may we follow the Apostle, and by faith "establish the law"?

I. 1. Let us, first, inquire, which are the most usual ways of making void the law through faith? Now the way for a Preacher to make it all void at a stroke is not to preach it at all. This is just the same thing as to blot it out of the oracles of God. More especially, when it is done with intent; when it is made a rule not to preach the law; and the very phrase "a Preacher of the law," is used as a term of reproach, as though it meant little less than an enemy of the gospel.

2. All this proceeds from the deepest ignorance of the nature, properties, and use of the law; and proves that those who act thus either know not Christ—are utter strangers to living faith—or at least that they are but babes in Christ and, as such, are "unskilled in the word of righteousness."

3. Their grand plea is this: preaching the gospel, that is, according to their judgment, speaking of nothing but the sufferings and merits of Christ, answers all the ends of the law. But this we utterly deny. It does not answer the very first end of the law, namely, convicting men of sin; awakening those who are still asleep on the brink of hell. There may have been here and there an exempt case. One in a thousand may have been awakened by the gospel, but this is no general rule. The ordinary method of God is to convict sinners by the law, and that only. The gospel is not the means which God has ordained, or which our Lord himself used, for this end. We have no authority in Scripture for applying it thus, nor any ground to think it will prove effectual. Nor have we any more ground to expect this, from the nature of the thing. "Those who are healthy," as our Lord himself observes, "do not need a physician, but those who are sick." It is absurd, therefore, to offer a physician to those who are whole, or at least imagine themselves to be so. You must first convince them that they are sick; otherwise they will not thank you for your labour. It is equally absurd to offer Christ to those whose heart is whole, having never yet been broken. It is, in the proper sense, "casting pearls before swine." Doubtless "they will trample them underfoot"; and it is no more than you have reason to expect, if they also "turn and rend you."

4. "But although there is no command in Scripture to offer Christ to the careless sinner, yet are there not scriptural precedents for it?" I think not: I know not any. I believe you cannot produce one, either from the four Evangelists or the Acts of the Apostles. Neither can you prove this to have been the practice of any of the Apostles, from any passage in all their writings.

5. "Does not even the Apostle Paul say, in his former Epistle to the Corinthians, 'We preach Christ crucified' (1:23), and in his latter, 'We preach not ourselves but Christ Jesus the Lord' (4:5)?" We consent to rest the cause on this issue; to tread in his steps, to follow his example. Preach just as Paul preached, and the dispute is at an end. For although we are certain he preached Christ in as perfect a manner as the very chief of the Apostles, yet who preached the law more than St. Paul? Therefore he did not think the gospel answered the same end.

6. The very first sermon of St. Paul's which is recorded concludes in these words: "By him all that believe are justified from all things, from which you could not be justified by the law of Moses. Beware therefore, lest that come upon you which is spoken of in the Prophets: "Behold, you despisers, and wonder, and perish: for I work a work in your days, a work which you will never believe, though a man declares it to you" (Acts 13:39–40). Now it is clear, all this is preaching the law in the sense in which you understand the term; even although great part, if not all, of his hearers were either Jews or religious proselytes (verse 43) and therefore probably many of them, in some degree at least, were convinced of sin already. He first reminds them that they could not be justified by the law of Moses but only by faith in Christ; and then severely threatens them with the judgments of God, which is in the strongest sense, preaching the law.

7. In his next discourse, that to the Heathens at Lystra (14:15ff), we do not find so much as the name of Christ. The whole purport of it is that they should "turn from those vain idols, to the living God." Now confess the truth. Do not you think, if you had been there, you could have preached much better than he? I should not wonder if you thought too, that his preaching so ill occasioned his being so ill treated; and that his being stoned was a just judgment upon him for not preaching Christ!

8. To the jailer, indeed, when "he sprang in, and came trembling, and fell down before Paul and Silas, and said, 'Sirs, what must I do to be saved?'" he immediately said, "Believe in the Lord Jesus Christ" (Acts 16:29, 30); and in the case of one so deeply convicted of sin, who would not have said the same? But to the men of Athens

you find him speaking in a quite different manner; reproving their superstition, ignorance, and idolatry; and strongly moving them to repent, from the consideration of a future judgment and of the resurrection from the dead (17:24–31). Likewise when Felix sent for Paul on purpose that he might "hear him concerning the faith in Christ"; instead of preaching Christ in your sense (which would probably have caused the Governor either to mock or to contradict and blaspheme), "he reasoned of righteousness, temperance, and judgment to come," until Felix (hardened as he was) "trembled" (24:24–25). Go you, and tread in his steps. Preach Christ to the careless sinner, by reasoning "of righteousness, temperance, and judgment to come"!

9. If you say, "But he preached Christ in a different manner in his Epistles," I answer, (1) He did not there preach at all, not in that sense in which we speak: for preaching, in our present question, means speaking before a congregation. But waiving this, I answer, (2) His Epistles are directed not to unbelievers, such as those of which we are now speaking, but "to the saints of God" in Rome, Corinth, Philippi, and other places. Now, unquestionably, he would speak more of Christ to these than to those who were without God in the world. And yet, (3) Every one of these is full of the law, even the Epistles to the Romans and the Galatians; in both of which he does what you term "preaching the law," and that to believers as well as unbelievers.

10. From this it is plain you do not know what it is to preach Christ in the sense of the Apostle. For doubtless St. Paul judged himself to be preaching Christ both to Felix, and at Antioch, Lystra, and Athens: From whose example every thinking man must infer that not only declaring the love of Christ to sinners, but also declaring that he will come from heaven in flaming fire, is, in the Apostle's sense, preaching Christ; yes, even in the full scriptural meaning of the word. To preach Christ is to preach what he has revealed, either in the Old or New Testament; so you are really preaching Christ when you are saying, "The wicked shall be sent into hell, and all the people that forget God," as when you are saying, "Behold the Lamb of God, who takes away the sin of the world!"

SERMON 30

11. Consider this well: to preach Christ is to preach all things that Christ has spoken; all his promises; all his threats and commands; all that is written in his book. Then you will know how to preach Christ without making void the law.

12. "But does not the greatest blessing attend those discourses in which we explicitly preach the merits and sufferings of Christ?"

Probably when we preach to a congregation of mourners, or of believers; these will be attended with the greatest blessing because such discourses are peculiarly suited to their state. At least, these will usually convey the most comfort. But this is not always the greatest blessing. I may sometimes receive a far greater by a discourse that cuts me to the heart and humbles me to the dust. Neither should I receive that comfort if I were to preach or to hear no discourses but on the sufferings of Christ. These, by constant repetition, would lose their force, and grow more and more flat and dead, till at length they would become a dull round of words, without any spirit, or life, or virtue. So to preach Christ in that way must, in time, make void the gospel as well as the law.

II. 1. A second way of making void the law through faith is to teach that faith supersedes the necessity of holiness. This divides itself into a thousand smaller paths, and many there are that walk in them. Indeed there are few that wholly escape it; few who are convinced that we are saved by faith but are sooner or later, more or less, drawn aside into this by-way.

2. All those are drawn into this by-way who, if not entirely convinced that faith in Christ entirely sets aside the necessity of keeping his law; nevertheless suppose it sets aside the necessity of keeping his law; and also suppose (1) That holiness is less necessary now than it was before Christ came; or (2) That a lesser degree of it is necessary; or (3) That it is less necessary for believers than for others. Yes, and so too are all those who, although their judgment is right in general, nevertheless think they may take more liberty in particular cases than they could have done before they believed. Indeed, the use of the term liberty in such a manner, meaning liberty from obedience or holiness, shows at once that their judgment is perverted and that they are guilty of what they imagined to be

far from them; namely, of making void the law through faith, by supposing faith to supersede holiness.

3. The first plea of those who teach this expressly is that we are now under the covenant of grace, not works; and therefore we are no longer under the necessity of performing the works of the law. But who was ever under the covenant of works? No one but Adam before the fall. He was fully and properly under that covenant which required perfect, universal obedience as the one condition of acceptance, and left no place for pardon upon the very least transgression. But no other man was ever under this, neither Jew nor Gentile; neither before Christ nor since. All his sons were and are under the covenant of grace. The manner of their acceptance is this: the free grace of God, through the merits of Christ, gives pardon to those who believe; who believe with such a faith as, working by love, produces all obedience and holiness.

4. The case is not therefore, as you suppose, that men were once more obliged to obey God, or to work the works of his law, than they are now. This is a supposition you cannot make good. But we should have been obliged, if we had been under the covenant of works, to have done those works before our acceptance. Whereas now all good works, though as necessary as ever, are not prior to our acceptance, but consequent upon it. Therefore the nature of the covenant of grace gives you no ground, no encouragement at all, to set aside any insistence or degree of obedience; any part or measure of holiness.

5. "But are we not justified by faith, without the works of the law?" Undoubtedly we are; without the works either of the ceremonial or the moral law. And would to God all men were convinced of this! It would prevent innumerable evils; antinomianism in particular: for generally speaking, the Pharisees are the ones who make the Antinomians. By running into an extreme so palpably contrary to Scripture, they give occasion for others to run into the opposite one. These, seeking to be justified by works, scare off those from allowing any place for them.

6. But the truth lies between. We are, doubtless, justified by faith. This is the cornerstone of the whole Christian building. We are

justified without the works of the law as any previous condition of justification; but they are an immediate fruit of that faith whereby we are justified. So if good works do not follow our faith, even all inward and outward holiness, it is plain our faith is worth nothing; we are still in our sins. Therefore, the fact that we are justified by faith, even by faith without works, is no ground for making void the law through faith; or for imagining that faith dispenses with any kind or degree of holiness.

7. "But does not St. Paul explicitly say, 'For the one who does no works, but believes on Him who justifies the ungodly, his faith is counted for righteousness?' And does it not follow from this that faith to a believer takes the role, the place, of righteousness? But if faith is in the role of righteousness or holiness, what need is there of this too?"

This, it must be acknowledged, comes home to the point, and is, indeed, the main pillar of antinomianism. And yet it needs not a long or laboured answer. We allow, (1) That God justifies the ungodly; those who, until that hour, are totally ungodly—full of all evil, empty of all good; (2) That he justifies the ungodly who do no works; who, until that moment, perform no good works—neither can they; for an evil tree cannot bring forth good fruit; (3) That he justifies them by faith alone, without any goodness or righteousness preceding; And (4) that faith is then counted to them for righteousness; namely, for preceding righteousness. That is, God, through the merits of Christ, accepts those who believe as if they had already fulfilled all righteousness. But what is all this to your point? The Apostle does not say, either here or elsewhere, that this faith is counted to them for subsequent righteousness. He does teach that there is no righteousness before faith, but where does he teach that there is none after it? He does assert that holiness cannot precede justification; but not that it need not follow it. St. Paul, therefore, gives you no help for making void the law by teaching that faith supersedes the necessity of holiness.

III. 1. There is yet another way of making void the law through faith which is more common than either of the former. And that is the doing it practically; the making it void in fact, though not in principle; the living as if faith was designed to excuse us from holiness.

How earnestly does the Apostle guard us against this, in those well-known words: "What then? Shall we sin, because we are not under the law but under grace? God forbid" (Rom. 6:15): a caution which it is needful thoroughly to consider, because it is of the greatest importance.

2. Being "under the law," may here mean, (1) Being obligated to observe the ceremonial law; (2) Being obligated to conform to the whole Mosaic institution; (3) Being obligated to keep the whole moral law as the condition of our acceptance with God; And, (4) Being under the wrath and curse of God; under sentence of eternal death; under a sense of guilt and condemnation, full of horror and slavish fear.

3. Now although a believer is "not without law to God, but under the law to Christ," yet from the moment he believes he is not "under the law" in any of the preceding senses. On the contrary, he is "under grace," under a more benign, gracious dispensation. As he is no longer under the ceremonial law, nor under the Mosaic institution; as he is not obliged to keep even the moral law as the condition of his acceptance; so he is delivered from the wrath and the curse of God, from all sense of guilt and condemnation, and from all that horror and fear of death and hell whereby he was all his life before subject to bondage. And he now performs (which he could not do while "under the law") a willing and complete obedience. He obeys not from the motive of slavish fear but on a nobler principle; namely, the grace of God ruling in his heart, and causing all his works to be done in love.

4. What then? Shall this evangelical principle of action be less powerful that the legal? Shall we be less obedient to God from filial love than we were from servile fear?

It is well if this is not a common case; if this practical antinomianism, this unobserved way of making void the law through faith, has not infected thousands of believers.

Has it not infected you? Examine yourself honestly and closely. Do you not do now what you would not have dared to do when you were "under the law," or (as we commonly call it) under conviction? For instance: you dared not then indulge yourself in food. You took just what was needful and that of the cheapest kind. Do you not allow yourself more latitude now? Do you not indulge yourself a little more than you did? O beware lest you "sin because you are not under the law, but under grace!"

5. When you were under conviction, you dared not indulge the lust of the eyes in any degree. You would not do anything, great or small, merely to gratify your curiosity. You regarded only cleanliness and necessity, or at most very moderate convenience, either in furniture or apparel; superfluity and finery of whatever kind, as well as fashionable elegance, were both a terror and an abomination to you.

Are they so still? Is your conscience as tender now in these things as it was then? Do you still follow the same rule both in furniture and apparel, trampling all finer, all superfluity, every thing useless, every thing merely ornamental, however fashionable, underfoot? Rather, have you not resumed what you had once laid aside, and what you could not then use without wounding your conscience? And have you not learned to say, "O, I am not so scrupulous now"? I would to God you were! Then you would not sin thus, "because you are not under the law, but under grace"!

6. You were once scrupulous too of commending any to their face; and still more, of suffering any to commend you. It was a stab to your heart; you could not bear it; you sought the honour that comes from God alone. You could not endure such conversation; nor any conversation which was not good to the use of edifying. All idle talk, all trifling discourse, you abhorred; you hated as well as feared it; being deeply sensible of the value of time, of every precious, fleeting moment. In the same way, you dreaded and abhorred idle expense; valuing your money only less than your time and trembling lest you should be found an unfaithful steward even of the mammon of unrighteousness.

Do you now look upon praise as deadly poison, which you can neither give nor receive except at the peril of your soul? Do you still dread and abhor all conversation which does not tend to the use of edifying; and labour to improve every moment, that it may not pass without leaving you better than it found you? Are not you less careful as to the expense both of money and time? Can you not now spend either freely, as you could not have done before? Alas, how has that "which should have been for your health, proved to you an occasion of falling"! How have you "sinned because you were not under the law, but under grace"!

7. God forbid you should any longer continue thus to "turn the grace of God into lasciviousness"! O remember how clear and strong a conviction you once had concerning all these things! And, at the same time, you were fully satisfied from whom that conviction came. The world told you that you were in a delusion, but you knew it was the voice of God. In these things you were not too scrupulous then; but now you are not scrupulous enough. God kept you longer in that painful school so that you might learn those great lessons the more perfectly. And have you forgotten them already? O recollect them before it is too late! Have you suffered so many things in vain? I trust, it is not yet in vain. Now use the conviction without the pain! Practice the lesson without the rod! Let not the mercy of God matter less to you now than his fiery indignation did before. Is love a less powerful motivation than fear? If not, let it be an invariable rule, "I will do nothing now that I am 'under grace' that I would not have dared to do when 'under the law.'"

8. I cannot conclude this section without exhorting you to examine yourself, likewise, concerning sins of omission. Are you as clear of these, now that you "are under grace," as you were when "under the law"? How diligent you were then in hearing the word of God! Did you neglect any opportunity? Did you not attend on them day and night? Would a small hindrance have kept you away? A little business? A visitor? A slight indisposition? A soft bed? A dark or cold morning? Did not you then fast often, or use abstinence to the uttermost of your power? Were not you often praying (cold and heavy as you were) while you were hanging over the mouth of hell? Did you not speak and not spare even for an unknown God? Did you not boldly plead his cause—reprove sinners—and avow the truth before an adulterous generation? And are you now a believer in Christ? Have you the faith that overcomes the world? What! and are less zealous for your Master now than you were when you did not know him? Less diligent in fasting, in prayer, in hearing his word, in calling sinners to God? O repent! See and feel your grievous loss! Remember from whence you are fallen!

Bewail your unfaithfulness! Now be zealous and do the first works; in case, if you continue to "make void the law through faith," God cuts you off, and gives you your portion with the unbelievers!

For Readers

Questions

1. Why does Christian teaching on justification faith tend to lead folks to deny the crucial role of law in the Christian life?
2. What are the three major ways in which we can undermine the place of law in the Christian life?
3. How do the examples of Paul help make the case for the place of law in our lives?
4. How are works the proper fruit of faith in logic and in experience?
5. How does our moral sensitivity before conversion help us develop greater sensitivity after conversion?

Helpful Information

After laying the intellectual foundations for understanding what law is, Wesley now devotes two sermons to practical questions. He divides the terrain neatly into those actions that show that we have abandoned the place of law in the Christian life and those that show that we take the place of law really seriously.

It is clear that he is here thinking of how preachers screw up in ministry, but it is not difficult to extend it beyond this restricted sphere. We are all tempted to think what is being preached here and need to examine ourselves rather than simply criticize what we hear from preachers. We can also extend the point made here by thinking through its import for personal witness.

The heart of the issue is clearly whether we take seriously all that Christ does and says or restrict ourselves to the more palatable elements of Christian witness. Wesley is psychologically very astute when he notices that what looks attractive at first can turn out to become boring and insipid. Thus, speaking only of the love of God or the promises of God can become flat and dead after a while. We need stronger medicine if we are to do justice to the disease that Christ has come to heal. For Wesley, there can be no healing if we ignore the role of law in convicting us of sin. Trying to please and not give offense leaves us bored and ineffective.

Wesley is exceptionally illuminating in drawing on experience of conviction of sin as a motivating element in driving us to deeper obedience to the law of God. If we have a sensitive conscience before we took Christ seriously, how much more sensitive should our conscience be after we have come to experience the extraordinary grace and love of God bestowed on us after we take Christ seriously as our Savior, Lord, and Friend?

SERMON 31

The Law Established through Faith: Discourse Two

"Do we then make void the law through faith? God forbid! Truly, we establish the law" (Rom. 3:31).

1. It has been shown in the preceding discourse which are the most usual ways of making void the law through faith; namely, First, not preaching it at all; which effectually makes it all void at a stroke; and this under the guise of preaching Christ and magnifying the gospel though it be, in truth, destroying both the one and the other; Secondly, teaching (whether directly or indirectly) that faith supersedes the necessity of holiness; that this is less necessary now, or a lesser degree of it necessary, than before Christ came; that it is less necessary to us, because we believe, than otherwise it would have been; or, that Christian liberty is a liberty from any kind or degree of holiness (thus perverting those great truths that we are now under the covenant of grace, and not of works; that a man is justified by faith, without the works of the law; and that "to him who does no works, but only believes, his faith is counted for righteousness"); or, Thirdly, doing this practically; making void the law in practice though not in principle; living or acting as if faith were designed to excuse us from holiness; allowing ourselves in sin "because we are not under the law but under grace." It remains to inquire how we may follow a better pattern, how we may be able to say, with the Apostle, "Do we then make void the law through faith? God forbid: truly, we establish the law."

2. We do not, indeed, establish the old ceremonial law: we know that is abolished forever. Much less do we establish the whole Mosaic dispensation: this we know our Lord has nailed to his cross. Nor yet do we so establish the moral law (which, it is to be feared, too many do) as if fulfilling it, keeping all the commandments, were the condition of our justification. If it were so, surely "in His sight should no man living be justified." But all this being allowed, we still, in the Apostle's sense, "establish the law," the moral law.

I. 1. We establish the law, first, by our doctrine; by endeavouring to preach it in its whole extent, to explain and enforce every part of it, in the same manner as our great Teacher did while upon earth. We establish it by following St. Peter's advice: "If any man speak, let him speak as the oracles of God"; as the holy men of old, moved by the Holy Spirit, spoke and wrote for our instruction; and as the Apostles of our blessed Lord, by the direction of the same Spirit. We establish it whenever we speak in his name, by keeping back nothing from those who hear; by declaring to them, without any limitation or reserve, the whole counsel of God. And in order the more effectually to establish it, here we use great plainness of speech. "We are not like many that corrupt the word of God," καπηλεύουσι ("mix," like artful men their bad wines); we do not adulterate or soften it to make it suit the taste of the hearers, "but like the sincere, as men of God, in the sight of God, we speak in Christ"; as having no other aim, except "by making known the truth to commend ourselves to every man's conscience in the sight of God."

2. We then, by our doctrine, establish the law when we thus openly declare it to all men; and that in the fullness in which it was delivered by our blessed Lord and his Apostles; when we publish it in all its height, and depth, and length, and breadth. We then establish the law when we declare every part of it, every commandment contained therein, not only in its full, literal sense but likewise in its spiritual meaning; not only with regard to the outward actions which it either forbids or enjoins, but also with respect to the inward principle, to the thoughts, desires, and intents of the heart.

3. And indeed this we do the more diligently, not only because it is of the deepest importance—inasmuch as all the fruit, every word and work, can only be evil continually if the tree is evil, if the dispositions and tempers of the heart are not right before God—but likewise because, as important as these things are, they are little considered or understood—so little, in fact, that we may truly say of the law too, when taken in its full spiritual meaning, it is "a mystery which was hidden from ages and generations since the world began." It was utterly hidden from the heathen world. They, with all their boasted wisdom, found neither God nor the law of God; not in the letter, much less in the spirit of it. "Their foolish hearts were" more and more "darkened"; while "professing themselves

wise, they became fools." And it was almost equally hidden, as to its spiritual meaning, from the bulk of the Jewish nation. Even these, who were so ready to declare upon others that, "these nations which know not the law are cursed," pronounced their own sentence there, as being under the same curse, the same dreadful ignorance. Witness our Lord's continual reproof of the wisest among them for their gross misinterpretations of it. Witness the supposition almost universally received among them that they needed only to make the outside of the cup clean; that the paying tithes of mint, anise, and cumin—outward exactness—would atone for inward unrighteousness, for the total neglect both of justice and mercy, of faith and the love of God. Indeed, so absolutely was the spiritual meaning of the law hidden from the wisest of them that one of their most eminent Rabbis comments thus on those words of the Psalmist, "If I incline to iniquity with my heart, the Lord will not hear me"; "that is," says he, "if it is only in my heart, if I do not commit outward wickedness, the Lord will not regard it; he will not punish me unless I proceed to the outward act"!

4. But alas! the law of God, as to its inward, spiritual meaning, is not hidden from the Jews or heathens only, but even from what is called the Christian world; at least, from a vast majority of them. The spiritual sense of the commandments of God is still a mystery to these also. Nor is this observable only in those lands which are overspread with Romish darkness and ignorance. But it is too sure that the far greater part even of those who are called Reformed Christians are utter strangers to this day to the law of Christ, in the purity and spirituality of it.

5. Hence it is that to this day, "the Scribes and Pharisees"—the men who have the form but not the power of religion, and who are generally wise in their own eyes and righteous in their own conceits—"hearing these things, are offended"; are deeply offended, when we speak of the religion of the heart; and particularly when we show that without this, were we to "give all our goods to feed the poor," it would profit us nothing. But offended they must be; for we cannot but speak the truth as it is in Jesus. It is our part, whether they will hear or whether they will forbear, to deliver our own soul. All that is written in the book of God we are to declare,

not as pleasing men, but the Lord. We are to declare not only all the promises, but all the warnings too, which we find there. At the same time that we proclaim all the blessings and privileges which God has prepared for his children; we are likewise to "teach all the things whatever he has commanded." And we know that all these have their use; either for awakening those that sleep, instructing the ignorant, comforting the feeble-minded, or building up and perfecting the saints. We know that "all Scripture, given by inspiration of God is profitable," either "for doctrine," or "for reproof," either "for correction or for instruction in righteousness"; and "that the man of God," in the process of the work of God in his soul, has need of every part of it that he may at length "be perfect, thoroughly furnished to do all good works."

6. It is our part thus to preach Christ, by preaching all things whatsoever he has revealed. We may indeed without blame, yes, even with a special blessing from God, declare the love of our Lord Jesus Christ; we may speak in a more particular manner of "the Lord our righteousness." We may expound upon the grace of God in Christ, "reconciling the world unto himself"; we may, at proper opportunities, dwell upon his praise as "bearing the iniquities of us all, as wounded for our transgressions, and bruised for our iniquities, that by his stripes we might be healed." But still we would not preach Christ, according to his word, if we were to confine ourselves entirely to this: we are not ourselves blameless before God unless we proclaim him in all his offices. To preach Christ as workmen who need not be ashamed is to preach him, not only as our great High Priest, "taken from among men, and ordained for men in things pertaining to God"; as such, "reconciling us to God by his blood," and "always living to make intercession for us"—but likewise as the Prophet of the Lord, "who of God is made wisdom for us," who, by his word and his Spirit, is with us always, "guiding us into all truth," yes, and even as remaining a King forever; as giving laws to all whom he has bought with his blood; restoring those to the image of God whom he had first reinstated in his favour; reigning in all believing hearts until he has "subdued all things to himself," until he has utterly cast out all sin and brought in everlasting righteousness.

II. 1. We establish the law, secondly, when we so preach faith in Christ as not to supersede but produce holiness; to produce all manner of holiness, negative and positive, of the heart and of the life.

To this end, we continually declare (which should be frequently and deeply considered by all "who would not make void the law through faith") that faith itself, even Christian faith, the faith of God's elect, the faith of the operation of God, is only the handmaiden of love. As glorious and honourable as it is, it is not the end of the commandment. God has given this honour to love alone: Love is the end of all the commandments of God. Love is the end, the sole end, of every dispensation of God, from the beginning of the world to the consummation of all things. And it will endure when heaven and earth flee away, for "love" alone "never fails." Faith will entirely fail; it will be swallowed up in sight, in the everlasting vision of God. But even then love

> Its nature and its office still the same,
> Lasting its lamp and unconsumed its flame,
> In deathless triumph shall forever live,
> And endless good diffuse, and endless praise receive.

2. Very excellent things are spoken of faith, and whoever is a partaker in it may well say with the Apostle, "Thanks be to God for his unspeakable gift." Yet still it loses all its excellence when brought into comparison with love. What St. Paul observes concerning the superior glory of the gospel above that of the law may with great propriety be spoken of the superior glory of love above that of faith: "Even that which was made glorious has no glory in this respect, by comparison to the exceeding glory. For if that which is done away is glorious, much more does that which remains exceed in glory"; truly, all the glory of faith, before it is done away, arises from this: that it ministers to love. It is the great temporary means which God has ordained to promote that eternal end.

3. Let those who magnify faith beyond all proportion, so as to swallow up everything else, and who so totally misapprehend the nature of it as to imagine it stands in the place of love, consider further, that as love will exist after faith, so it did exist long before it. The angels who, from the moment of their creation, beheld the face of their Father that is in heaven, had no occasion for faith, in its general

notion, as it is the evidence of things not seen. Neither had they need of faith in its more particular meaning, faith in the blood of Jesus: for he did not take upon himself the nature of angels, but only the seed of Abraham. There was therefore no place before the foundation of the world for faith either in the general or particular sense. But there was for love. Love existed from eternity in God, the great ocean of love. Love had a place in all the children of God, from the moment of their creation. They received at once from their gracious Creator to exist, and to love.

4. Nor is it certain (as ingeniously and plausibly as many have descanted upon this) that faith, even in the general sense of the word, had any place in paradise. It is highly probable, from that short and uncircumstantial account which we have in Holy Writ, that Adam, before he rebelled against God, walked with him by sight and not by faith.

> For then his reason's eye was strong and clear,
>   And (as an eagle can behold the sun)
> Might have beheld his Maker's face as near,
>   As the intellectual angels could have done.

He was then able to talk with him face to face whose face we cannot now see and live; and consequently had no need of that faith whose office it is to supply the want of sight.

5. On the other hand, it is absolutely certain that faith, in its particular sense, had then no place. For in that sense it necessarily presupposes sin and the wrath of God declared against the sinner; without which there is no need of an atonement for sin to bring about the sinner's reconciliation with God. Consequently, as there was no need of an atonement before the fall, so there was no place for faith in that atonement; man being then pure from every stain of sin; holy as God is holy. But love even then filled his heart; it reigned in him without rival, and it was only when love was lost by sin that faith was added, not for its own sake, nor with any design that it should exist any longer than until it had answered the end for which it was ordained—namely, to restore man to the love from which he had fallen. At the fall, therefore, was added this evidence of things unseen, which before was utterly needless;

this confidence in redeeming love, which could not possibly have any place till the promise was made, that "the Seed of the woman should bruise the serpent's head."

6. Faith, then, was originally designed by God to re-establish the law of love. Therefore, in speaking thus, we are not undervaluing it or robbing it of its due praise; but on the contrary showing its real worth, exalting it in its just proportion, and giving it that very place which the wisdom of God assigned it from the beginning. It is the grand means of restoring that holy love wherein man was originally created. It follows, that although faith is of no value in itself (as neither is any other means whatsoever), yet as it leads to that end, the establishing anew the law of love in our hearts, and as, in the present state of things, it is the only means under heaven for effecting it; it is on that account an unspeakable blessing to man, and of unspeakable value before God.

III. 1. And this naturally brings us to observe, thirdly, the most important way of establishing the law; namely, the establishing it in our own hearts and lives. Indeed, without this, what would all the rest avail? We might establish it by our doctrine; we might preach it in its whole extent; might explain and enforce every part of it. We might open it in its most spiritual meaning, and declare the mysteries of the kingdom; we might preach Christ in all his offices, and faith in Christ as opening all the treasures of his love; and yet, all this time, if the law we preached were not established in our hearts, we should be of no more account before God than "sounding brass or tinkling cymbals." All our preaching would be so far from profiting ourselves that it would only increase our damnation.

2. This is, therefore, the main point to be considered. How may we establish the law in our own hearts so that it may have its full influence on our lives? And this can only be done by faith. Faith alone it is which effectively serves this purpose, as we learn from daily experience. For as long as we walk by faith, not by sight, we go swiftly on in the way of holiness. While we steadily look, not at the things which are seen, but at those which are not seen, we are more and more crucified to the world and the world crucified to us. Simply let the eye of the soul be constantly fixed, not on the things which are temporal, but on those which are eternal, and

SERMON 31

our affections are more and more loosened from earth, and fixed on things above. So that faith, in general, is the most direct and effective means of promoting all righteousness and true holiness; of establishing the holy and spiritual law in the hearts of those who believe.

3. And by faith, taken in its more particular meaning as confidence in a pardoning God, we establish his law in our own hearts in a still more effectual manner. For there is no motive which so powerfully inclines us to love God as the sense of the love of God in Christ. Nothing enables us like a piercing conviction of this to give our hearts to him who was given for us. And from this principle of grateful love to God arises love to our brother also. Neither can we avoid loving our neighbour, if we truly believe the love with which God has loved us. Now this love to man, grounded on faith and love to God, "does no evil to" our "neighbour." Consequently it is, as the Apostle observes, "the fulfilling of the" whole negative "law." "For: you shall not commit adultery; you shall not kill; you shall not steal; you shall not bear false witness; you shall not covet; and if there is any other commandment, it is briefly comprehended in this saying, 'You shall love your neighbour as yourself.'" Neither is love content with barely working no evil to our neighbour. It continually incites us to do good as we have time and opportunity; to do good, in every possible kind, and in every possible degree, to all men. It is therefore, the fulfilling of the positive as well as of the negative law of God.

4. Nor does faith fulfill either the negative or positive law, as to the external part only; but it works inwardly by love, to the purifying of the heart, the cleansing it from all vile affections. Everyone that has this faith in himself, "purifies himself, even as he is pure"— purifies himself from every earthly, sensual desire, from all vile and inordinate affections; yes, even from the whole of that carnal mind which is enmity against God. At the same time, if it does its perfect work, it fills him with all goodness, righteousness, and truth. It brings all heaven into his soul; and causes him to walk in the light, even as God is in the light.

5. Let us thus endeavour to establish the law in ourselves; not by sinning "because we are under grace," but rather by using all the power we

receive thereby "to fulfill all righteousness." Calling to mind what light we received from God while his Spirit was convincing us of sin, let us beware we do not put out that light; what we had then attained let us hold fast. Let nothing induce us to build again what we have destroyed; to resume anything, small or great, which we then clearly saw was not for the glory of God or the profit of our own soul; or to neglect anything, small or great, which we could not then neglect without a rebuke from our own conscience. To increase and perfect the light which we had before, let us now add the light of faith. We confirm the former gift of God by a deeper sense of what he had then shown us, by a greater tenderness of conscience and a more exquisite sensibility of sin. Walking now with joy, and not with fear, in a clear, steady sight of things eternal, we shall look on pleasure, wealth, praise—all the things of earth, as on bubbles upon the water; counting nothing important, nothing desirable, nothing worth a deliberate thought, but only what is "within the veil," where Jesus "sits at the right hand of God."

6. Can you say, "You are merciful to my unrighteousness; my sins you remember no more"? Then for the time to come see that you flee from sin as from the bite of a serpent! For how very sinful does it appear to you now! How heinous above all expression! On the other hand, in how amiable a light do you now see the holy and perfect will of God! Now, therefore, labour that it may be fulfilled, both in you, by you, and upon you! Now watch and pray that you may sin no more, that you may see and shun the least transgression of his law! You see the motes which you could not see before, when the sun shines into a dark place. In like manner you see the sins which you could not see before, now the Sun of Righteousness shines in your heart. Now, then, do all diligence to walk, in every respect, according to the light you have received! Now be zealous to receive more light daily, more of the knowledge and love of God, more of the Spirit of Christ, more of his life, and of the power of his resurrection! Now use all the knowledge, and love, and life, and power you have already attained: so you shall continually go on from faith to faith; so shall you daily increase in holy love, till faith is swallowed up in sight, and the law of love established to all eternity!

SERMON 31

For Readers

Questions

1. What is the inward spiritual meaning of the law, and why is it important?
2. How is the excoriation of "heathens" and Jews used to bring home the failure of Christians in their understanding of the law?
3. How can faith, law, and love be integrated into a deep synthesis, so that law cannot then be set against love in the moral thinking of the Christian?
4. How can faith as a practice of trust in God drive the Christian to deeper obedience to God?
5. How can faith as an experience of the piercing love of God drive us into deeper obedience to God?

Helpful Information

Not surprisingly, Wesley structures this second sermon on the relation between faith and law in a way that mirrors what he does in the previous sermon. He simply follows the logic of the text of Scripture. Yet, we should not move too quickly, or we will miss the subtlety of his exposition.

Moreover, it would be easy to charge Wesley with anti-Judaism here. He did not wrestle with the new issues we must face today because of a richer relationship between Jews and Christians and because of the appearance of Messianic Jews on the scene. This issue comes up all through these three sermons in his treatment of the ceremonial law and the Mosaic dispensation. However, if Wesley is tough on "heathens" and Jews, he is even tougher on Christians. In fact, he elegantly builds on the former to tackle the serious failure of Christians.

In this sermon, his deft way of developing both conceptual and experiential links between law and love and between faith and love are striking in the extreme. So, law is connected to holiness, which is the handmaiden of love. And there is a deep experiential link between faith seen in terms of trust in God as its object, who is described as the great ocean of love, and the actual practice of love. This is taken one step further, when he insists that our experience of the piercing love of God provides vivid motivation for obeying the law of God.

Wesley is also clever when he brings out that we stand in a better relation to God than Adam did precisely because we now know a level of divine love through redemption that is only available to those who have known the reality of sin. It is no accident that he exhorts us at the end to receive more light. As we gain deeper knowledge and insight into the nature of faith and law and love, we are drawn deeper into the life of heaven on earth.

Editor's Introduction to Sermon 32

In his three sermons on law Wesley is clearly concerned about the temptation to set aside the will of God as given in divine law. This is a natural temptation for those who pay attention to the fact that we are justified by grace through faith in Jesus Christ rather than by works of the law. Of course, there is no necessity to set aside divine law given this vision of justification. However, human agents are not mere calculating machines governed by logic; they think all too often in a very loose and undisciplined fashion. So, they hear that they are not under law; immediately they jump to the conclusion that they no longer need law in order to discern the will of God. The nasty, technical term for this position is *antinomianism*.

We can surely add that if one takes religion to be first and foremost a matter of the heart, the temptation to go down this false trail is greatly increased. It would appear that in a religion of the heart one should rely first and foremost on one's feelings rather than law to figure out the difference between right and wrong. Equally, if one takes religion to be a matter of love (love for God and neighbor), it is easy to conclude that love is all you need. You do not need law. If you insist on law, then you are a legalist, and legalism is bad.

However, lurking in the wings is a very different temptation for those committed to the religion of the heart. The religion of the heart is not in fact a religion of feeling; this is a lazy caricature. It is a religion that sets enormous store by the work of the Holy Spirit to bring us to faith, to convince us of the amazing significance of the life and work of Christ, and to provide the moral energy to become truly holy. These themes set one up for a very different spiritual challenge. The challenge now is the temptation to use the Holy Spirit as a labor-saving device. So, rather than use one's good sense and reason to figure out what to do, one looks to the Holy Spirit to provide daily guidance for even the most trivial decisions one has to make. One develops a lopsided super-piety in which one ceases to listen to the voice of reason. At its worst, one becomes utterly gullible and credulous, ready to act upon any inward impression that happens to show up. As a result, the moral life becomes entirely arbitrary, subject to all sorts of projection in which radical mistakes are made about the will of God. The danger now is delusion.

In Wesley's time, the term *enthusiasm* was the standard term for this whole way of thinking. It was a common criticism directed at the Methodists. That criticism posed two distinct problems. First, there was a public relations problem in that if this criticism was not answered, the mission of Methodism would be seriously impeded. Second, there was an acute pastoral problem in that Methodists were indeed prone to become radically unbalanced in their spiritual lives. Sermon 32 is a carefully constructed essay intended to deal with both of these challenges.

SERMON 32

The Nature of Enthusiasm

"And Festus said with a loud voice, 'Paul, you are beside yourself'" (Acts 26:24).

1. And so say all the world, the men who know not God, regarding all who are of Paul's religion: of everyone who is so a follower of him as he was of Christ. It is true, there is a sort of religion, and it is even called Christianity too, which may be practised without any such imputation, which is generally allowed to be consistent with common sense, that is, a religion of form, a round of outward duties, performed in a decent, regular manner. You may add orthodoxy to this, a system of right opinions; yes, even some amount of heathen morality; and few will pronounce that "much religion has made you mad." But if you aim at the religion of the heart, if you talk of "righteousness, and peace, and joy in the Holy Spirit," then it will not be long before your sentence is passed, "You are beside yourself."

2. And it is no compliment which the men of the world pay you here. They, for once, mean what they say. They not only affirm, but cordially believe, that every man is beside himself who says, "the love of God is shed abroad in" his "heart by the Holy Spirit given to him"; and that God has enabled him to rejoice in Christ "with joy unspeakable and full of glory." If a man is indeed alive to God and dead to all things here below; if he continually sees Him that is invisible, and accordingly walks by faith, and not by sight; then they account it a clear case: beyond all dispute, "much religion has made him mad."

3. It is easy to observe that the determinate thing which the world accounts madness is that utter contempt of all temporal things, and steady pursuit of things eternal; that divine conviction of things not seen; that rejoicing in the favour of God, that happy, holy love of God and that testimony of His Spirit with our spirit, that we are the children of God—that is, in truth, the whole spirit, and life, and power of the religion of Jesus Christ.

4. They will, however, allow that in other respects the man acts and talks like one in his senses. In other things, he is a reasonable man, it is in

49

SERMON 32

these instances only his head is touched. It is therefore acknowledged, that the madness under which he labours is of a particular kind; and accordingly they are accustomed to distinguish it by a particular name, "enthusiasm."

5. A term this, which is exceeding frequently used, which is scarcely ever out of some men's mouths; and yet it is exceeding rarely understood, even by those who use it most. It may be, therefore, not unacceptable to serious men, to all who desire to understand what they speak or hear, if I endeavour to explain the meaning of this term—to show what enthusiasm is. It may be an encouragement to those who are unjustly charged with it; and may possibly be of use to some who are justly charged with it; at least to others who might be so, were they not cautioned against it.

6. As to the word itself, it is generally allowed to be of Greek extraction. But whence the Greek word ἐνθουσιασμός is derived, no one has yet been able to show. Some have endeavoured to derive it from ἐν Θεῷ—"in God"; because all enthusiasm has reference to Him. But this is quite forced; there being little resemblance between the word derived and those they strive to derive it from. Others would derive it from ἐν θυσίᾳ—"in sacrifice"; because many of the enthusiasts of old were affected in the most violent manner during the time of sacrifice. Perhaps it is a fictitious word, invented from the noise which some of those made who were so affected.

7. It is not improbable that one reason why this uncouth word has been retained in so many languages was because men were not better agreed concerning the meaning than concerning the derivation of it. They therefore adopted the Greek word, because they did not understand it: they did not translate it into their own tongues because they knew not how to translate it; it having been always a word of a loose, uncertain sense, to which no determinate meaning was fixed.

8. It is not, therefore, at all surprising that it is so variously taken at this day; different persons understanding it in different senses, quite inconsistent with each other. Some take it in a good sense, as a divine impulse or impression, superior to all the natural faculties, and suspending, for the time, either in whole or in part, both the reason and the outward senses. In this meaning of the word, both the Prophets of old and the

50

Apostles were proper enthusiasts; being, at diverse times, so filled with the Spirit and so influenced by Him who dwelt in their hearts, that the exercise of their own reason, their senses, and all their natural faculties, being suspended, they were wholly actuated by the power of God, and "spoke" only "as they were moved by the Holy Spirit."

9. Others take the word in a neutral sense, neither morally good nor evil; thus they speak of the enthusiasm of the poets; of Homer and Virgil in particular. And this a late eminent writer extends so far as to assert, that there is no man who excels in his profession, whatever it be, who has not in his temper a strong strain of enthusiasm. By enthusiasm these appear to mean an uncommon vigour of thought, a peculiar fervour of spirit, a vivacity and strength not to be found in common men; elevating the soul to greater and higher things than cold reason could have attained.

10. But neither of these is the sense wherein the word "enthusiasm" is most usually understood. The generality of men, if no farther agreed, at least agree thus far concerning it, that it is something evil: and this is plainly the sentiment of all those who call the religion of the heart "enthusiasm." Accordingly, I shall take it in the following pages as an evil; a misfortune, if not a fault.

11. As to the nature of enthusiasm, it is, undoubtedly a disorder of the mind; and such a disorder which greatly hinders the exercise of reason. Sometimes it even sets it aside entirely: it not only dims but shuts the eyes of the understanding. It may, therefore, well be accounted a species of mindlessness; of insanity rather than of folly: since a fool is properly one who draws wrong conclusions from right premises; whereas a madman draws right conclusions from wrong premises. And so does an enthusiast suppose his premises true, and his conclusions would necessarily follow. But here lies his mistake: his premises are false. He imagines himself to be what he is not: and therefore, having set out wrong, the farther he goes the more he wanders out of the way.

12. Every enthusiast, then, is properly a madman. Yet his is not an ordinary, but a religious, madness. By "religious," I do not mean that it is any part of religion: quite the reverse. Religion is the spirit of a sound mind and, consequently, stands in direct opposition to madness of every kind. But I mean it has religion for its object; it is conversant about religion.

SERMON 32

And so the enthusiast is generally talking of religion, of God or of the things of God, but talking in such a manner that every reasonable Christian may discern the disorder of his mind. Enthusiasm in general may then be described in some such manner as this: a religious madness arising from some falsely imagined influence or inspiration of God; at least, from imputing something to God which should not be imputed to Him, or expecting something from God which should not be expected from Him.

13. There are innumerable sorts of enthusiasm. Those which are most common, and for that reason most dangerous, I shall endeavour to reduce under a few general heads, that they may be more easily understood and avoided.

The first sort of enthusiasm which I shall mention, is that of those who imagine they have grace when they have not. Thus some imagine, when it is not so, that they have redemption through Christ, "even the forgiveness of sins." These are usually those who "have no root in themselves"; no deep repentance or thorough conviction. "Therefore they receive the word with joy." And "because they have no depth of ground," no deep work in their hearts, therefore the seed "immediately springs up." There is immediately a superficial change which, together with that light joy, striking in with the pride of their unbroken heart, and with their inordinate self-love, easily persuades them they have already "tasted the good word of God, and the powers of the world to come."

14. This is properly an instance of the first sort of enthusiasm: it is a kind of madness, arising from the imagination that they have that grace which, in truth, they have not: so that they only deceive their own souls. Madness it may be justly termed: for the reasoning of these poor men would be right, if their premises were good; but since those are a mere creation of their own imagination, all that is built on them falls to the ground. The foundation of all their reveries is this: they imagine themselves to have faith in Christ. If they had this, they would be "kings and priests to God," possessed of a "kingdom which cannot be moved"; but they do not have it; consequently, all their following behaviour is as far from truth and soberness as that of the ordinary madman who, fancying himself an earthly king, speaks and acts in that character.

15. There are many other enthusiasts of this sort. Such, for instance, is the fiery zealot for religion; or, more properly, for the opinions and modes

THE NATURE OF ENTHUSIASM

of worship which he dignifies with that name. This man also strongly imagines himself to be a believer in Jesus; indeed, a champion for the faith which was once delivered to the saints. Accordingly, all his conduct is formed upon that vain imagination. And allowing his supposition to be just, he would have some tolerable plea for his behaviour; whereas now it is evidently the effect of a distempered brain, as well as of a distempered heart.

16. But the most common of all the enthusiasts of this kind are those who imagine themselves Christians and are not. These abound, not only in all parts of our land, but in most parts of the habitable earth. That they are not Christians is clear and undeniable, if we believe the oracles of God. For Christians are holy, these are unholy; Christians love God, these love the world; Christians are humble, these are proud; Christians are gentle, these are passionate; Christians have the mind which was in Christ, these are at the utmost distance from it. Consequently, they are no more Christians than they are archangels. Yet they imagine themselves so to be; and they can give several reasons for it: for they have been called so ever since they can remember; they were christened many years ago; they embrace the Christian opinions, commonly termed the Christian or catholic faith; they use the Christian modes of worship, as their fathers did before them; they live what is called a good Christian life, as the rest of their neighbours do. And who shall presume to think or say that these men are not Christians—though they do not have one grain of true faith in Christ or of real, inward holiness; though they have never tasted the love of God or been "made partakers of the Holy Spirit"!

17. Ah poor self-deceivers! Christians you are not. But you are enthusiasts in a high degree. Physicians, heal yourselves! But first diagnose your disease: your whole life is enthusiasm; as being all based upon the supposition that you have received that grace of God when you have not. As a result of this great mistake, you blunder on, day after day, speaking and acting under a character which in no way belongs to you. Hence arises that palpable, glaring inconsistency that runs through your whole behaviour; which is an awkward mixture of real Heathenism and imaginary Christianity. Yet still, as you have so vast a majority on your side, you will always carry it by mere strength of numbers "that you are the only men in your senses, and all are lunatics who are not

53

as you are." But this does not change the nature of things. In the sight of God, and His holy angels, yes, and all the children of God upon earth too, you are mere madmen, mere enthusiasts all! Are you not? Are you not "walking in a vain shadow, a shadow of religion, a shadow of happiness"? Are you not still "troubling yourselves in vain" with misfortunes as imaginary as your happiness or religion? Do you not fancy yourselves great or good, to be very knowing and very wise? How long? Perhaps until death brings you back to your senses, to bewail your folly forever and ever!

18. A second sort of enthusiasm is that of those who imagine they have such gifts from God as they have not. Thus some have imagined themselves to be endued with a power of working miracles, of healing the sick by a word or a touch, of restoring sight to the blind: even of raising the dead, a notorious instance of which is still fresh in our own history. Others have undertaken to prophesy, to foretell things to come, and that with the utmost certainty and exactness. But a little time usually convinces these enthusiasts. When plain facts run counter to their predictions, experience performs what reason could not, and knocks them back down to their senses.

19. To the same class belong those who, in preaching or prayer, imagine themselves to be influenced by the Spirit of God when, in fact, they are not. I am sensible, indeed, that without Him we can do nothing, more especially in our public ministry; that all our preaching is utterly vain unless His power goes with it; and all our prayer, unless His Spirit helps our infirmities. I know that if we do not both preach and pray by the Spirit, it is all wasted effort; since the help that is done on earth He Himself does, who accomplishes all in all. But this does not affect the case before us. Though there is a real influence of the Spirit of God, there is also an imaginary one; and there are many who mistake the one for the other. Many suppose themselves to be under that influence when they are not, when it is far from them. And many others suppose they are more under that influence than they really are. Of this number, I fear, are all those who imagine that God dictates the very words they speak; and that, consequently, it is impossible for them to speak anything amiss, either as to the matter or manner of it. It is well known how many enthusiasts of this sort also have appeared during the present century; some of

THE NATURE OF ENTHUSIASM

whom speak in a far more authoritative manner than St. Paul or any of the Apostles.

20. The same sort of enthusiasm, though in a lower degree, is frequently found in men of a private character. They may likewise imagine themselves to be influenced or directed by the Spirit when they are not. I allow, "if any man have not the Spirit of Christ, he is none of His"; and that if ever we either think, speak, or act rightly, it is through the assistance of that blessed Spirit. But how many impute things to Him, or expect things from Him, without any rational or scriptural ground! Such persons imagine that they either do or shall receive particular directions from God, not only in points of importance, but in things of no moment; in the most trifling circumstances of life. Whereas in these cases God has given us our own reason for a guide; though never excluding the secret assistance of His Spirit.

21. To this kind of enthusiasm they are peculiarly exposed who expect to be directed by God, either in spiritual things or in common life, in what is justly called an extraordinary manner: I mean, by visions or dreams, by strong impressions or sudden impulses on the mind. I do not deny that God has, of old times, manifested His will in this manner; or that He can do so now: I truly believe He does, in some very rare instances. But how frequently do men go wrong here! How are they misled by pride and a fertile imagination, to ascribe the kinds of impulses or impressions, dreams or visions, to God, which are utterly unworthy of Him! Now this is all pure enthusiasm; all as wide of religion as it is of truth and sobriety.

22. Perhaps some may ask, "Should we not then inquire what is the will of God in all things? And should not His will be the rule of our practice?" Unquestionably it should. But how is a sober Christian to make this inquiry; to know what is the will of God? Not by waiting for supernatural dreams; not by expecting God to reveal it in visions; not by looking for any particular impressions or sudden impulses on his mind: no; but by consulting the oracles of God. "To the law and to the testimony!" This is the general method of knowing what is "the holy and acceptable will of God."

23. "But how shall I know what is the will of God in such and such a particular case? The thing proposed is, in itself, of an indifferent nature,

SERMON 32

and so left undetermined in Scripture." I answer, the Scripture itself gives you a general rule, applicable to all particular cases: "The will of God is our sanctification." It is His will that we should be inwardly and outwardly holy; that we should be good, and do good, in every kind and in the highest degree of which we are capable. Thus far we tread upon firm ground. This is as clear as the shining of the sun. In order, therefore, to know what is the will of God in a particular case, we have only to apply this general rule.

24. Suppose, for instance, it were proposed to a reasonable man to marry, or to enter into a new business. In order to know whether this is the will of God, being assured, "It is the will of God concerning me, that I should be as holy and do as much good as I can," he has only to enquire, "In which of these states can I be most holy, and do the most good?" And this is to be determined partly by reason and partly by experience. Experience tells him what advantages he has in his present state, either for being or doing good; and reason is to show what he certainly or probably will have in the state proposed. By comparing these, he is to judge which of the two may most conduce to his being and doing good; and as far as he knows this, so far he is certain what is the will of God.

25. Meantime, the assistance of His Spirit is supposed during the whole process of the inquiry. Indeed it is not easy to say in how many ways that assistance is conveyed. He may bring many circumstances to our remembrance; may place others in a stronger and clearer light; may imperceptibly open our mind to receive conviction and fix that conviction upon our heart. And to a concurrence of many circumstances of this kind, in favour of what is acceptable in His sight, He may also add such an unutterable peace of mind, and so uncommon a measure of His love, as will leave us no possibility of doubting that this, even this, is His will concerning us.

26. This is the plain, scriptural, rational way to know what is the will of God in a particular case. But considering how seldom this way is taken, and what a flood of enthusiasm inevitably breaks in on those who endeavour to know the will of God by unscriptural, irrational ways; it were to be wished that the expression itself were far more sparingly used. Using it, as some do, on the most trivial occasions, is a plain breach of the third commandment. It is a gross way of taking the name

of God in vain and betrays great irreverence toward Him. Would it not be far better, then, to use other expressions which are not liable to such objections? For example: instead of saying, on any particular occasion, "I want to know what the will of God is"; would it not be better to say, "I want to know what will be most for my improvement; and what will make me most useful?" This way of speaking is clear and unexceptionable: it is putting the matter on a plain, scriptural issue, and that without any danger of enthusiasm.

27. A third very common sort of enthusiasm (if it does not coincide with the former) is that of those who think to attain the end without using the means, by the immediate power of God. If, indeed, those means were providentially withheld, they would not fall under this charge. God can and sometimes does, in cases of this nature, exert His own immediate power. But those who expect this when they have those means and will not use them are proper enthusiasts. Such are they who expect to understand the holy Scriptures without reading them and meditating upon them; indeed, without using all such assistance as they can and may probably put to that purpose. These are the ones who deliberately speak in the public assembly without any preparation. I say "deliberately" because there may be circumstances which, sometimes, make it unavoidable. But whoever despises that great means of speaking profitably is so far an enthusiast.

28. It may be expected that I should mention what some have accounted a fourth sort of enthusiasm; namely, imagining those things to be due to the providence of God which are not due to it. But I doubt: I do not know what things they are which are not owing to the providence of God; in ordering, or at least in governing, of which, this is not either directly or remotely concerned. I except nothing but sin; and even in the sins of others, I see the providence of God to me. I do not say His general providence; for this I take to be an impressive word which means just nothing. And if there be a particular providence, it must extend to all persons and all things. So our Lord understood it, or He could never have said, "Even the hairs of your head are all numbered"; and, "Not even a sparrow falls to the ground except by" the will of "your Father" in heaven. But if it be so, if God presides *universis tanquam singulis, et singulis tanquam universis*, "over the whole universe as over every single person, and over every single person as over the whole

SERMON 32

universe"; what is it (except only our own sins) which we are not to ascribe to the providence of God? So I cannot apprehend there is any room here for the charge of enthusiasm.

29. If it be said that the charge lies here: "When you impute this to Providence, you imagine yourself the peculiar favourite of heaven," I answer, you have forgot some of the last words I spoke: *praesidet universis tanquam singulis*, "His providence is over all persons in the universe, as much as over any single person." Do you not see that he who, believing this, imputes anything which befalls him to Providence, does not by this make himself any more the favourite of heaven than he supposes every man under heaven to be? Therefore you have no pretence, upon this ground, to charge him with enthusiasm.

30. Against every sort of this it behooves us to guard with the utmost diligence; considering the dreadful effects it has so often produced, and which, indeed, naturally result from it. Its immediate offspring is pride; it continually increases this source from whence it flows; and by this it alienates us more and more from the favour and from the life of God. It dries up the very springs of faith and love, of righteousness and true holiness; seeing all these flow from grace: but "God opposes the proud and gives grace" only "to the humble."

31. Together with pride there will naturally arise an unadvisable and obstinate spirit. So that into whatever error or fault the enthusiast falls, there is small hope of his recovery. For reason will have little weight with him (as has been frequently and justly observed) who imagines he is led by a higher guide—by the immediate wisdom of God. And as he grows in pride, so he must grow in hard-headedness and in stubbornness also. He must be less and less capable of being convinced, less susceptible of persuasion; more and more attached to his own judgment and his own will, until he is entirely set and immobile.

32. Being thus fortified against both the grace of God and all advice and help from man, he is wholly left to the guidance of his own heart and of the king of the children of pride. No marvel, then, that he is daily more rooted and grounded in contempt of all mankind, in furious anger, in every unkind disposition, in every earthly and devilish temper. Neither can we wonder at the terrible outward effects which have flowed from such dispositions in all ages; even all manner of wickedness,

THE NATURE OF ENTHUSIASM

all the works of darkness, committed by those who call themselves Christians, while they wrought with greediness such things as were hardly named even among the Heathens. Such is the nature, such the dreadful effects, of that many-headed monster, Enthusiasm! From the consideration of which we may now draw some plain inferences, with regard to our own practice.

33. First, if enthusiasm be a term frequently used yet rarely understood, take care not to talk whereof you do not know. Do not use the word before you understand it. As in all other points, so likewise in this: learn to think before you speak. First, know the meaning of this hard word, and then use it, if need require.

34. But if so few, even among men of education and learning, much more among the common sort of men, understand this dark, ambiguous word or have any fixed notion of what it means; then, secondly, beware of judging or calling any man an enthusiast on the basis of common report. This is by no means a sufficient ground for giving a name of reproach to any man; least of all is it a sufficient ground for so black a term of reproach as this. The more evil it contains, the more cautious you should be how you apply it to anyone; to bring so heavy an accusation without full proof being consistent neither with justice nor mercy.

35. But if enthusiasm is so great an evil, beware you are not entangled with it yourself. Watch and pray, that you do not fall into the temptation. It easily besets those who fear or love God. O beware you do not think of yourself more highly than you ought. Do not imagine you have attained that grace of God which you have not attained. You may have much joy; you may have a measure of love, and yet not have living faith. Cry out to God that He would not allow you, blind as you are, to go astray; that you may never fancy yourself a believer in Christ until Christ is revealed in you and His Spirit witnesses with your spirit that you are a child of God.

36. Beware you are not a fiery, persecuting enthusiast. Do not imagine that God has called you (in exact contrast to the spirit of Him you call your Master) to destroy men's lives, and not to save them. Never dream of forcing men into the ways of God. You think and let others think. Use no constraint in matters of religion. Even those who are farthest

SERMON 32

out of the way, never compel them to come in by any other means but reason, truth, and love.

37. Beware you do not run with the common herd of enthusiasts, fancying you are a Christian when you are not. Do not presume to assume that venerable name unless you have a clear, scriptural title to it; unless you have the mind which was in Christ, and walk as He also walked.

38. Beware you do not fall into the second sort of enthusiasm—fancying you have those gifts from God which you have not. Trust not in visions or dreams; in sudden impressions, or strong impulses of any kind. Remember, it is not by these you are to know what is the will of God on any particular occasion but by applying the plain Scripture rule, with the help of experience and reason, and the ordinary assistance of the Spirit of God. Do not take the name of God in your mouth lightly; do not talk of the will of God on every trifling occasion, but let your words, as well as your actions, be all tempered with reverence and godly fear.

39. Beware, lastly, of imagining you shall obtain the end without using the means which lead to it. God can give the end without any means at all; but you have no reason to think He will. Therefore constantly and carefully use all those means which He has appointed to be the ordinary channels of His grace. Use every means which either reason or Scripture recommends, as conducive (through the free love of God in Christ) either to the obtaining or increasing any of the gifts of God. Thus expect a daily growth in that pure and holy religion which the world always did, and always will, call "enthusiasm"; but which, to all who are saved from real enthusiasm, from merely nominal Christianity, is "the wisdom of God, and the power of God"; the glorious image of the Most High; "righteousness and peace"; a "fountain of living water, springing up into everlasting life"!

For Readers

Questions

1. What is the core problem with enthusiasm properly understood? What vice is in play in enthusiasm?

2. What are the three varieties of enthusiasm enumerated here?

3. Read as a short essay on divine guidance, what useful advice is offered in this sermon?
4. How does this sermon deal with the public relations problems related to defending the crucial work of the Holy Spirit in the Christian life?
5. What vision of providence is in play here?

Helpful Information

This is a very clever sermon designed to get readers to think clearly about a difficult issue; to offer a defense of the work of the Holy Spirit in early Christianity and today; and to avoid the pitfalls of using the Holy Spirit as a holy, labor-saving device.

Having carefully defined *enthusiasm*, Wesley undercuts the criticism of his opponents by suggesting that it is they who are the real enthusiasts, for as mere nominal Christians, they claim to be inspired by the Holy Spirit when they are not. In the process, he makes it clear that one cannot take the prophets and apostles of old seriously and reject a vital place for the work of the Holy Spirit in the Christian life. Early Methodists would have been pleased to see the tables turned against their hostile opponents in the public relations campaign lodged against them.

However, the meat of the sermon is directed at ensuring that believers develop a balanced spirituality that integrates the guidance of the Holy Spirit with the guidance of Scripture, reason, and experience understood as concurring circumstances. So, the crucial vice that shows up in enthusiasm is mindlessness. There is the real danger of cognitive malfunction. Serious Christians are prone to send their brains on a holiday, all too ready to follow impulses, impressions, and dreams. They are also prone to immaturity by not taking seriously their God-given ability to think things through, opting instead to look for special divine guidance to deal with all sorts of daily trivialities.

At the edge of this sermon Wesley drops in his very robust doctrine of providence in which God works through everything that happens. He rightly notes that providence will not help solve the problem of divine guidance precisely because God will continue to work in lives even when we are intellectually careless and spiritually unbalanced. Hence, he rightly looks to other considerations to help us truly discern what God wants us to do. As a footnote, Wesley provided timely advice for those who are wrestling with those special gifts of the Holy Spirit in ministry that became central to the heirs of Wesley in later generations.

Editor's Introduction to Sermons 33–34

These two sermons can naturally be grouped together because they address challenges that only arise if one is really serious about one's religious commitments. Put differently, they do not arise in the case of believers who are half-hearted, or who are lukewarm, or who could not care less about the specifics of religious commitment so long as they are somehow committed in general to being religious. Those who claim to be spiritual but are not religious, or who dismiss institutional religion in the name of spirituality, will not be troubled by the challenges taken up here. It is those who seek a deep spirituality in the life of the church who are in danger at this point. Given that Wesley holds out for the possibility of a very high level of assurance before God, it is entirely fitting that he addresses this network of challenges.

Sermon 33 deals with the challenge of bigotry, and Sermon 34 deals with the temptation to attack or undermine the ministry of Christians who disagree with us on crucial points of doctrine and practice. We can see immediately that both sermons arise for a simple reason. The kind of assurance that Wesley expects Christians to have as a matter of course can lead them to develop poisonous and dysfunctional relations with others. So, in the first case, assurance leads to a sense that we—and we alone—have the franchise on Christian ministry. Hence, we forbid others or undermine their work. In the second case, our sense of assurance leads to a sense of intellectual superiority in which we refuse to acknowledge the good work that other Christian groups, and even non-Christian groups, do in all sincerity and integrity.

Wesley shows astonishing prescience in taking up these challenges. I suspect that much of this prescience was deeply intuitive in nature rather than worked out by some kind of explicit analysis. His ruminations constitute a wellspring of wisdom that has had a deep impact on the lives of generations of Methodists. They also make a distinct contribution to any effort to think through the deep divisions that have been within Christianity from the beginning.

SERMON 33

A Caution against Bigotry

"And John answered him, saying, 'Master, we saw one casting out devils in Your name: and he does not follow us: and we rebuked him because he does not follow us.' But Jesus said, 'Forbid him not'" (Mark 9:38–39).

1. In the preceding verses we read that after the Twelve had been disputing "which of them should be the greatest," Jesus took a little child, and set him in the midst of them, and taking him in his arms, said to them, "Whoever shall welcome one of these little children in My name welcomes me; and whoever welcomes me does not welcome me" alone, "but also the one who sent me." Then "John answered," that is, said with reference to what our Lord had just said, "Master, we saw one casting out devils in Your name, and we rebuked him because he does not follow us." It is as if he had said, "Should we have welcomed him? In welcoming him, would we have welcomed you? Should we not rather have forbidden him? Did not we do well there?" "But Jesus said, 'Forbid him not.'"

2. The same passage is recorded by St. Luke, and almost in the same words. But it may be asked, "What is this to us, since no one now 'casts out devils'? Has not the power of doing this been withdrawn from the church for twelve or fourteen hundred years? How then are we concerned in the case here proposed, or in our Lord's decision of it?"

3. Perhaps more closely than is commonly imagined; the case proposed being no uncommon case. That we may reap our full advantage from it, I design to show, first, in what sense men may, and do, now cast out devils: secondly, what we may understand by, "He is not one of us." I shall, thirdly, explain our Lord's direction, "Forbid him not"; and conclude with an inference from the whole.

I. 1. I am, in the first place, to show in what sense men may, and do now cast out devils.

In order to have the clearest view of this, we should remember that (according to the scriptural account) as God dwells and works in the children of light, so the Devil dwells and works in the children of darkness. As the Holy Spirit possesses the souls of good men, so the evil spirit possesses the souls of the wicked. Hence it is that the Apostle terms him "the god of this world"; from the unchecked power he holds over worldly men. Hence our blessed Lord styles him "the prince of this world"; so absolute is his dominion over it. And hence St. John: "We know that we are of God, and" all who are not of God, "the whole world," "ἐν τῷ πονηρῷ κεῖται," not "lies in wickedness," but "lies in the wicked one"; lives and moves in him, as they who are not of the world do in God.

2. For the Devil is not to be considered only as "a roaring lion going about seeking whom he may devour"; nor merely as a subtle enemy who comes unawares upon poor souls and "leads them captive at his will"; but as he who dwells in them, and walks in them; who rules the darkness or wickedness of this world (of worldly men and all their dark intentions and actions), by keeping possession of their hearts, setting up his throne there and bringing every thought into obedience to himself. Thus the "strong one armed guards his house"; and if this "unclean spirit" sometimes "goes out of a man," yet he often returns with "seven spirits worse than himself, and they enter in and dwell there." Nor can he be idle in his dwelling. He is continually "working in" these "children of disobedience": he works in them with power, with mighty energy, transforming them into his own likeness, effacing all the remains of the image of God and preparing them for every evil word and work.

3. It is, therefore, an unquestionable truth that the god and prince of this world still possesses all who know not God. Only the manner in which he now possesses them differs from that in which he did it of old. Then he frequently tormented their bodies as well as souls, and that openly, without any disguise: now he torments their souls only (except in some rare cases), and that as covertly as possible. The reason of this difference is plain: it was then his aim to drive mankind into superstition; therefore, he wrought as openly as he could. But it is his aim to drive us into infidelity; therefore, he works as privately as he can: for the more secret he is, the more he prevails.

4. Yet, if we may credit historians, there are countries even now where he works as openly as before. "But why in savage and barbarous countries only? Why not in Italy, France, or England?" For a very

plain reason: he knows his men, and he knows what he has to do with each. To Laplanders he appears barefaced; because he is to sink them in superstition and gross idolatry. But with you he is pursuing a different point. He is to make you idolize yourselves; to make you wiser in your own eyes than God himself, than all the oracles of God. Now, in order to do this, he must not appear in his own shape: that would frustrate his design. No: he uses all his art to make you deny his existence until he has you safe in his own place.

5. He reigns, therefore, although in a different way, yet as absolute in one land as in the other. He has the carefree Italian infidel in his teeth as surely as the wild Tartar. But he is fast asleep in the mouth of the lion, who is too wise to wake him up. So he only plays with him for the present, and when he pleases, swallows him up!

    The god of this world holds his English worshippers just as securely as those in Lapland. But it is not his business to jar them, lest they should flee to the God of heaven. The prince of darkness, therefore, does not show himself while he rules over these his willing subjects. The conqueror holds his captives so much the safer because they imagine themselves free. Thus "the strong one armed guards his house, and his goods are secure"; neither the Deist nor nominal Christian suspects he is there: so he and they are perfectly at peace with each other.

6. All this while he works with power in them. He blinds the eyes of their understanding so that the light of the glorious gospel of Christ cannot shine upon them. He chains their souls down to earth and hell with the chains of their own vile affections. He binds them down to the earth by love of the world, love of money, of pleasure, of praise. And by pride, envy, anger, hate, revenge, he causes their souls to draw close to hell; acting the more secure and uncontrolled because they do not know he acts at all.

7. But how easily may we know the cause from its effects! These are sometimes gross and palpable. So they were in the most refined of the heathen nations. Go no farther than the admired, the virtuous Romans; and you will find these, when at the height of their learning and glory, "filled with all unrighteousness, fornication, wickedness, covetousness, maliciousness; full of envy, murder, debate, deceit, malignity; whisperers, backbiters, despiteful, proud, boasters,

disobedient to parents, covenant-breakers, without natural affection, implacable, unmerciful."

8. The strongest parts of this description are confirmed by one whom some may think a more unexceptionable witness. I mean their brother heathen, Dion Cassius. He observed that before Caesar's return from Gaul, not only were gluttony and lewdness of every kind open and barefaced; not only did falsehood, injustice, and ruthlessness abound, in public courts as well as private families; but the most outrageous robberies, rapes, and murders were so frequent in all parts of Rome that few men went out of doors without making their wills, not knowing if they should return alive!

9. The works of the Devil among many (if not all) the modern heathens are as gross and palpable. The natural religion of the Creeks, Cherokees, Chickasaws, and all other Indians bordering on our southern settlements (not of a few single men but of entire nations), is to torture all their prisoners from morning until night, until at last they roast them to death; and to come up behind and shoot any of their own countrymen upon the slightest accidental provocation! It is even a common thing among them for the son, if he thinks his father has lived too long, to knock out his brains; and for a mother, if she is tired of her children, to fasten stones about their necks and throw three or four of them into the river, one after another!

10. It were to be wished that none but heathens practise such gross, palpable works of the Devil. But we dare not say so. Even in cruelty and bloodshed, how little have the Christians fallen short of them! And not the Spaniards or Portuguese alone, butchering thousands in South America: not the Dutch only in the East Indies, or the French in North America, following the Spaniards step by step: our own countrymen, too, have wallowed in blood, and exterminated whole nations; plainly proving by this what spirit it is that dwells and works in the children of disobedience.

11. These monsters might almost make us overlook the works of the Devil that are wrought in our own country. But, alas, we cannot open our eyes even here without seeing them on every side. Is it a small proof of his power that common swearers, drunkards, whoremongers, adulterers, thieves, robbers, sodomites, murderers, are still

12. He less openly, but no less effectually, works in dissemblers, gossips, liars, slanderers; in oppressors and extortionists, in the one who lies under oath, the seller of his friend, his honour, his conscience, his country. And yet these may talk of religion or conscience still; of honour, virtue, and public spirit! But they can no more deceive Satan than they can God. He also knows those that are his, and a great multitude they are, out of every nation and people, of whom he has full possession at this day.

13. If you consider this, you cannot but see in what sense men may now also cast out devils: yes, and every Minister of Christ does cast them out, if his Lord's work prospers in his hand.

    By the power of God attending his word, he brings these sinners to repentance; a comprehensive inward as well as outward change, from all evil to all good. And this is, in a sound sense, to exorcise devils out of the souls in which they had until that moment dwelt. The strong one can no longer keep his house. A stronger than he has come upon him, and has cast him out and taken possession for himself, and made it a habitation of God through his Spirit. Here, then, the power of Satan ends, and the Son of God "destroys the works of the Devil." The understanding of the sinner is now enlightened, and his heart sweetly drawn to God. His desires are refined, his affections purified; and, being filled with the Holy Spirit, he grows in grace till he is not only holy in heart, but in all manner of conversation.

14. All this is indeed the work of God. It is God alone who can cast out Satan. But he is generally pleased to do this by man as an instrument in his hand: who is then said to cast out devils in his name by his power and authority. And he sends whom he will send upon this great work; but usually such as man would never have thought of: for "His ways are not as our ways, neither his thoughts as our thoughts." Accordingly, he chooses the weak to confound the mighty; the foolish to confound the wise; for this plain reason, that he may secure the glory to himself; that "no flesh may glory in his sight."

II. 1. But shall we not forbid one who thus "casts out devils," if "he does not follow us"? This, it seems, was both the judgment and practice

— found in every part of our land? How triumphant does the prince of this world reign in all these children of disobedience!

of the Apostle until he referred the case to his Master. "We rebuked him," he says, "because he does not follow us," which he supposed to be a very sufficient reason. What we may understand by this expression, "he does not follow us," is the next point to be considered.

The most basic circumstance we can understand by that is that he has no outward connexion with us. We do not labour in conjunction with each other. He is not our fellow-helper in the gospel. And indeed whenever our Lord is pleased to send many labourers into his harvest, they cannot all act in subordination to, or in connexion with, each other. Nay, they cannot be personal acquaintances with, nor be so much as known to, one another. Many there will necessarily be, in different parts of the harvest, so far from having any mutual intercourse, that they will be as absolute strangers to each other as if they had lived in different ages. And concerning any of these whom we know not, we may doubtless say, "He does not follow us."

2. A second meaning of this expression may be he is not of our party. It has long been matter of melancholy consideration to all who pray for the peace of Jerusalem, that so many several parties are still subsisting among those who are all called Christians. This has been particularly notable in our own countrymen, who have been continually dividing from each other upon points of no importance, and many times those with which religion was not concerned. The most trifling circumstances have given rise to different parties, which have continued for many generations; and each of these would be ready to object to one who was on the other side, "He does not follow us."

3. That expression may mean, thirdly, he differs from us in our religious opinions. There was a time when all Christians were of one mind as well as of one heart, so great grace was upon them all when they were first filled with the Holy Spirit! But how short a time did this blessing last! How soon was that unanimity lost, and differences of opinion sprang up again, even in the church of Christ—and that not in nominal but in real Christians; nay, in the very chief of them, the Apostles themselves! Nor does it appear that the differences which then began were ever entirely removed. We do not find that even those pillars in the temple of God, as long as they remained on the earth, were ever brought to think alike, to be of one mind, particularly with regard to the ceremonial law. It is therefore not surprising that

infinite varieties of opinion should now be found in the Christian church. A very probable consequence of this is, that whenever we see anyone "casting out devils," he will be one who, in this sense, "does not follow us"—who is not of our opinion. It is scarcely to be imagined he will be of our mind in all points, even of religion. He may very probably think in a different manner from us even on several subjects of importance; such as the nature and use of the moral law, the eternal decrees of God, the sufficiency and efficacy of his grace, and the perseverance of his children.

4. He may differ from us, fourthly, not only in opinion but likewise in some point of practice. He may not approve of that manner of worshipping God which is practised in our congregation; and may judge that to be more profitable for his soul which took its rise from Calvin or Martin Luther. He may have many objections to that Liturgy which we approve of beyond all others; many doubts concerning that form of church government which we esteem both apostolic and scriptural. Perhaps he may go farther from us yet: he may, from a principle of conscience, refrain from several of those which we believe to be the ordinances of Christ. Or, if we both agree that they are ordained of God, there may still remain a difference between us either as to the manner of administering those ordinances, or the persons to whom they should be administered. Now the unavoidable consequence of any of these differences will be, that he who thus differs from us must separate himself, with regard to those points, from our society. In this respect, therefore, "he does not follow us": he is not (as we phrase it) "of our Church."

5. But in a far stronger sense "he does not follow us," who is not only of a different Church, but of such a Church as we account to be in many respects anti-scriptural and anti-Christian, a Church which we believe to be utterly false and erroneous in her doctrines, as well as very dangerously wrong in her practice; guilty of gross superstition as well as idolatry; a Church that has added many articles to the faith which was once delivered to the saints; that has dropped one whole commandment of God, and made void several of the rest by her traditions; and that, pretending the highest veneration for, and strictest conformity to, the ancient Church, has nevertheless brought in numberless innovations, without any warrant either from

antiquity or Scripture. Now, most certainly, "he does not follow us," who stands at so great a distance from us.

6. Yet there may be a still wider difference than this. He who differs from us in judgment or practice, may possibly stand at a greater distance from us in affection than in judgment. And this indeed is a very natural and a very common effect of the other. The differences which begin in points of opinion seldom end there. They generally spread into the affections, and then separate best friends. Nor are any animosities so deep and irreconcilable as those which spring from disagreement in religion. For this cause the bitterest enemies of a man are those of his own household. For this the father rises against his own children, and the children against the father; and perhaps they persecute each other even unto death, thinking all the time they are serving God. It is therefore nothing more than we may expect if those who differ from us, either in religious opinions or practice, soon contract a sharpness, yes, even a bitterness towards us; if they are more and more prejudiced against us, till they conceive as ill an opinion of our persons as of our principles. An almost necessary consequence of this will be that they will speak in the same manner as they think of us. They will set themselves in opposition to us, and, as far as they are able, hinder our work; seeing it does not appear to them to be the work of God, but either of man or of the Devil. He that thinks, speaks, and acts in such a manner as this, in the highest sense, "does not follow us."

7. I do not indeed conceive that the person of whom the Apostle speaks in the text (although we have no particular account of him, either in the context, or in any other part of holy writ) went so far as this. We have no reason to suppose that there was any material difference between him and the Apostles, much less that he had any prejudice either against them or their Master. It seems we may gather thus much from our Lord's own words, which immediately follow the text: "There is no man who does a miracle in My name, that can lightly speak evil of me." But I purposely put the case in the strongest light, adding all the circumstances which can well be conceived, that, being forewarned of the temptation in its full strength, we may in no case yield to it, and fight against God.

III. 1. Suppose, then, a man has no interaction with us, suppose he be not of our party, suppose he separates from our Church, and even widely differs from us in judgment, practice, and affection; yet if we see even this man "casting out devils," Jesus says, "Forbid him not." This important instruction from our Lord, I am, in the third place, to explain.

2. If we see this man casting out devils, it is better if, in such a case, we would believe what we saw with our eyes, if we did not give the lie to our own senses. He must be little acquainted with human nature who does not immediately perceive how extremely unready we should be to believe that any man does cast out devils who "does not follow us" in all or most of the senses above recited: I had almost said, in any of them, seeing we may easily learn even from what passes in our own breasts how unwilling men are to recognize anything good in those who do not in all things agree with themselves.

3. "But what is a sufficient, reasonable proof that a man does (in the sense above) cast out devils?" The answer is easy. Is there full proof, (1) That a person before us was a gross, open sinner? (2) That he is not so now that he has broken from his sins, and lives a Christian life? And (3) That this change was wrought by his hearing this man preach? If these three points be plain and undeniable, then you have sufficient, reasonable proof, such as you cannot resist without willingly sinning, that this man casts out devils.

4. Then "forbid him not." Beware how you attempt to hinder him, either by your authority, or arguments, or persuasions. Do not in any way strive to prevent his using all the power which God has given him. If you have authority with him, do not use that authority to stop the work of God. Do not furnish him with reasons why he ought not speak in the name of Jesus any more. Satan will not fail to supply him with these, if you do not second him therein. Persuade him not to depart from the work. If he should give place to the devil and you, many souls might perish in their iniquity, but their blood would God require at your hands.

5. "But what if he is only a layman who casts out devils? Should I not forbid him then?"

Is the fact allowed? Is there reasonable proof that this man has or does cast out devils? If there is, forbid him not; no, not at the peril of your soul. Shall not God work by whom he will work? No man can do these works unless God is with him; unless God has sent him for this very thing. But if God has sent him, will you call him back? Will you forbid him to go?

6. "But I do not know that he is sent of God." "Now here is a marvelous thing" (may any of the seals of his mission say, any whom he has brought from Satan to God), "that you know not from where this man comes, but see, he has opened my eyes! If this man were not of God, he could do nothing." If you doubt the fact, send for the parents of the man: send for his brethren, friends, acquaintance. But if you cannot doubt this, if you must acknowledge "that a notable miracle has been wrought" then with what conscience, with what face, can you charge him whom God has sent "not to speak any more in his name"?

7. I allow, that it is highly expedient, whoever preaches in his name should have an outward as well as an inward call, but that it is absolutely necessary, I deny.

"Surely not; is not the Scripture explicit? 'No man takes this honour upon himself, but only those who are called by God, as was Aaron'" (Heb. 5:4).

Numberless times has this text been quoted on the occasion, as containing the very strength of the cause; but surely never was so unhappy a quotation. For, first, Aaron was not called to preach at all: he was called "to offer gifts and sacrifices for sin." That was his special employment. Secondly, these men do not offer sacrifices at all, but only preach; which Aaron did not. Therefore it is not possible to find one text in all the Bible which is more wide of the point than this.

8. "But what was the practice of the apostolic age?" You may easily see in the Acts of the Apostles. In the eighth chapter we read, "There was a great persecution against the church which was at Jerusalem; and they were all scattered abroad throughout the regions of Judea and Samaria, except the Apostles" (verse 1). "Therefore they that were scattered abroad went everywhere preaching the word" (verse 4). Now, were all these outwardly called to preach? No man in his senses can think so. Here, then, is an undeniable proof, what

was the practice of the apostolic age. Here you see not one, but a multitude of lay preachers, men that were sent only by God.

9. Indeed, so far is the practice of the apostolic age from inclining us to think it was unlawful for a man to preach before he was ordained, that we have reason to think it was then accounted necessary. Certainly the practice and the direction of the Apostle Paul was to examine a man before he was ordained at all. "Let these" (the deacons), he says, "first be examined; then let them use the office of a deacon" (1 Tim. 3:10). Tested how? By setting them to construe a sentence of Greek and asking them a few commonplace questions? O amazing proof of a Minister of Christ! No; instead by making a clear, open trial (as is still done by most of the Protestant Churches of Europe) not only whether their lives be holy and blameless, but whether they have such gifts as are absolutely and indispensably necessary in order to edify the church of Christ.

10. But what if a man has these, and has brought sinners to repentance, and yet the Bishop will not ordain him? Then the Bishop does forbid him to cast out devils. But I dare not forbid him: I have published my reasons to all the world. Yet it is still insisted I ought to do it. You who insist upon it must answer those reasons. I do not know that any have done this yet, or even made an attempt of doing it. Some have spoken of them as very weak and trifling, and this was prudent enough; for it is far easier to despise, or at least to seem to despise, an argument, than to answer it. Yet until this is done I must say that when I have reasonable proof that any man does cast out devils, whatever others do, I dare not forbid him, lest I be found even to fight against God.

11. And whoever you are who fear God, forbid him not, either directly or indirectly. There are many ways of doing this. You indirectly forbid him if you either wholly deny, or despise and make little account of, the work which God has wrought by his hands. You indirectly forbid him, when you discourage him in his work, by drawing him into disputes concerning it, by raising objections against it, or frightening him with consequences which very possibly will never be. You forbid him when you show any unkindness toward him either in language or behaviour; and much more when you speak of him to others either in an unkind or a contemptuous manner; when you

SERMON 33

endeavour to represent him to any either in an odious or a despicable light. You are forbidding him all the time you are speaking evil of him or making no account of his labours. O forbid him not in any of these ways; nor by forbidding others to hear him—by discouraging sinners from hearing that word which is able to save their souls!

12. Indeed, if you would observe our Lord's direction in its full meaning and extent, then remember his words: "He who is not for us is against us; and he who does not gather with me scatters." He who does not gather men into the kingdom of God assuredly scatters them from it. For there can be no neutrality in this war. Everyone is either on God's side, or on Satan's. Are you on God's side? Then you will not only not forbid any man that casts out devils, but you will labour, to the uttermost of your power, to forward him in the work. You will readily acknowledge the work of God and confess the greatness of it. You will remove all difficulties and objections, as far as may be, out of his way. You will strengthen his hands by speaking honourably of him before all men and avowing the things which you have seen and heard. You will encourage others to attend upon his word, to hear him whom God has sent. And you will omit no actual proof of tender love, which God gives you an opportunity of showing him.

IV. 1. If we willingly fail in any of these points, if we either directly or indirectly forbid him, "because he does not follow us," then we are bigots. This is the inference I draw from what has been said. But the term "bigotry," I fear, as frequently as it is used, is almost as little understood as "enthusiasm." It is a too-strong attachment to, or fondness for, our own party, opinion, church, and religion. Therefore he is a bigot who is so fond of any of these, so strongly attached to them, as to forbid anyone who casts out devils because he differs from himself in any or all these particulars.

2. Do you beware of this. Take care (1) That you do not convict yourself of bigotry, by your reluctance to believe that any man does cast out devils who differs from you. And if you are clear thus far, if you acknowledge the fact, then examine yourself, (2) Am I not guilty of bigotry in this, in forbidding him directly or indirectly? Do I not directly forbid him on this ground, because he is not of my party, because he does not fall in with my opinions, or because he does

not worship God according to that scheme of religion which I have received from my fathers?

3. Examine yourself: Do I not at least indirectly forbid him on any of these grounds? Am I not sorry that God should thus own and bless a man that holds such erroneous opinions? Do I not discourage him, because he is not of my Church, by disputing with him concerning it, by raising objections, and by perplexing his mind with distant consequences? Do I show no anger, contempt, or unkindness of any sort, either in my words or actions? Do I not mention behind his back his (real or supposed) faults—his defects or infirmities? Do not I hinder sinners from hearing his word? If you do any of these things, you are a bigot to this day.

4. "Search me, O Lord, and prove me. Try out my reins and my heart! Look well if there be any way of" bigotry "in me and lead me in the way everlasting." In order to examine ourselves thoroughly, let the case be proposed in the strongest manner. What if I were to see a Papist, an Arian, a Socinian casting out devils? If I did, I could not forbid even him without convicting myself of bigotry. Yes, if it could be supposed that I should see even a Jew, a Deist, or a Turk doing the same, and I were to forbid him either directly or indirectly, I should be no better than a bigot still.

5. O stand clear of this! But be not content with not forbidding any that casts out devils. It is well to go thus far; but do not stop here. If you will avoid all bigotry, go on. In every instance of this kind, whatever the instrument may be, acknowledge the finger of God. And not only acknowledge, but rejoice in his work, and praise his name with thanksgiving. Encourage whomever God is pleased to employ to give himself wholly up to the work. Speak well of him wherever you are; defend his character and his mission. Enlarge, as far as you can, his sphere of action; show him all kindness in word and deed; and cease not to cry to God in his behalf, that he may save both himself and them that hear him.

6. I need add but one caution: Do not imagine that the bigotry of another is any excuse for your own. It is not impossible that one who casts out devils himself may yet forbid you to do so. You may observe that this is the very case mentioned in the text. The Apostles forbade

SERMON 33

another to do what they did themselves. But beware of retorting. It is not your part to return evil for evil. Another not observing the direction of our Lord is no reason why you should neglect it. No, just let him have all the bigotry to himself. If he forbids you, do not you forbid him. Rather labour and watch and pray all the more, to confirm your love toward him. If he speaks all manner of evil of you, speak all manner of good (that is true) of him. Imitate here that glorious saying of a great man (O that he had always breathed the same spirit!), "Let Luther call me a hundred devils; I will still reverence him as a messenger of God."

For Readers

Questions

1. What extended vision of the demonic is developed in this sermon? How does this vision lead to the very specific description of exorcism in play?
2. Identify the catalogue of differences that are used to capture the variety of agents doing the work of God in tackling evil. How deep do these differences run?
3. How is the ministry of the laity introduced and defended here?
4. How exactly is bigotry defined? What kind of vice is it?
5. How is being bigoted against bigots handled here?

Helpful Information

This sermon makes our hair stand on head for at least two reasons. First, it takes with radical seriousness the reality of the devil. Second, as an exegesis of the text it so extends the concept of the demonic that we find it strained if not utterly misleading. Yet Wesley's use of the language of the demonic to tackle a perennial problem in the history of religion is ingenious.

The problem is this: we become so sure of ourselves that we are convinced that God works through us and only us in tackling the evil we see all around us. In short, we become exclusivists who cannot stand the fact that God brings people to salvation without asking our permission or without limiting himself to our work in ministry. So, we do all we can to prevent them from doing the good that they do. At the very least we treat other workers in the vineyard of the Lord with suspicion.

On the one hand, given that early Methodism was enthusiastically committed to evangelism and other forms of ministry—given that they were sure that God had called them to this work—this was an obvious challenge that needed to be addressed. On the other hand, given Wesley's vision of radical evil (that the world was not neutral territory but enemy territory), he implicitly recognized that it was vital to support all who were doing what they could to further the work of God. To make his case in the strongest possible terms, he is fully prepared to support the work not just of Christian heretics but the work of Jews and Muslims.

As part of this he manages to provide a quiet defense of the ministry of lay preaching, and he manages to explain why the best way to deal with bigoted bishops is to ignore their exclusivism. Even then, he hints at why Methodists test candidates for the ministry in terms of both an inward call from God and an outward call from the church they will serve.

Ever the egghead, Wesley traces the fundamental problem back to cognitive malfunction. The intellectual vice that is at the root of bigotry is being too strongly attached to one's own opinions. Even as we cannot avoid having opinions, we need to bear in mind our fallibility and develop an appropriate sense of intellectual and spiritual humility. Thus, his parting shot is that we need to be careful not to be bigots when we attack bigotry!

SERMON 34

Catholic Spirit

"And when he had set out from there, he saw Jehonadab the son of Rechab coming to meet him, and he saluted him, and said to him, 'Is your heart right, as my heart is with your heart?' And Jehonadab answered: 'It is.' 'If it is, give me your hand'" (2 Kings 10:15).

1. It is acknowledged even by those who do not pay this great debt that love is due to all mankind, the royal law, "You shall love your neighbour as yourself," being self-evident to all that hear it: and that not according to the miserable construction put upon it by the zealots of old times, "You shall love your neighbour"—your relation, acquaintance, friend—"and hate your enemy." Not so; "I say unto you," said our Lord, "love your enemies, bless those who curse you, do good to those who hate you, and pray for those who despitefully treat you and persecute you; that you may be the children," may appear so to all mankind, "of your Father in heaven; who makes the sun rise on the evil and on the good, and sends rain on the just and on the unjust."

2. But it is certain that there is a peculiar love which we owe to those that love God. So David: "All my delight is in the saints that are in the earth, and upon such as excel in virtue." And so a greater than he: "A new commandment I give unto you, Love one another, as I have loved you, so you also love one another. By this shall all men know that you are My disciples, if you have love for one another" (John 13:34–35). This is that love on which the Apostle John so frequently and strongly insists: "This," he says, "is the message that you heard from the beginning, that we should love one another" (1 John 3:11). "By this we recognize the love of God, because he laid down his life for us: and we ought," if love should call us to it, "to lay down our lives for the brethren" (verse 16). And again: "Beloved, let us love one another: for love is of God. He that does not love does not know God; for God is love" (4:7–8). "Not that we loved God, but that he loved us, and sent his Son to be the propitiation for our sins. Beloved, if God so loved us, we ought also to love one another" (verses 10–11).

81

SERMON 34

3. All men approve of this, but do all men practise it? Daily experience shows the contrary. Where are even the Christians who "love one another as he has commanded"? How many hindrances lie in the way! The two grand, general hindrances are, first, that they cannot all think alike and in consequence of this, secondly, they cannot all walk alike; but in several smaller points their practice must differ in proportion to the difference of their sentiments.

4. But although a difference in opinions or modes of worship may prevent an entire external union, yet need it prevent our union in affection? Though we cannot think alike, may we not love alike? May we not be of one heart, though we are not of one opinion? Without all doubt, we may. Here all the children of God may unite, notwithstanding these smaller differences. These remaining as they are, we may agree with one another in love and in good works.

5. Surely in this respect the example of Jehu himself, as mixed of character as he was, is well worthy of both the attention and imitation of every serious Christian. "And when he had set out from there, he saw Jehonadab the son of Rechab coming to meet him; and he saluted him, and said to him, 'Is your heart right, as my heart is with your heart?' And Jehonadab answered, 'It is.' 'If it is, give me your hand.'"

The text naturally divides itself into two parts: First, a question proposed by Jehu to Jehonadab: "Is your heart right, as my heart is with your heart?" Secondly, an offer made upon Jehonadab's answer, "It is": "If it is, give me your hand."

I. 1. And, first, let us consider the question proposed by Jehu to Jehonadab, "Is your heart right, as my heart is with your heart?"

The very first thing we may observe in these words is that here is no inquiry concerning Jehonadab's opinions. And yet it is certain he held some which were very uncommon, indeed quite particular to himself; and some which had a close influence upon his practice; on which, likewise, he laid so great a stress as to entail them upon his children's children, to their last generation. This is evident from the account given by Jeremiah many years after his death: "I took Jaazaniah and his brethren and all his sons, and the whole house of the Rechabites, . . . and set before them pots full of wine, and cups, and said to them, 'Drink some wine.' But they said, 'We will drink no wine: for Jonadab,'" or Jehonadab, "'the son of Rechab,

CATHOLIC SPIRIT

our father'" (it would be less ambiguous, if the words were placed thus: "Jehonadab our father, the son of Rechab," out of love and reverence to whom he probably desired his descendants might be called by his name), "'commanded us, saying, "You shall drink no wine, neither you nor your sons forever. Neither shall you build houses, nor sow the seed; nor plant a vineyard, nor have any of these things: but all your days you shall dwell in tents." And we have obeyed and done according to all that Jonadab our father commanded us'" (Jer. 35:3–10).

2. And yet Jehu (although it seems to have been his manner both in things secular and religious, to drive furiously) does not concern himself at all with any of these things but lets Jehonadab abound in his own sense. And neither of them appears to have given the other the least disturbance touching the opinions which he maintained.

3. It is very possible, that many good men now also may entertain peculiar opinions; and some of them may be as peculiar in this as even Jehonadab was. And it is certain, as long as we know but "in part," that no men will see all things alike. It is an unavoidable consequence of the present weakness and shortness of human understanding that several men will be of several minds, in religion as well as in common life. So it has been from the beginning of the world, and so it will be "till the restitution of all things."

4. To go even further: although every man necessarily believes that every particular opinion which he holds is true (for to believe any opinion is not true is the same thing as not to hold it); yet no man can be certain that all his own opinions, taken together, are true. In fact, every thinking man is assured they are not, since *humanum est errare et nescire*, "to be ignorant of many things, and to mistake in some, is the necessary condition of humanity." This, therefore, he is sensible, is his own case. He knows, in general, that he himself is mistaken; although in what particulars he is mistaken he does not, perhaps cannot, know.

5. I say "perhaps he cannot know"; for who can tell how far invincible ignorance (or—which amounts to the same thing—invincible prejudice) may extend, which is often so planted in tender minds that it is afterwards impossible to tear up what has taken so deep

SERMON 34

a root. And who can say, unless he knew every circumstance attending it, how far any mistake is culpable, since all guilt must suppose some agreement in the will; which he alone can judge who searches the heart?

6. Every wise man, therefore, will allow others the same liberty of thinking which he desires they should allow him; and will no more insist on their embracing his opinions than he would have them to insist on his embracing theirs. He bears with those who differ from him, and only asks him with whom he desires to unite in love that single question, "Is your heart right, as my heart is with your heart?"

7. We may, secondly, observe that here is no inquiry made concerning Jehonadab's mode of worship, even though it is highly probable there was, in this respect also, a very wide difference between them. For we may well believe Jehonadab, as well as all his posterity, worshipped God at Jerusalem, whereas Jehu did not: he had more regard to state policy than religion. And therefore, although he slew the worshippers of Baal and "eradicated Baal out of Israel," yet from the convenient sin of Jeroboam, the worship of the "golden calves," he "departed not" (2 Kings 10:29).

8. But even among men of an upright heart, men who desire to "have a conscience void of offence," it must necessarily be that, as long as there are various opinions, there will be various ways of worshipping God; since a variety of opinion necessarily implies a variety of practice. And as in all ages men have differed in nothing more than in their opinions concerning the Supreme Being, so in nothing have they more differed from each other than in the manner of worshipping him. Had this been only in the heathen world, it would not have been at all surprising: for we know, these "through" their "wisdom did not know God"; nor, therefore, could they know how to worship him. But is it not strange that even in the Christian world, although they all agree in the general, "God is Spirit; and they that worship him must worship him in spirit and in truth"; yet the particular modes of worshipping God are almost as varied as among the heathens?

9. And how shall we choose among so much variety? No man can choose for, or prescribe to, another. But everyone must follow the

dictates of his own conscience, in simplicity and godly sincerity. He must be fully persuaded in his own mind and then act according to the best light he has. Nor has any creature power to constrain another to walk by his own rule. God has given no right to any of the children of men thus to lord it over the conscience of his brothers; but every man must judge for himself, as every man must give an account of himself to God.

10. Therefore, although every follower of Christ is obliged, by the very nature of the Christian institution, to be a member of some particular congregation or other, some Church, as it is usually termed (which implies a particular manner of worshipping God; for "two cannot walk together unless they be agreed"); yet none can be obliged by any power on earth but that of his own conscience to prefer this or that congregation to another, this or that particular manner of worship. I know it is commonly supposed that the place of our birth fixes the Church to which we ought to belong; that one, for instance, who is born in England ought to be a member of that which is styled the Church of England, and consequently, to worship God in the particular manner which is prescribed by that Church. I was once a zealous maintainer of this; but I find many reasons to back off from this zeal. I fear it is attended with such difficulties as no reasonable man can get over. Not the least of which is, that if this rule had taken precedence, there could have been no Reformation from Roman Catholicism, since it entirely destroys the right of private judgment on which that whole Reformation stands.

11. I dare not, therefore, presume to impose my mode of worship on any other. I believe it is truly primitive and apostolic: but my belief is no rule for another. I ask not, therefore, of him with whom I would unite in love, "Are you of my church, of my congregation? Do you receive the same form of church government and allow the same church officers with me? Do you join in the same form of prayer in which I worship God?" I do not ask, "Do you receive the supper of the Lord in the same posture and manner that I do?" Nor whether, in the administration of baptism, you agree with me in admitting sureties for the baptized, in the manner of administering it; or the age of those to whom it should be administered. I do

not even ask of you (as clear as I am in my own mind), whether you allow baptism and the Lord's Supper at all. Let all these things stand by: we will talk of them, if need be, at a more convenient season; my only question at present is this: "Is your heart right, as my heart is with your heart?"

12. But what is properly implied in the question? I do not mean, "What did Jehu imply in it?" but, "What should a follower of Christ understand by it when he proposes it to any of his brethren?" The first thing implied is this: Is your heart right with God? Do you believe his being and his perfections? His eternity, immensity, wisdom, power? His justice, mercy, and truth? Do you believe that he now "maintains all things by the word of his power," and that he governs even the most minute, even the most noxious, to his own glory, and the good of them that love him? Have you a divine evidence, a supernatural conviction, of the things of God? Do you "walk by faith not by sight," looking not at temporal things, but things eternal?

13. Do you believe in the Lord Jesus Christ, "God over all, blessed forever"? Is he revealed in your soul? Do you know Jesus Christ and him crucified? Does he dwell in you and you in him? Is he formed in your heart by faith? Having absolutely relinquished all your own works, your own righteousness, have you "submitted yourself to the righteousness of God which is by faith in Christ Jesus"? Are you "found in him, not having your own righteousness, but the righteousness which is by faith"? And are you, through him, "fighting the good fight of faith, and laying hold of eternal life"?

14. Is your faith ἐνεργουμένη δἰ ἀγάπης—"filled with the energy of love"? Do you love God (I do not say "above all things," for it is both an unscriptural and an ambiguous expression, but) "with all your heart, and with all your mind, and with all your soul, and with all your strength"? Do you seek all your happiness in him alone? And do you find what you seek? Does your soul continually "magnify the Lord, and your spirit rejoice in God your Saviour"? Having learned "in everything to give thanks," do you find "it is a joyful and a pleasant thing to be thankful"? Is God the centre of your soul, the sum of all your desires? Are you accordingly laying up your treasure in heaven, and counting everything else dung

and dross? Has the love of God cast the love of the world out of your soul? Then you are "crucified to the world"; you are dead to all below; and your "life is hid with Christ in God."

15. Are you employed in doing not your own will, but the will of him that sent you; of him that sent you down to sojourn here a while, to spend a few days in a strange land until, having finished the work he has given you to do, you return to your Father's house? Is it your food and drink to do the will of your Father which is in heaven? Is your eye single in all things? always fixed on him? always looking to Jesus? Do you point at him in whatever you do? in all your labour, your business, your conversation? aiming only at the glory of God in all, "whatever you do, either in word or deed, doing it all in the name of the Lord Jesus; giving thanks unto God, even the Father, through him"?

16. Does the love of God constrain you to serve him with fear, to "rejoice before him with reverence"? Are you more afraid of displeasing God than of either death or hell? Is nothing so terrible to you as the thought of offending the eyes of his glory? For this reason, do you "hate all evil ways," every transgression of his holy and perfect law; and thus "make every effort to have a conscience clear of offence toward God, and toward man"?

17. Is your heart right toward your neighbour? Do you love as yourself, all mankind, without exception? "If you love those only that love you, what does that merit you"? Do you "love your enemies"? Is your soul full of good-will, of tender affection, toward them? Do you love even the enemies of God, the unthankful and unholy? Does your heart ache for them? Could you "wish yourself" temporally "cursed" for their sake? And do you show this by "blessing those who curse you, and praying for those who spitefully treat you, and persecute you"?

18. Do you show your love by your works? While you have time, as you have opportunity, do you in fact "do good to all men," neighbours or strangers, friends or enemies, good or bad? Do you do them all the good you can; endeavouring to supply all their needs; assisting them both in body and soul, to the uttermost of your power? If you are thus minded, may every Christian say, even if you only

sincerely desire it and are going on until you attain it, then "your heart is right, as my heart is with your heart."

II. 1. "If it be, give me your hand." I do not mean, "Be of my opinion." You need not: I do not expect or desire it. Neither do I mean, "I will be of your opinion." I cannot, it does not depend on my choice: I can no more think, than I can see or hear, as I will. You keep your opinion; I mine; and that as steadily as ever. You need not even try to come over to me or bring me over to you. I do not ask you to argue for those points, or to hear or speak one word concerning them. Let all opinions alone on one side and the other: only "give me your hand."

2. I do not mean, "Embrace my modes of worship," or, "I will embrace yours." This also is a thing which does not depend either on your choice or mine. We must both act as each is fully persuaded in his own mind. You hold fast that which you believe is most acceptable to God, and I will do the same. I believe the Episcopal form of church government to be scriptural and apostolic. If you think the Presbyterian or Independent is better, think so still, and act accordingly. I believe infants ought to be baptized; and that this may be done either by dipping or sprinkling. If you are otherwise persuaded, be so still, and follow your own persuasion. It appears to me, that forms of prayer are of excellent use, particularly in the great congregation. If you judge extemporaneous prayer to be of more use, act according to your own judgment. My sentiment is that I ought not to forbid water in which persons may be baptized; and that I ought to eat bread and drink wine as a memorial of my dying Master; however, if you are not convinced of this, act according to the light you have. I have no desire to debate with you one minute upon any of the preceding heads. Let all these smaller points stand aside. Let them never come into sight "If your heart is as my heart," if you love God and all humankind, I ask no more: "give me your hand."

3. I mean, first, love me: and that not only as you love all mankind; not only as you love your enemies or the enemies of God, those that hate you, that "spitefully treat you and persecute you"; not only as a stranger, as one of whom you know neither good nor evil—I am not satisfied with this—no; "if your heart be right, as

mine with your heart," then love me with a very tender affection, as a friend that is closer than a brother; as a brother in Christ, a fellow citizen of the New Jerusalem, a fellow soldier engaged in the same warfare, under the same Captain of our salvation. Love me as a companion in the kingdom and patience of Jesus, and a joint heir of his glory.

4. Love me (but in a higher degree than you do the bulk of mankind) with the love that is long-suffering and kind; that is patient—if I am ignorant or out of the way, bearing and not increasing my burden; and is tender, soft, and compassionate still; that is not envious if at any time it pleases God to prosper me in his work even more than you. Love me with the love that is not easily provoked, either at my follies or infirmities; or even at my acting (if it should sometimes so appear to you) not according to the will of God. Love me so as to think no evil of me; to put away all jealousy and evil-surmising. Love me with the love that covers over all things; that never reveals either my faults or infirmities—that believes all things; is always willing to think the best, to put the fairest construction on all my words and actions—that hopes all things; either that the thing related was never done; or not done with such circumstances as are related; or, at least, that it was done with a good-intention, or in a sudden stress of temptation. And hopes to the end that whatever is amiss will, by the grace of God, be corrected; and whatever is wanting, supplied through the riches of his mercy in Christ Jesus.

5. I mean, secondly, commend me to God in all your prayers; wrestle with him on my behalf that he would speedily correct what he sees amiss, and supply what is wanting in me. In your nearest access to the throne of grace, beg of him who is then very present with you that my heart may be more as your heart, more right both toward God and toward man; that I may have a fuller conviction of things not seen, and a stronger view of the love of God in Christ Jesus; may more steadily walk by faith, not by sight; and more earnestly grasp eternal life. Pray that the love of God and of all mankind may be more largely poured into my heart; that I may be more fervent and active in doing the will of my Father which is in heaven, more zealous of good works, and more careful to abstain from all appearance of evil.

SERMON 34

6. I mean, thirdly, provoke me to love and to good works. Second your prayer, as you have opportunity, by speaking to me, in love, whatever you believe to be for my soul's health. Quicken me in the work which God has given me to do and instruct me how to do it more perfectly. Yes, even "smite me as a friend, and reprove me," whenever I appear to you to be doing my own will rather than the will of him that sent me. O speak and spare not, whatever you believe may conduce to amending my faults, strengthening my weakness, building me up in love, or making me more fit, in any way, for the Master's use.

7. I mean, lastly, love me not in word only, but in deed and truth. As far as you can in good conscience (retaining still your own opinions and your own manner of worshipping God), join with me in the work of God; and let us go on hand in hand. And thus far, it is certain, you may go. Speak honourably of the work of God wherever you are, by whomsoever he works, and kindly of his messengers. And, if it is in your power, not only sympathize with them when they are in any difficulty or distress, but give them a cheerful and effectual assistance, that they may glorify God on your behalf.

8. Two things should be observed with regard to what has been spoken under this last head: One, that whatever love, whatever offices of love, whatever spiritual or temporal assistance, I claim from him whose heart is right, as my heart is with his, the same I am ready, by the grace of God, according to my measure, to give him: Two, that I have not made this claim on behalf of myself alone, but of all whose heart is right toward God and man, that we may all love one another as Christ has loved us.

III. 1. One inference we may make from what has been said. We may learn from hence, what is a catholic spirit.

There is scarcely any expression which has been more grossly misunderstood, and more dangerously misapplied, than this: but it will be easy for any who calmly consider the preceding observations to correct any such misapprehensions of it, and to prevent any such misapplication.

For from hence we may learn, first, that a catholic spirit is not speculative latitudinarianism. It is not an indifference to all opinions:

this is the spawn of hell, not the offspring of heaven. This unsettledness of thought, this being "driven to and fro, and tossed about with every wind of doctrine," is a great curse, not a blessing; an irreconcilable enemy, not a friend, to true catholicism. A man of a truly catholic spirit has not now his religion to seek. He is fixed as the sun in his judgment concerning the main branches of Christian doctrine. It is true, he is always ready to hear and weigh whatever can be offered against his principles; but as this does not show any wavering in his own mind, so neither does it occasion any. He does not stand between two opinions, nor vainly endeavour to blend them into one. Observe this, you who know not of what spirit you are: who call yourselves men of a catholic spirit only because you are of a muddy understanding; because your mind is all in a mist; because you have no settled, consistent principles but are for jumbling all opinions together. Be convinced that you have quite missed your way; you know not where you are. You think you have come into the very spirit of Christ; when in truth, you are nearer the spirit of Antichrist. Go, first, and learn the first elements of the gospel of Christ, and then you shall learn to be of a truly catholic spirit.

2. From what has been said, we may learn, secondly, that a catholic spirit is not any kind of practical latitudinarianism. It is not indifference as to public worship, or as to the outward manner of performing it. This, likewise, would not be a blessing but a curse. Far from being a help to those, it would, so long as it remained, be an unspeakable hindrance to the worshipping of God in spirit and in truth. But the man of a truly catholic spirit, having weighed all things in the balance of the sanctuary, has no doubt, no scruple at all, concerning that particular mode of worship in which he joins. He is clearly convinced that this manner of worshipping God is both scriptural and rational. He knows none in the world which is more scriptural, none which is more rational. Therefore, without rambling hither and thither, he cleaves close to it, and praises God for the opportunity of so doing.

3. Hence we may, thirdly, learn that a catholic spirit is not indifference to all congregations. This is another sort of latitudinarianism, no less absurd and unscriptural than the former. But it is far from a

man of a truly catholic spirit. He is fixed in his congregation as well as his principles. He is united to one, not only in spirit, but by all the outward ties of Christian fellowship. There he partakes of all the ordinances of God. There he receives the supper of the Lord. There he pours out his soul in public prayer and joins in public praise and thanksgiving. There he rejoices to hear the word of reconciliation, the gospel of the grace of God. With these his nearest, his best-beloved brethren, on solemn occasions, he seeks God by fasting. These particularly he watches over in love, as they do over his soul; admonishing, exhorting, comforting, reproving, and every way building up each other in the faith. These he regards as his own household; and therefore, according to the ability God has given him, naturally cares for them, and provides that they may have all the things that are needful for life and godliness.

4. But while he is steadily fixed in his religious principles in what he believes to be the truth as it is in Jesus; while he firmly adheres to that worship of God which he judges to be most acceptable in his sight; and while he is united by the most tender and close ties to one particular congregation, his heart is enlarged toward all mankind, those he knows and those he does not; he embraces with strong and cordial affection both neighbours and strangers, friends and enemies. This is catholic or universal love. And he that has this is of a catholic spirit. For love alone gives the title to this character: catholic love is a catholic spirit.

5. If, then, we take this word in the strictest sense, a man of a catholic spirit is one who, in the manner above-mentioned, gives his hand to all whose hearts are right with his heart: one who knows how to value, and praise God for, all the advantages he enjoys with regard to the knowledge of the things of God, the true scriptural manner of worshipping him, and, above all, his union with a congregation fearing God and working righteousness: one who, retaining these blessings with the strictest care, keeping them as the apple of his eye, at the same time loves—as friends, as brothers in the Lord, as members of Christ and children of God, as joint partakers now of the present kingdom of God, and fellow heirs of his eternal kingdom—all, of whatever opinion or worship, or congregation,

CATHOLIC SPIRIT

who believe in the Lord Jesus Christ; who love God and man; who, rejoicing to please and fearing to offend God, are careful to abstain from evil, and zealous of good works. He is the man of a truly catholic spirit who bears all these continually upon his heart; who, having an unspeakable tenderness for their persons, and longing for their welfare, does not cease to commend them to God in prayer, as well as to plead their cause before men; who speaks encouragement to them, and labours, by all his words, to strengthen their hands in God. He assists them to the uttermost of his power in all things, spiritual and temporal. He is ready "to spend and be spent for them"; yes, even to lay down his life for their sake.

6. You, O man of God, think on these things! If you are already in this way, go on. If you have until now mistaken the path, thank God who has brought you back! And now run the race which is set before you, in the royal way of universal love. Take heed, lest you be either wavering in your judgment or hardened in your sympathies: but keep an even pace, rooted in the faith once delivered to the saints, and grounded in love, in true catholic love, till you are swallowed up in love for ever and ever!

> Weary of all this wordy strife,
> These notions, forms, and modes, and names,
> To You, the way, the Truth, the Life,
> Whose love my simple heart inflames,
> Divinely taught, at last I fly,
> With You and Yours to live and die.
> Forth from the midst of Babel brought,
> Parties and sects I cast behind;
> Enlarged my heart, and free my thought,
> Where'er the latent truth I find
> The latent truth with joy to own,
> And bow to Jesus' name alone.
> Redeemed by Your almighty grace,
> I taste my glorious liberty,
> With open arms the world embrace,
> But cleave to those who cleave to You;
> But only in Your saints delight,

Who walk with God in purest white.
One with the little flock I rest,
The members sound who hold the head.
The chosen few, with pardon blest
And by th' anointing Spirit led
Into the mind that was in You
Into the depths of Deity.
My brethren, friends, and kinsmen these
Who do my heavenly Father's will;
Who aim at perfect holiness,
And all Your counsels to fulfil,
Athirst to be whate'er You are,
And love their God with all their heart.
For these, howe'er in flesh disjoined,
Where'er dispersed o'er earth abroad,
Unfeigned, unbounded love I find
And constant as the life of God
Fountain of life, from thence it sprung,
As pure, as even, and as strong.
Joined to the hidden church unknown
In this sure bond of perfectness
Obscurely safe, I dwell alone
And glory in th' uniting grace,
To me, to each believer given,
To all Your saints in earth and heaven.
—Charles Wesley

For Readers

Questions

1. What exactly is the problem that this sermon attempts to address?

2. Why is it impossible to reach agreement on matters of opinion in religion?

3. How should we relate to those who disagree deeply with us?

4. What areas of agreement does Wesley use as a limit on diversity of opinion?

5. Does diversity of opinion apply within a Christian denomination or across denominations? Is the issue one of interdenominational dispute or cross-denominational dispute?

Helpful Information

The scriptural text used in Sermon 34 is clearly a pretext. It is in fact a crazy text to use if read in its original context. However, this is beside the point. Wesley has other fish to fry, and, like many preachers, he uses the text as a clever tagline.

The problem he is seeking to address is an acute one. Christians cannot agree on crucial issues relative to being together in one organic body. They lack complete knowledge, they are fallible in their thinking, and they are shaped by radically different backgrounds. So, what should we do? In the end, Wesley resorts to an appeal to the royal law of love. But this is a very general solution. We need something more concrete.

The basic solution is to allow for liberty of opinion and practice, freedom of conscience, and private judgment within a broader framework of agreement about God, Jesus, faith, readiness to serve God, and enacted love of the neighbor. There is no point in trying to impose your opinions across the board. Instead let us love each other, be patient and long-suffering, and provoke one another to love and good works. So, abandon the game of denominational one-upmanship and cross-border strife. Let there be the royal law of love.

This in no way means that you stand alone on the sidelines of church life. You get clear on what you believe, and you belong wholeheartedly to one denomination or another. You subject yourself to its beliefs, practices, and disciplines. In this arena, there will be no pluralism; there will be definitive beliefs and practices. However, across the denominations you allow for lots of tolerance and do all you can to exercise understanding and love.

In the twentieth century, Christian leaders rejected this vision and worked tirelessly to secure one organic church. This has failed, as we can see with the new divisions that have developed in all major forms of Christianity. So, Wesley's advice deserves a fresh run for its money in our day. We might improve on excellence at this point by seeking out the gifts of the Holy Spirit across the Christian churches and making sure we are open to all that the Holy Spirit wants us to be.

Editor's Introduction to Sermons 35–37

These three sermons very clearly belong together. In different ways they deal with serious difficulties that arise because of the high calling that Wesley sees as central to real Christianity. The whole thrust of Wesley's vision of the gospel centers on the real possibility of radical transformation here and now through the work of grace. The term he uses for this is *Christian perfection*, clearly a notion is that is bound to generate skepticism. We should not be distracted by the language. Wesley defends it because it is biblical, and he inherited a tradition that spoke naturally as he does. However, this is a matter of semantics. He is happy to substitute other language: holiness, entire sanctification, perfect love, the restoration of the image of God, and the like. He will not for a moment abandon his deep conviction that God can do more for our sins than forgive them. We do not have to live morally and spiritually defeated lives. Genuine sanctity is possible. The argument for this is not drawn from abstract principles, but from detailed exegesis of the New Testament, not least from the teaching of Christ himself.

Here's the rub. What should be done if this high calling fails to pan out? What if these great expectations turn out to be illusory or exaggerated? What if the expectations paradoxically become a spiritual snare and handicap? Clearly, all these options are not just likely; they actually show up in our experience. At this point Wesley could abandon his claim, or he could make transformation an impossible ideal, or he might confine it to a select few who are lucky enough or spiritually strenuous enough to become truly transformed from top to bottom. Wesley does not take any of these relatively easy ways to solve the problems that naturally arise. So, he charts his own response in the three sermons under review.

In Sermon 35, he provides a careful overview of what is and is not possible. In this case, he sets out to correct misunderstandings and to provide a more realistic account of what is possible. In Sermon 36, he tackles the problem of wandering thoughts. If the Christian life is marked by the single intention to please God, what should we make of the wandering thoughts that inevitably arise? Are these incompatible with the practice of

Christian holiness? In Sermon 37, he shows amazing psychological insight for dealing with the effects of failure by tackling head on the obvious gap between aspiration and actuality. In a throwaway comment, he even notes the danger of envy. Here is a person who has been a believer for years and feels nothing but abject failure in dealing with sin. Then, along comes a recent convert who seems to be making incredible progress. So, envy sets in, and murmuring against God, and maybe even anger at those who have presented him with this whole vision of transformation.

One of the interesting features that stand out in these sermons is the strong emphasis on the Christian life as one of progress driven by high expectations and hopes. Some later Methodists, drawing on other material in Wesley, were tempted by a kind of big-bang conception of change. They looked for a single moment when they could become all that God wanted them to be. Clearly in these sermons, this is not the vision that is in play, even though that vision does not exclude moments of crisis or a kind of second conversion. Wesley even notes at one point that we should leave issues of timing entirely up to God.

SERMON 35

Christian Perfection

"Not as though I had already attained it or were already perfect" (Phil. 3:12).

1. There is scarcely any expression in Holy Writ which has given more offence than this. The word "perfect" is what many cannot bear. The very sound of it is an abomination to them. And whoever "preaches perfection" (as the phrase goes); that is, asserts that it is attainable in this life, runs the great hazard of being accounted by them worse than a heathen man or a publican.

2. And hence some have advised to completely lay aside the use of those expressions, "because they have given so great offence." But are they not found in the oracles of God? If so, by what authority can any Messenger of God lay them aside, even though all men should be offended? We have not so learned from Christ; neither may we thus give place to the Devil. Whatever God has spoken, that will we speak, whether men will hear or not; knowing that then alone can any Minister of Christ be "innocent of the blood of all men," when he has "not refused to declare to them all the counsel of God" (Acts 20:26–27).

3. We may not, therefore, lay these expressions aside, since they are the words of God and not of man. But we may and ought to explain the meaning of them, that those who are sincere of heart may not go wide to the right or to the left, from the mark of the prize of their high calling. And this is all the more necessary because in the verse already repeated the Apostle speaks of himself as not perfect: "Not," says he, "as though I were already perfect." And yet immediately after, in the fifteenth verse, he speaks of himself, indeed and many others too, as perfect. "Let us," says he, "as many as are perfect, be thus minded" (Phil. 3:15).

4. In order, therefore, to remove the difficulty arising from this seeming contradiction, as well as to give light to those who are pressing forward to the mark, and that those who are lame be not turned out of the way, I shall endeavour to show,

>First, in what sense Christians are not; and,
>Secondly, in what sense they are, perfect.

SERMON 35

I. 1. In the first place I shall endeavour to show in what sense Christians are not perfect. And both from experience and Scripture it appears, first, that they are not perfect in knowledge: they are not so perfect in this life as to be free from ignorance. They know, it may be, in common with other men, many things relating to the present world; and they know, with regard to the world to come, the general truths which God has revealed. They know, likewise (which the natural man does not comprehend, for these things are spiritually discerned) "what manner of love" it is with which "the Father" has loved them, "that they should be called the sons of God" (1 John 3:1). They know the mighty working of his Spirit in their hearts (Eph. 3:16); and the wisdom of his providence, directing all their paths (Prov. 3:6), and causing all things to work together for their good (Rom. 8:28). Yes, they know in every circumstance of life what the Lord requires of them, and how to keep a conscience void of offence toward both God and man (Acts 24:16).

2. But numberless are the things which they do not know. Concerning the Almighty himself, they cannot search him out to perfection. "Look, these are but a part of his ways; but the thunder of his power who can understand?" (Job 26:14). They cannot understand, I will not say, how "there are Three that bear record in heaven, the Father, the Son, and the Holy Spirit, and these three are one" (1 John 5:7); or how the eternal Son of God "took upon himself the form of a servant" (Phil. 2:7); but not any one attribute, not any one circumstance of the divine nature. Neither is it for them to know the times and seasons when God will work his great works upon the earth; no, not even those which he has in part revealed by his servants and Prophets since the world began. Much less do they know when God, having "accomplished the number of his elect, will hasten his kingdom"; when "the heavens shall pass away with a great noise, and the elements shall melt with fervent heat" (2 Pet. 3:10).

3. They know not the reasons even of many of his present dealings with the sons of men; but are constrained to rest here—though "clouds and darkness are round about him, righteousness and judgment are the habitation of his seat" (Ps. 97:2). Indeed, often with regard to his dealings with themselves, their Lord will say to

them, "What I do, you do not understand now; but later you shall understand" (John 13:7). And how little do they know of what is ever before them, of even the visible works of his hands!—how "he spreads the North over the empty place and hangs the earth from nothing" (Job 26:7); how he unites all the parts of this vast machine by a secret chain which cannot be broken? So great is the ignorance, so very little the knowledge, of even the best of men!

4. No one, then, is so perfect in this life as to be free from ignorance. Nor, secondly, from mistake; which indeed is almost an unavoidable consequence of it; seeing as those who "know only in part" (1 Cor. 13:12) are always prone to error concerning the things which they do not know. It is true, the children of God do not make mistakes concerning the things essential to salvation: they do not "take darkness for light or light for darkness" (Isa. 5:20); nor "seek death in the error of their life" (Wisdom 1:12). For they are "taught by God," and the way which he teaches them, the way of holiness, is so plain that "the wayfaring man, though a fool, does not go wrong in it" (Isa. 35:8). But in things unessential to salvation they do go wrong, and that frequently. The best and wisest of men are frequently mistaken even with regard to facts; believing those things not to have been which really were, or those to have been done which were not. Or, supposing they are not mistaken as to the fact itself, they may be with regard to its circumstances; believing them, or many of them, to have been quite different from what in truth they were. And from this cannot but arise many further mistakes. Hence they may believe either past or present actions which were or are evil to be good; and such as were or are good to be evil. Hence also they may judge not according to truth with regard to the characters of men; and that not only by supposing good men to be better, or wicked men to be worse, than they are, but by believing them to have been or to be good men who were or are very wicked; or perhaps those to have been or to be wicked men, who were or are holy and blameless.

5. Even with regard to the Holy Scriptures themselves, as careful as they are to avoid it, the best of men are prone to mistakes, and do make mistakes every day; especially with respect to those parts which less directly relate to practice. Hence even the children of

SERMON 35

God are not agreed as to the interpretation of many places in holy writ: nor is their difference of opinion any proof that they are not the children of God on either side; but it is a proof that we are no more to expect any living man to be infallible than to be omniscient.

6. If it be objected to what has been observed under this and the preceding head, that St. John, speaking to his brethren in the faith says, "You have an anointing from the Holy One, and you know all things" (1 John 2:20), the answer is plain: "You know all things that are needful for your souls' health" (cf. 3 John 2). That the Apostle never intended to extend this further, that he could not speak it in an absolute sense, is clear, first, from hence—that otherwise he would describe the disciple as "above his Master"; seeing Christ himself, as a man, knew not all things: "Of that hour," says he, "no one knows; not even the Son, but the Father only" (Mark 13:32). It is clear, secondly, from the Apostle's own words that follow: "These things have I written to you concerning them that deceive you" (cf. 1 John 3:7); as well as from his frequently repeated caution, "Let no man deceive you"; which would have been altogether unnecessary had not those very persons who had that anointing from the Holy One (1 John 2:20) been liable not to ignorance only, but also to mistake.

7. Even Christians, therefore, are not so perfect as to be free either from ignorance or error. We may, thirdly, add, nor from infirmities. Only let us take care to understand this word rightly: only let us not give that soft title to known sins, as the manner of some is. So, one man tells us, "Every man has his weakness, and mine is drunkenness." Another has the infirmity of uncleanness; another of taking God's holy name in vain; and yet another has the infirmity of calling his brother, "You fool" (Matt. 5:22), or returning "insult for insult" (1 Pet. 3:9). It is plain that all of you who thus speak, if you do not repent, shall, with your infirmities, go alive into hell! But I mean here not only those which are properly termed bodily infirmities, but all those inward or outward imperfections which are not of a moral nature. Such are the weakness or slowness of understanding, dullness or confusedness of apprehension, incoherence of thought, unusual quickness or heaviness of imagination. Such (to mention no more of this kind) is the lack of a ready or retentive memory.

CHRISTIAN PERFECTION

Such in another kind are those which are commonly, in some measure, consequent upon these; namely, slowness of speech, impropriety of language, ungracefulness of pronunciation; to which one might add a thousand nameless defects, either in conversation or behaviour. These are the infirmities which are found in the best of men in a larger or smaller proportion. And from these none can hope to be perfectly freed until the spirit returns to God who gave it (Eccles. 12:7).

8. Nor can we expect, till then, to be wholly free from temptation. Such perfection does not belong to this life. It is true, there are those who, being given up to work all uncleanness with greediness (Eph. 4:19), scarcely perceive the temptations which they do not resist and so seem to be without temptation. There are also many whom the wise enemy of souls, seeing to be fast asleep in the dead form of godliness, will not tempt to gross sin, lest they should awake before they drop into everlasting burnings. I know there are also children of God who, being now justified freely (Rom. 5:1), having found redemption in the blood of Christ (Eph. 1:7), for the present feel no temptation. God has said to their enemies, "Do not touch my anointed, and do my children no harm." And for this season, it may be for weeks or months, he causes them to "ride on high places" (Deut. 32:13); he bears them as on eagles' wings (Exod. 19:4), above all the fiery darts of the wicked one (Eph. 6:16). But this state will not last forever; as we may learn from that single consideration—that the Son of God himself, in the days of his flesh, was tempted even to the end of his life (Heb. 2:18; 4:15; 6:7). Therefore, so let his servant expect to be; for "it is enough that he be as his Master" (Luke 6:40).

9. Christian perfection, therefore, does not imply (as some men seem to have imagined) an exemption either from ignorance or mistake, or infirmities or temptations. Indeed, it is only another term for holiness. They are two names for the same thing. Thus every one that is perfect is holy, and every one that is holy is, in the Scripture sense, perfect. Yet we may, lastly, observe that neither in this respect is there any absolute perfection on earth. There is no perfection of degrees, as it is termed; none which does not admit of a continual increase. So however much any man has attained, or in however high a degree he is perfect, he still has need to "grow in grace"

103

SERMON 35

(2 Pet. 3:18) and daily to advance in the knowledge and love of God his Saviour.

II. 1. In what sense, then, are Christians perfect? This is what I shall endeavour, in the second place, to show. But it should be premised that there are several stages in the Christian life, as in the natural; some of the children of God being but newborn babies; others having attained to more maturity. And accordingly St. John, in his first Epistle (1 John 2:12, etc.), applies himself differently to those he terms little children, those he styles young men, and those whom he entitles fathers. "I write to you, little children," says the Apostle, "because your sins are forgiven": because you have attained thus far, being "justified freely," you "have peace with God, through Jesus Christ" (Rom. 5:1). "I write to you, young men, because you have overcome the wicked one"; or (as he afterwards adds), "because you are strong, and the word of God abides in you" (1 John 2:13–14). You have quenched the fiery darts of the wicked one (Eph. 6:16), the doubts and fears with which he disturbed your first peace; and the witness of God, that your sins are forgiven, now abides in your heart. "I write to you, fathers, because you have known him that is from the beginning" (1 John 2:13). You have known both the Father and the Son and the Spirit of Christ, in your innermost soul. You are "perfect men, being grown up to the measure of the stature of the fullness of Christ" (Eph. 4:13).

2. It is of these chiefly I speak in the latter part of this discourse: for these alone are properly Christians. But even babes in Christ are in such a sense perfect or born of God (an expression also taken in diverse senses) as, first, not to commit sin. If any doubt of this privilege of the sons of God, the question is not to be decided by abstract arguments, which may be drawn out to an endless length and leave the point just as it was before. Neither is it to be determined by the experience of this or that particular person. Many may suppose they do not commit sin when they do; but this proves nothing either way. To the law and to the testimony we appeal. "Let God be true, and every man a liar" (Rom. 3:4). By his Word will we abide, and that alone. By it we should be judged.

3. Now the Word of God plainly declares that even those who are justified, who are born again in the lowest sense, "do not continue

CHRISTIAN PERFECTION

in sin"; that they cannot "live in it any longer" (Rom. 6:1–2); that they are "planted together in the likeness of the death" of Christ (Rom. 6:5); that their "old man is crucified with him," the body of sin being destroyed, so that henceforth they do not serve sin; that being dead with Christ, they are free from sin (Rom. 6:6–7); that they are "dead unto sin, and alive unto God" (Rom. 6:11); that "sin has no more dominion over them," who are "not under the law, but under grace"; but that these, "being freed from sin, have been made the servants of righteousness" (Rom. 6:14–18).

4. The very least which can be implied in these words is that the persons spoken of there, namely, all real Christians, or believers in Christ, are made free from outward sin. And the same freedom, which St. Paul here expresses in such variety of phrases, St. Peter expresses in that one (1 Pet. 4:1–2): "He who has suffered in the flesh has ceased from sin—that he no longer should live according to the desires of men, but to the will of God." For this "ceasing from sin," if interpreted in the lowest sense, as regarding only the outward behaviour, must denote the ceasing from the outward act, from any outward transgression of the law.

as opposed to inward ?

5. But most direct are the well-known words of St. John, in the third chapter of his First Epistle, verse 8, etc.: "He who commits sin is of the Devil; for the Devil was a sinner from the beginning. For this purpose the Son of God was manifested, that he might destroy the works of the Devil. Whoever is born of God does not commit sin; for his seed remains in him: And he cannot sin because he is born of God" (1 John 3:8–9). And those in the fifth: "We know that whoever is born of God does not sin; but he who is begotten of God is kept safe and that wicked one does not touch him" (1 John 5:18).

6. Indeed it is said this means only "He does not sin willfully"; or "he does not commit sin habitually; or, not as other men do; or, not as he did before." But by whom is this said? By St. John? No. There is no such word in the text; nor in the whole chapter; nor in all his Epistle; nor in any part of his writings whatsoever. Why then, the best way to answer a bold assertion is simply to deny it. And if any man can prove it from the Word of God, let him bring forth his strong reasons.

105

SERMON 35

7. And a sort of reason there is, which has been frequently brought to support these strange assertions, drawn from the examples recorded in the Word of God: "What!" say they, "did not Abraham himself commit sin, lying, and denying his marriage? Did not Moses commit sin when he provoked God at the waters of strife? Indeed, to produce one for all, did not even David, 'the man after God's own heart,' commit sin in the matter of Uriah the Hittite; even murder and adultery?" It is most sure he did. All this is true. But what is it you would infer from this? It may be granted, first, that David in the general course of his life was one of the holiest men among the Jews; and, secondly, that the holiest men among the Jews did sometimes commit sin. But if you would infer from this that all Christians do and must commit sin as long as they live, this consequence we utterly deny; it will never follow from those premises.

8. Those who argue thus seem never to have considered that declaration of our Lord (Matt. 11:11): "Truly I say to you, among those who are born of women there has not risen a greater than John the Baptist; nevertheless, the least person in the kingdom of heaven is greater than he." I fear, indeed, there are some who have imagined "the kingdom of heaven," here, to mean the kingdom of glory; as if the Son of God had just revealed to us that the least glorified saint in heaven is greater than any man on earth! To mention this is sufficiently to refute it. There can, therefore, no doubt be made, but "the kingdom of heaven," here (as in the following verse, where it is said to be taken by force) (Matt. 11:12) or "the kingdom of God," as St. Luke expresses it, is that kingdom of God on earth to which all true believers in Christ, all real Christians, belong. In these words, then, our Lord declares two things. First, that before his coming in the flesh, among all the children of men there had not been one greater than John the Baptist; from which it evidently follows that neither Abraham, David, nor any Jew was greater than John. Our Lord, secondly, declares that he who is least in the kingdom of God (in that kingdom which he came to set up on earth, and which the violent now began to take by force) is greater than he: not a greater prophet as some have interpreted the word; for this is palpably false in fact; but greater in the grace of God and the

knowledge of our Lord Jesus Christ. Therefore, we cannot measure the privileges of real Christians by those formerly given to the Jews. Their "ministration" (or dispensation), we allow "was glorious"; but ours "exceeds in glory" (2 Cor. 3:7–9). So whoever would bring down the Christian dispensation to the Jewish standard, whoever gleans up the examples of weakness recorded in the Law and the Prophets, and thence infers that they who have "put on Christ" (Gal. 3:27) are endued with no greater strength, seriously err, neither "knowing the Scriptures nor the power of God" (Matt. 22:29).

9. "But are there not assertions in Scripture which prove the same thing, if it cannot be inferred from those examples? Does not the Scripture say expressly, 'Even a just man sins seven times a day'?" I answer, No; the Scripture says no such thing. There is no such text in all the Bible. That which seems to be intended is the sixteenth verse of the twenty-fourth chapter of the Proverbs, the words of which are these: "A just man falls seven times and rises up again" (Prov. 24:16). But this is quite another thing. For, first, the words "a day" are not in the text. So if a just man falls seven times in his life, it is as much as is affirmed here. Secondly, here is no mention of "falling into sin" at all; what is here mentioned is "falling into temporal affliction." This plainly appears from the verse before, the words of which are these: "Do not lie in wait, O wicked man, against the dwelling of the righteous; do not raid his resting place" (Prov. 24:15). It follows, "For a just man falls seven times, and rises up again; but the wicked shall fall into trouble." It is as if he had said, "God will deliver him out of his trouble; but when you fall, there shall be none to deliver you."

10. "But, however, in other places," continue the objectors, "Solomon does assert plainly, 'There is no man who does not sin' (1 Kings 8:46; 2 Chron. 6:36); and even, 'There is not a just man on earth that does what is good, and does not sin'" (Eccles. 7:20). I answer, without doubt, thus it was in the days of Solomon. Indeed, thus it was from Adam to Moses, from Moses to Solomon, and from Solomon to Christ. There was then no man who did not sin. Even from the day that sin entered into the world, there was not a just man upon earth who did good and did not sin, until the Son of God was manifested to take away our sins. It is unquestionably

SERMON 35

true that "the heir, as long as he is a child, is no different from a servant" (Gal. 4:1). And that even so they (all the holy men of old, who were under the Jewish dispensation) were, during that infant state of the Church, "in bondage under the elements of the world" (Gal. 4:3). "But when the fullness of the time had come, God sent forth his Son, born under the law, to redeem them that were under the law, that they might receive the adoption of sons" (Gal. 4:4); that they might receive that "grace which is now made manifest by the appearing of our Saviour, Jesus Christ, who has abolished death and brought life and immortality to light through the gospel" (2 Tim. 1:10). Now, therefore, they "are no longer servants, but sons" (Gal. 4:7). So whatever was the case of those under the law, we may safely affirm with St. John that, since the gospel was given, "he who is born of God does not sin" (1 John 5:18).

11. It is of great importance to observe, and that more carefully than is commonly done, the wide difference there is between the Jewish and the Christian dispensation; and the basis for it which the same Apostle assigns in the seventh chapter of his Gospel (John 7:38, etc.). After he had there related those words of our blessed Lord, "He that believes in me, as the Scripture has said, rivers of living water shall flow out of him," he immediately subjoins, "This he spoke concerning the Spirit," οὗ ἔμελλον λαμβάνειν οἱ πιστεύοντες εἰς αὐτόν, "which they who would believe in him were to receive at a later time." "For the Holy Spirit had not yet been given, because Jesus had not yet been glorified" (John 7:39). Now, the Apostle cannot mean here (as some have taught) that the miracle-working power of the Holy Spirit had not yet been given. For this had been given; our Lord had given it to all the Apostles when he first sent them forth to preach the gospel. He then gave them power over unclean spirits to cast them out; power to heal the sick; yes, even to raise the dead. But the Holy Spirit had not yet been given in his sanctifying graces, as he was after Jesus was glorified. It was then when "he ascended up on high and led captivity captive," that he "received" those "gifts for men; even for the rebellious, that the Lord God might dwell among them" (Ps. 68:18). And when the day of Pentecost had fully come, then for the first time it was that they who "waited for the promise of the Father" (Acts 1:4) were

made more than conquerors (Rom. 8:37) over sin by the Holy Spirit given unto them.

12. That this great salvation from sin was not given until Jesus was glorified, St. Peter also plainly testifies; where, speaking of his brethren in the flesh as now "receiving the goal of their faith, the salvation of their souls," he adds (1 Peter 1:9–10, etc.), "Of which salvation the Prophets inquired and searched diligently, who prophesied of the grace," that is, the gracious dispensation, "that should come to you: looking for what, or what manner of time the Spirit of Christ which was in them did signify, when he testified ahead of time about the sufferings of Christ and the glory," the glorious salvation, "that should follow. Unto whom it was revealed that not to themselves, but to us they did minister the things which are now reported to you by those who have preached the gospel unto you with the Holy Spirit sent down from heaven" (1 Pet. 1:12); namely, at the day of Pentecost, and so to all generations, into the hearts of all true believers. For this reason, even "the grace which was brought down to them by the revelation of Jesus Christ" (1 Pet. 1:13), the Apostle might well set down that strong exhortation, "As he who has called you is holy, be holy in all manner of conversation" (1 Pet. 1:13).

13. Those who have duly considered these things must allow that the privileges of Christians are in no way to be measured by what the Old Testament records concerning those who were under the Jewish dispensation, since the fullness of times has now come; the Holy Spirit is now given; the great salvation of God is brought down to men by the revelation of Jesus Christ. The kingdom of heaven is now set up on earth, concerning which the Spirit of God declared of old (so far is David from being the pattern or standard of Christian perfection), "He that is feeble among them at that day shall be like David; and the house of David shall be like God, as the angel of the Lord before them" (Zech. 12:8).

14. If, therefore, you would prove that the Apostle's words, "He that is born of God does not commit sin" (1 John 5:18), are not to be understood according to their plain, natural, obvious meaning, it is from the New Testament you are to bring your proofs, else you will fight as one beating the air. And the first of these which is usually brought is taken from the examples recorded in the New

SERMON 35

Testament. "The Apostles themselves," it is said, "committed sin; even the greatest among them, Peter and Paul: St. Paul, by his sharp contention with Barnabas; and St. Peter, by his dissimulation at Antioch." Well: suppose both Peter and Paul did then commit sin; what is it you would infer from that? That all the other Apostles committed sin sometimes? There is no shadow of proof in this. Or would you infer from it that all the other Christians of the apostolic age committed sin? Worse and worse: this is such an inference as one would imagine, a man in his senses could never have thought of. Or will you argue thus: "If two of the Apostles did once commit sin, then all other Christians, in all ages, do and will commit sin as long as they live?" Alas, my brother! a child of common understanding would be ashamed of reasoning such as this. Least of all can you with any colour of argument infer that any man must commit sin at all. No: God forbid we should speak thus! No necessity of sinning was laid upon them. The grace of God was surely sufficient for them. And it is sufficient for us at this day. With the temptation which fell on them there was a way to escape; as there is to every soul of man in every temptation. So that whoever is tempted to any sin need not yield; for no man is tempted above that which he is able to bear (1 Cor. 10:13).

15. "But St. Paul begged the Lord three times and yet he could not escape from his temptation." Let us consider his own words literally translated: "There was given to me a thorn to the flesh, an angel" (or messenger) "of Satan, to buffet me. Concerning this, I begged the Lord three times, that it" (or he) "might depart from me. But he said to me, 'My grace is sufficient for you: for my strength is made perfect in weakness.' Most gladly, therefore, I will instead glory in" these "my weaknesses, that the strength of Christ may rest upon me. Therefore I take pleasure in weaknesses; for when I am weak, then am I strong" (2 Cor. 12:7–10).

16. As this scripture is one of the strongholds of the patrons of sin, it may be proper to weigh it thoroughly. Let it be observed then, first, it does by no means appear that this thorn, whatever it was, occasioned St. Paul to commit sin; much less laid him under any necessity of doing so. Therefore, from this it can never be proven that any Christian must commit sin.

Secondly, the ancient Fathers inform us, it was bodily pain: "a violent headache, says Tertullian, to which both Chrysostom and St. Jerome agree. St. Cyprian expresses it a little more generally, in these terms: "Many and grievous torments of the flesh and of the body."

Thirdly, to this exactly agree the Apostle's own words, "A thorn to the flesh to smite, beat, or buffet me." "My strength is made perfect in weakness"—this same word occurs no less than four times in these two verses alone.

But, fourthly, whatever it was, it could not be either inward or outward sin. It could no more be inward stirrings than outward expressions of pride, anger, or lust. This is manifest, beyond all possible exception, from the words that immediately follow: "Most gladly will I glory in" these "my weaknesses, that the strength of Christ may rest upon me" (2 Cor. 12:9). What! Did he glory in pride, in anger, in lust? Was it through these weaknesses that the strength of Christ rested upon him? He goes on: "Therefore I take pleasure in weaknesses; for when I am weak, then am I strong" (2 Cor. 12:10); that is, when I am weak in body, then am I strong in spirit. But will any man dare say, "When I am weak by pride or lust, then am I strong in spirit"? I call you all to record this day who find the strength of Christ resting upon you, can you glory in anger, or pride, or lust? Can you take pleasure in these infirmities? Do these weaknesses make you strong? Would you not leap into hell, if it were possible, to escape them? Even by yourselves, then, judge whether the Apostle could glory and take pleasure in them!

Let it, lastly, be observed, that this thorn was given to St. Paul over fourteen years before he wrote this Epistle; which itself was written several years before he finished his course. So he had after this a long course to run, many battles to fight, many victories to gain, and great increase to receive in all the gifts of God, and the knowledge of Jesus Christ. Therefore from any spiritual weakness (if such it had been) which he at that time felt, we could by no means infer that he was never made strong; that Paul the aged, the father in Christ, still laboured under the same weaknesses; that he was in no higher state till the day of his death. From all which it appears that this instance of St. Paul is quite foreign to the question and does in no way clash with the assertion of St. John, "He that is born of God does not sin."

17. "But does not St. James directly contradict this? His words are, 'In many things we offend all' (Jas. 3:2:). And is not offending the same as committing sin?" In this place, I allow it is. I allow the persons here spoken of did commit sin; indeed, that they all committed many sins. But who are the persons here spoken of? Why, those many masters or teachers whom God had not sent (probably the same vain men who taught faith without works, which is so sharply reproved in the preceding chapter); not the Apostle himself, nor any real Christian. That in the word we (used by a figure of speech common in all other, as well as the inspired, writings) the Apostle could not possibly include himself or any other true believer, appears evidently, first, from the same word in the ninth verse: "With this," he says, "we bless God and with this we curse men. Blessing and cursing proceed from the same mouth" (Jas. 3:9). True; but not from the mouth of the Apostle, nor of anyone who is in Christ a new creature.

Secondly, from the verse immediately preceding the text, and manifestly connected with it: "My brethren, let not many of us be masters" (or teachers), "knowing that we shall receive the greater condemnation." "For in many things we offend all." We! Who? Not the Apostles, not true believers; but those who know they would "receive the greater condemnation" because of those many offences. But this could not be spoken of the Apostle himself, nor of any who trod in his steps, since "there is no condemnation to them who walk not after the flesh, but after the Spirit" (Rom. 8:2).

Nay, thirdly, the very verse itself proves that "we offend all" cannot be spoken either of all men or of all Christians: For in it there immediately follows the mention of a man who "does not offend," as the "we" first mentioned did; from whom, therefore, he is professedly contradistinguished, and pronounced a "perfect man."

18. So clearly does St. James explain himself and set the meaning of his own words. Yet, lest anyone should still remain in doubt, St. John, writing many years after St. James, puts the matter entirely out of dispute by the explicit declarations above recited. But here a fresh difficulty may arise: How shall we reconcile St. John with himself? In one place he declares, "Whoever is born of God does not commit sin" (1 John 3:9); and again, "We know that he who

is born of God does not sin" (1 John 5:18). And yet in another he says, "If we say that we have no sin, we deceive ourselves, and the truth is not in us" (1 John 1:8); and again, "If we say that we have not sinned, we make him a liar, and his word is not in us" (1 John 1:10).

19. As great a difficulty as this may at first appear, it vanishes away if we observe, firstly, that the tenth verse determines the meaning of the eighth: "If we say we have no sin," in the former, being explained by, "If we say we have not sinned," in the latter verse. Secondly, the point under present consideration is not whether we have or have not sinned before now; and neither of these verses asserts that we do sin or commit sin now. Thirdly, that the ninth verse explains both the eighth and tenth. "If we confess our sins, he is faithful and just to forgive us our sins, and to cleanse us from all unrighteousness." It is as if he had said, "I have before affirmed, 'The blood of Jesus Christ cleanses us from all sin'; but let no man say, 'I do not need it; I have no sin to be cleansed from.'" "If we say that we have no sin, that we have not sinned, we deceive ourselves, and make God a liar. But if we confess our sins, he is faithful and just," not only "to forgive our sins," but also "to cleanse us from all unrighteousness" (1 John 1:8–10) that we may "go and sin no more" (John 8:11).

20. St. John, therefore, is consistent with himself, as well as with the other holy writers; as will yet more evidently appear if we place all his assertions touching this matter in one view: He declares, first, the blood of Jesus Christ cleanses us from all sin. Secondly, no man can say, "I have not sinned; I have no sin to be cleansed from." Thirdly, God is ready both to forgive our past sins and to save us from them for the time to come (1 John 1:7–10). Fourthly, "These things I write to you," says the Apostle, "that you may not sin. But if any man" should "sin," or "has sinned" (as the word might be rendered), he need not continue in sin; since "we have an Advocate with the Father, Jesus Christ the righteous" (1 John 2:1–2). Thus far all is clear. But lest any doubt should remain in a point of such great importance, the Apostle resumes this subject in the third chapter and explains his own meaning at length. "Little children," he says, "do not let anyone deceive you" (as though I had given any encouragement to those that continue in sin): "He

SERMON 35

who does what is righteous is righteous, even as He is righteous. He who commits sin is of the Devil; for the Devil was a sinner from the beginning. For this purpose the Son of God was manifested, that he might destroy the works of the Devil. Whoever is born of God does not commit sin: For his seed remains in him; and he cannot sin, because he is born of God. In this we see who the children of God are, and who the children of the Devil are" (1 John 3:7–10). Here the point, which until then might possibly have admitted of some doubt in weak minds, is purposely settled by the last of the inspired writers and decided in the clearest manner. In conformity, therefore, both to the doctrine of St. John, and to the whole tenor of the New Testament, we fix this conclusion—A Christian is so far perfect as not to commit sin.

21. This is the glorious privilege of every Christian; yes, even if he is only a babe in Christ. But it is only of those who are strong in the Lord, and "have overcome the wicked one," or rather of those who "have known him that is from the beginning," that it can be said they are in such a sense perfect, as, secondly, to be freed from evil thoughts and evil tempers. First, from evil or sinful thoughts. But here let it be observed that thoughts concerning evil are not always evil thoughts; that a thought concerning sin and a sinful thought are widely different. A man, for instance, may think of a murder which another has committed and yet this is no evil or sinful thought. So our blessed Lord himself doubtless thought of, or understood, the thing spoken by the Devil when he said, "All these things will I give you, if you will fall down and worship me" (Matt. 4:9). Yet had he no evil or sinful thought; nor indeed was capable of having any. And it even follows from this that neither have real Christians: for "everyone who is perfect is like his Master" (Luke 6:40). Therefore, if He was free from evil or sinful thoughts, so are they likewise.

22. And indeed, from what should evil thoughts proceed, in the servant who is like his Master? "Out of the heart of man" (if at all) "proceed evil thoughts" (Mark 7:21). If, therefore, his heart is no longer evil, then evil thoughts can no longer proceed out of it. If the tree were corrupt, so would be the fruit: but the tree is good; the fruit therefore is good also (Matt. 22:33); as our Lord himself bears witness. "Every good tree brings forth good fruit. A good tree cannot bring

forth evil fruit," just as "an evil tree cannot bring forth good fruit" (Matt 7:17–18).

23. The same happy privilege of real Christians, St. Paul asserts from his own experience. "The weapons of our warfare," he says, "are not carnal, but mighty through God for pulling down strongholds; casting down imaginings" (or "reasonings" rather, for so the word λογισμούς signifies; all the reasonings of pride and unbelief against the declarations, promises, or gifts of God) "and every high thing that exalts itself over the knowledge of God, and bringing into captivity every thought to the obedience of Christ" (2 Cor. 10:4, etc.).

24. And as Christians indeed are freed from evil thoughts, so are they, secondly, freed from evil tempers. This is evident from the above-mentioned declaration of our Lord himself: "The disciple is not above his Master; but everyone that is perfect shall be like his Master" (Luke 6:40). He had been delivering, just before, some of the most sublime doctrines of Christianity, and some of the most grievous on flesh and blood. "I say to you, love your enemies, do good to those who hate you; and to him who strikes you on the one cheek, offer also the other" (Luke 6:29). Now he well knew the world would not receive these; and, therefore he immediately adds, "Can the blind lead the blind? Will they not both fall into the ditch?" (Luke 6:39). It is as if he had said, "Do not confer with flesh and blood about these things—with men void of spiritual discernment, the eyes of whose understanding God has not opened—lest they and you perish together." In the next verse he removes the two grand objections with which these wise fools meet us at every turn: "These things are too harsh to be borne," or, "They are too high to be attained" (Matt. 23:4), saying, "'The disciple is not above his Master'; therefore, if I have suffered, be content to tread in my steps. And do not doubt that I will fulfill my word: 'For everyone that is perfect shall be like his Master.'" But the Master was free from all sinful tempers. So, therefore, is his disciple, even every real Christian.

25. Every one of these can say, with St. Paul, "I am crucified with Christ: nevertheless I live; yet not I, but Christ lives in me" (Gal. 2:20): words that manifestly describe a deliverance from inward as well as from outward sin. This is expressed both negatively, I live not (my evil

nature, the body of sin, is destroyed); and positively, Christ lives in me; and, therefore, all that is holy, and just, and good. Indeed, both these, Christ lives in me, and I live not, are inseparably connected; for "what communion has light with darkness, or Christ with Belial?" (2 Cor. 6:15).

26. He, therefore, who lives in true believers, has "purified their hearts by faith" (Acts 15:9); to the extent that everyone who has Christ in him, the hope of glory (Col. 1:27), "purifies himself, even as he is pure" (1 John 3:3). He is purified from pride; for Christ was lowly of heart. He is pure from self-will or desire; for Christ desired only to do the will of his Father and to finish his work. And he is pure from anger, in the common sense of the word; for Christ was meek and gentle, patient and long-suffering. I say, in the common sense of the word; for not all anger is evil. We read of our Lord himself (Mark 3:5), that he once "looked round with anger." But with what kind of anger? The next word shows συλλυπούμενος, "grieving for the hardness of their hearts" (Mark 3:6). So then he was angry at the sin and in the same moment grieving for the sinners; angry or displeased at the offence, but sorry for the offenders. With anger—yes, even hatred—he looked upon the thing; with grief and love upon the person. Go, you that are perfect, and do likewise. Be thus angry and you have not sinned; feeling outrage at every offence against God but only love and tender compassion to the offender.

27. Thus does Jesus "save his people from their sins" (Matt. 1:21). And not only from outward sins but also from the sins of their hearts; from evil thoughts and from evil tempers. "True," say some, "we shall thus be saved from our sins; but not until death; not in this world." But how are we to reconcile this with the direct words of St. John?—"In this is our love made perfect, that we may have confidence on the day of judgment. Because as he is, so are we in this world." The Apostle here, beyond all contradiction, speaks of himself and other living Christians, of whom (as though he had foreseen this very evasion and set himself to overturn it from the foundation) he flatly affirms that not only at or after death but in this world they are like their Master (1 John 4:17).

28. Exactly agreeable to this are his words in the first chapter of this Epistle (1 John 1:5, etc.), "God is light, and in him is no darkness at

all. If we walk in the light, we have fellowship one with another, and the blood of Jesus Christ his Son cleanses us from all sin." And again, "If we confess our sins, he is faithful and just to forgive us our sins and to cleanse us from all unrighteousness" (1 John 1:9). Now it is evident that the Apostle here also speaks of a deliverance wrought in this world. For he does not say that the blood of Christ will cleanse at the hour of death, or in the day of judgment, but, it "cleanses," at the present moment, "us," living Christians, "from all sin." And it is equally evident, that if any sin remains, we are not cleansed from all sin: if any unrighteousness remains in the soul, it is not cleansed from all unrighteousness. Neither let any sinner against his own soul say that this relates to justification only, or the cleansing us from the guilt of sin. First, because this is muddling together what the Apostle clearly distinguishes, who mentions first "to forgive us our sins," and then "to cleanse us from all unrighteousness." Secondly, because this is asserting justification by works in the strongest sense possible; it is making all inward as well as outward holiness necessarily previous to justification. For if the cleansing here spoken of is no other than the cleansing us from the guilt of sin, then we are not cleansed from guilt; that is, are not justified, unless on condition of "walking in the light, as he is in the light" (1 John 1:7). It remains, then, that Christians are saved in this world from all sin, from all unrighteousness; that they are now in such a sense perfect as not to commit sin, and to be freed from evil thoughts and evil tempers.

29. Thus has the Lord fulfilled the things he spoke by his holy prophets, which have been since the world began—by Moses in particular, saying (Deut. 30:6), I "will circumcise your heart, and the heart of your descendants, to love the Lord your God with all your heart, and with all your soul"; by David, crying out, "Create in me a clean heart, and renew a right spirit within me" (Ps. 51:10);—and most remarkably by Ezekiel, in those words: "Then will I sprinkle clean water upon you, and you shall be clean; from all your filthiness, and from all your idols, will I cleanse you. A new heart also will I give you, and a new spirit will I put within you; and cause you to walk in my statutes, and you shall keep my judgments, and do them. You shall be my people, and I will be your God. I will also

SERMON 35

save you from all your uncleanliness. Thus says the Lord your God, 'In the day that I shall have cleansed you from all your iniquities; the Heathen shall know that I the Lord rebuild the ruined places; I the Lord have spoken it, and I will do it" (Ezek. 36:25, etc.).

30. "Having therefore these promises, dearly beloved," both in the Law and in the Prophets, and having the prophetic word confirmed unto us in the Gospel, by our blessed Lord and his Apostles; "let us cleanse ourselves from all filthiness of flesh and spirit, perfecting holiness in the fear of God" (2 Cor. 7:1). "Let us fear, lest" so many "promises being made us of entering into his rest," which he that has entered into, has ceased from his own works, "any of us should come short of it" (Heb. 4:1). "This one thing let us do, forgetting those things which are behind, and reaching forth to those things which are before, let us press toward the mark, for the prize of the high calling of God in Christ Jesus" (Phil. 3:13–14); crying out to him day and night, until we also are "delivered from the bondage of corruption into the glorious liberty of the sons of God!" (Rom. 8:21).

The promise of sanctification (Ezek. 36:25, etc.)

[1] God of all power, and truth, and grace,
  Which shall from age to age endure;
Whose word, when heaven and earth shall pass,
  Remains, and stands for ever sure:

[2] Calmly to you my soul looks up,
  And waits your promises to prove;
The object of my steadfast hope,
  The seal of your eternal love.

[3] That I your mercy may proclaim,
  That all mankind your truth may see,
Hallow your great and glorious name,
  And perfect holiness in me.

[4] Chose from the world, if now I stand
  Adorn'd in righteousness divine;
If, brought unto the promised land,
  I justly call the Saviour mine;

CHRISTIAN PERFECTION

5 Perform the work you have begun,
    My inmost soul to you convert:
Love me, for ever love your own,
    And sprinkle with your blood my heart.

6 Your sanctifying Spirit pour,
    To quench my thirst, and wash me clean;
Now, Father, let the gracious shower
    Descend, and make me pure from sin.

7 Purge me from every sinful blot;
    My idols all be cast aside:
Cleanse me from every evil thought,
    From all the filth of self and pride.

8 Give me a new, a perfect heart,
    From doubt, and fear, and sorrow free;
The mind which was in Christ impart,
    And let my spirit cleave to you.

9 O take this heart of stone away,
    (Your rule it doth not, cannot own);
In me no longer let it stay:
    O take away this heart of stone.

10 The hatred of my carnal mind
    Out of my flesh at once remove;
Give me a tender heart, resign'd,
    And pure, and fill'd with faith and love.

11 Within me your good Spirit place,
    Spirit of health, and love and power;
Plant in me your victorious grace,
    And sin shall never enter more.

12 Cause me to walk in Christ my Way,
    And I your statutes shall fulfill;
In every point your law obey.
    And perfectly perform your will.

13 Have you not said, who cannot lie,
    That I your law shall keep and do?
Lord, I believe, though men deny;
    They all are false, but you are true.

SERMON 35

¹⁴ O that I now, from sin released,
>   Your word might to the utmost prove!
> Enter into the promised rest,
>   The Canaan of your perfect love!

¹⁵ There let me ever, ever dwell;
>   By you my God, and I will be
> Your servant: O set to your seal!
>   Give me eternal life in you.

¹⁶ From all remaining filth within
>   Let me in You salvation have:
> From actual, and from inbred sin
>   My ransom'd soul persist to save.

¹⁷ Wash out my old original stain:
>   Tell me no more "It cannot be,"
> Demons or men! The Lamb was slain
>   His blood was all poured out for me!

¹⁸ Sprinkle it, Jesu, on my heart:
>   One drop of your all-cleansing blood
> Shall make my sinfulness depart,
>   And fill me with the life of God.

¹⁹ Father, supply my every need:
>   Sustain the life yourself Have given;
> Call for the corn, the living bread,
>   The manna that comes down from heaven.

²⁰ The gracious fruits of righteousness,
>   Your blessings' unexhausted store,
> In me abundantly increase;
>   Nor let me ever hunger more.

²¹ Let me no more in deep complaint
>   "My leanness, O my leanness!" cry;
> Alone consumed with pining want,
>   Of all my Father's children I!

²² The painful thirst, the fond desire,
>   Your joyous presence shall remove;
> While my full soul doth still require
>   Your whole eternity of love.

²³ Holy, and true, and righteous Lord,
> I wait to prove your perfect will;
> Be mindful of your gracious word,
> > And stamp me with your Spirit's seal!

²⁴ Your faithful mercies let me find,
> In which you causest me to trust;
> Give me the meek and lowly mind,
> > And lay my spirit in the dust.

²⁵ Show me how foul my heart has been,
> When all renew'd by grace I am:
> When you have emptied me of sin,
> > Show me the fullness of my shame.

²⁶ Open my faith's interior eye,
> Display your glory from above;
> And all I am shall sink and die,
> > Lost in astonishment and love.

²⁷ Confound, o'erpower me with your grace:
> I would be by myself abhorr'd;
> (All might, all majesty, all praise,
> > All glory be to Christ my Lord!)

²⁸ Now let me gain perfection's height!
> Now let me into nothing fall!
> Be less than nothing in your sight,
> > And feel that Christ is all in all!
>
> —Charles Wesley (Ezek. 36:25ff)

For Readers

Questions

1. Why should we retain the notion of Christian perfection in order to avoid limiting the possibilities of grace in this life?
2. Are there better contemporary concepts with less baggage?
3. How can we sort out carefully and objectively what we can and cannot expect God to do for us as sinners in this life?
4. What is radically new in the arrival of the New Testament as contrasted with the Old Testament with respect to our lives as Christians?

5. How should we understand the meaning and significance of 1 John 3:7–10?

Helpful Information

Wesley is adamant about not cutting down to our measure the possibilities of radical moral transformation here and now. His deepest reason for this is his reading of the New Testament, not least the teaching of Christ. He is not going to quibble over the language; however, he will hold to the substance. If we disagree with him, we have to deal with a higher authority, nothing less than God and his teaching as given through Christ.

The text he uses from Philippians suggests that he is prepared to work at the level of aspiration and expectation. This strategy is confirmed in his distinction between babies, young men, and fathers. He is holding out for moving through stages of the Christian life, even as he wants to insist on privileging fathers as the proper Christians.

While the divisions of the sermon come across as artificial at first, the actual content is surely helpful. He leaves lots of room for factors that can naturally help us deal with the glaring gap between aspiration and reality. He is totally ruling out any notion of absolute perfection. He is also providing a relatively rich account of the kind of everyday frustrations that constantly challenge our efforts to love God and love our neighbors as ourselves. Once we know these, we are better prepared to handle their impact on our growth in grace.

Even so, he will not allow this lowering of expectations to a much more realistic level to undermine the promises he sees scattered throughout the New Testament. *Expectations*, however, is not quite the right word. What drives the quest for change is the promise of God. Human expectations like divine commands are veiled promises. And promises from God, unlike human promises, are such that we will never be disappointed if we take them seriously.

SERMON 36

Wandering Thoughts

"Bringing into captivity every thought to the obedience of Christ" (2 Cor. 5:5).

1. But will God so "bring every thought into captivity to the obedience of Christ," that no wandering thought will find a place in the mind, even while we remain in the body? So some have vehemently maintained; yes, have even affirmed that none are perfected in love unless they are so far perfected in understanding that all wandering thoughts are done away; unless not only every affection and temper be holy and just and good, but every individual thought which arises in the mind be wise and regular.

2. This is a question of no small importance. For how many of those who fear God; indeed, and love him, perhaps with all their hearts, have been greatly distressed on this account! How many, by not understanding it right, have not only been distressed but greatly hurt in their souls—cast into unprofitable, even mischievous reasonings, which slackened their motion towards God, and weakened them in running the race set before them! No, many, through misapprehensions of this very thing, have even cast away the precious gift of God. They have been induced, first, to doubt of, and then to deny, the work God had wrought in their souls; and by this have grieved the Spirit of God until he withdrew and left them in utter darkness!

3. How is it then, that amidst the abundance of books which have been recently published almost on all subjects, we should have none upon wandering thoughts? At least none that will at all satisfy a calm and serious mind? In order to do this in some degree, I purpose to inquire,

   I. What are the various kinds of wandering thoughts?
   II. What are the general occasions of them?
   III. Which of them are sinful, and which not?
   IV. Which of them may we expect and pray to be delivered from?

I. 1. I purpose to inquire, first, "What are the various kinds of wandering thoughts?" The particular kinds are innumerable; but in general they are of two sorts: Thoughts that wander from God; and thoughts that wander from the particular point we have in hand.

SERMON 36

2. With regard to the former, all our thoughts are naturally of this kind: for they are continually wandering from God. We think nothing about him; God is not in all our thoughts; we are, one and all, as the Apostle observes, "without God in the world." We think of what we love; but we do not love God; therefore, we do not think of him. Or, if we are now and then constrained to think of him for a time, yet because we take no pleasure in it; no, worse, because these thoughts are not only insipid but distasteful and irritating to us, we drive them out as soon as we can and return to what we love to think of. So the world, and the things of the world—what we shall eat, what we shall drink, what we shall put on; what we shall see, what we shall hear, what we shall gain; how we shall please our senses or our imagination—these take up all our time and engross all our thought. As long, therefore, as we love the world; that is, as long as we are in our natural state; all our thoughts, from morning to evening and from evening to morning, are none other than wandering thoughts.

3. But many times we are not only "without God in the world" but also fighting against him; as there is in every man by nature a "carnal mind which is enmity against God." No wonder, therefore, that men abound with unbelieving thoughts; either saying in their hearts, "There is no God," or questioning, if not denying, his power or wisdom, his mercy, or justice, or holiness. No wonder that they so often doubt of his providence, at least, that it extends to all events; or that, even though they allow it, they still entertain murmuring or complaining thoughts. Closely related to these, and frequently connected with them, are proud and vain imaginations. Again: sometimes they are taken up with angry, malicious, or vengeful thoughts; at other times, with airy scenes of pleasure, whether of sense or imagination; by which the earthly, sensual mind becomes even more earthy and sensual. Now by all these they make flat war with God: These are wandering thoughts of the highest kind.

4. Widely different from these are the other sort of wandering thoughts; in which the heart does not wander from God but the understanding wanders from the particular point it had then in view. For instance: I sit down to consider those words in the verse preceding the text: "The weapons of our warfare are not carnal, but mighty through

WANDERING THOUGHTS

God." I think, "This ought to be the case with all that are called Christians. But how far is it otherwise! Look round into almost every part of what is termed the Christian world. What manner of weapons are they using? In what kind of warfare are they engaged;

> While men, like fiends, each other tear;
> In all the hellish rage of war?

See how these Christians love one another! In what are they preferable to Turks and Pagans? What abomination can be found among Mahometans or Heathens which is not found among Christians also?" And thus my mind runs off, before I am aware, from one circumstance to another. Now, all these are, in some sense, wandering thoughts: For although they do not wander from God, much less fight against him, yet they do wander from the particular point I had in view.

II. Such is the nature, such are the sorts (to speak rather usefully than philosophically) of wandering thoughts. But what are the general occasions of them? This we are, in the second place, to consider.

1. And it is easy to observe that the occasion of the former sort of thoughts, which oppose or wander from God, are, in general, sinful tempers. For instance, why is not God in all the thoughts, in any of the thoughts of a natural man? For a plain reason: whether he is rich or poor, learned or unlearned, he is an Atheist (though not as commonly so called); he neither knows nor loves God. Why are his thoughts continually wandering after the world? Because he is an idolater. He does not worship an image or bow down to the stock of a tree, yet he is sunk into equally damnable idolatry: He loves, that is, worships, the world. He seeks happiness in the things that are seen, in the pleasures that perish in the having. Why is it that his thoughts are perpetually wandering from the very purpose of his being, the knowledge of God in Christ? Because he is an unbeliever; because he has no faith; or at least, no more than a devil. So all these wandering thoughts easily and naturally spring from that evil root of unbelief.

2. The case is the same in other instances: pride, anger, revenge, vanity, lust, covetousness, every one of them brings about thoughts suitable to its own nature. And so does every sinful temper of which the

SERMON 36

human mind is capable. The particulars it is hardly possible, nor is it necessary, to enumerate; it suffices to observe that as many evil tempers as find a place in any soul, so many ways that soul will depart from God, by the worst kind of wandering thoughts.

3. The occasions of the latter kind of wandering thoughts are exceedingly various. Multitudes of them are occasioned by the natural union between the soul and body. How immediately and how deeply is the understanding affected by a diseased body! Let but the blood move irregularly in the brain and all regular thinking is at an end. Raging madness ensues; and then farewell to all consistency of thought. Indeed, let only the spirits be hurried or agitated to a certain degree and a temporary madness, a delirium, prevents all settled thought. And is not the same irregularity of thought, in a measure, occasioned by every nervous disorder? So does the "corruptible body press down the soul and cause it to muse about many things."

4. But does it only cause this in the time of sickness or preternatural disorder? No, but more or less, at all times, even in a state of perfect health. Let a man be ever so healthy, he will be more or less delirious every four-and-twenty hours. For does he not sleep? And while he sleeps, is he not liable to dream? And who then is master of his own thoughts, or able to preserve the order and consistency of them? Who can then keep them fixed to any one point, or prevent their wandering from pole to pole?

5. But suppose we are awake, are we always so awake that we can steadily govern our thoughts? Are we not unavoidably exposed to contrary extremes by the very nature of this machine, the body? Sometimes we are too heavy, too dull and languid, to pursue any chain of thought. Sometimes, on the other hand, we are too lively. The imagination, without leave, leaps to and fro and carries us away hither and thither, whether we will or not; and all this from the purely natural motion of the spirits or vibration of the nerves.

6. Further: how many wanderings of thought may arise from those various associations of our ideas which are made entirely without our knowledge, and independently of our choice? How these connections are formed, we cannot tell, but they are formed in

a thousand different ways. Nor is it in the power of the wisest or holiest of men to break those associations, or to prevent what is the necessary consequences of them, and matter of daily observation. Let the fire but touch one end of the train, and it immediately runs on to the other.

7. Once more: let us fix our attention as studiously as we are able on any subject, yet let either pleasure or pain arise, especially if it is intense, and it will demand our immediate attention, and attach our thought to itself. It will interrupt the steadiest contemplation and divert the mind from its favourite subject.

8. These occasions of wandering thoughts lie within, are built into our very nature. But they will likewise naturally and necessarily arise from the various impulses of outward objects. Whatever strikes upon the organ of sense, the eyes or ears, will raise a perception in the mind. And, accordingly, whatever we see or hear will break in upon our former train of thought. Every man, therefore, who does anything in our sight, or speaks anything in our hearing, occasions our mind to wander, more or less, from the point we were thinking of before.

9. And there is no question but that those evil spirits who are continually seeking whom they may devour make use of all the foregoing occasions to harry and distract our minds. Sometimes by one, sometimes by another of these means, they will harass and perplex us, and, as far as God permits, interrupt our thoughts, particularly when they are engaged on the best subjects. Nor is this at all strange: they understand the very springs of thought and know on which of the bodily organs the imagination, the understanding, and every other faculty of the mind more immediately depends. And thus they know how, by affecting those organs, to affect the operations dependent on them. Add to this, that they can interject a thousand thoughts without any of the preceding means; it being as natural for spirit to act upon spirit as for matter to act upon matter. These things being considered, we cannot be surprised that our attention so often wanders from any point which we have in view.

III. 1. What kind of wandering thoughts are sinful, and what not, is the third thing to be inquired into. First, all those thoughts which wander

SERMON 36

from God, which leave him no room in our minds, are undoubtedly sinful. For all these imply practical Atheism; and by these we are without God in the world. And so much more are all those which are contrary to God, which imply opposition or enmity to him. Such are all murmuring, discontented thoughts, which say, in effect, "We will not have you to rule over us"; all unbelieving thoughts, whether with regard to his being, his attributes, or his providence. I mean his particular providence over all things, as well as all persons, in the universe; that without which "not a sparrow falls to the ground," by which "the hairs of our head are all numbered"; for as to a general providence (commonly so called), as distinct from a particular, it is only a decent, well-sounding word, which means just nothing.

2. Again: all thoughts which spring from sinful tempers are undoubtedly sinful. Such, for instance, are those that spring from a vengeful temper, from pride, or lust, or vanity. "An evil tree cannot bring forth good fruit": therefore if the tree is evil, so must the fruit be also.

3. And so must those be which either produce or feed any sinful temper; those which either give rise to pride or vanity, to anger or love of the world, or confirm and increase these or any other unholy temper, passion, or affection. For not only whatever flows from evil is evil; but also whatever leads to it; whatever tends to alienate the soul from God, and to make or keep it earthly, sensual, and devilish.

4. Hence even those thoughts which are occasioned by weakness or disease, by the natural mechanism of the body, or by the laws of vital union, however innocent they may be in themselves, do nevertheless become sinful when they either produce or cherish and increase in us any sinful temper; suppose the desire of the flesh, the desire of the eyes, or the pride of life. In like manner, the wandering thoughts which are occasioned by the words or actions of other men, if they cause or feed any wrong disposition, then become sinful. And the same we may observe of those which are suggested or interjected by the Devil. When they minister to any earthly or devilish temper (which they do, whenever we give place to them and thus make them our own), then they are equally sinful with the tempers to which they minister.

5. But abstracting from these cases, wandering thoughts, in the latter sense of the word, that is, thoughts in which our understanding wanders from the point it has in view, are no more sinful than the motion of the blood in our veins, or of the spirits in our brain. If they arise from an infirm constitution, or from some accidental weakness or distemper, they are as innocent as it is to have a weak constitution or a distempered body. And surely no one doubts that a bad state of nerves, a fever of any kind, and either a transient or a lasting delirium, may be consistent with perfect innocence. And if they should arise in a soul which is united to a healthful body, either from the natural union between the body and soul, or from any of ten thousand changes which may occur in those organs of the body that minister to thought—in any of these cases they are as perfectly innocent as the causes from which they spring. And so they are when they spring from the casual, involuntary associations of our ideas.

6. If our thoughts wander from the point we had in view by means of other men variously affecting our senses, they are equally innocent still: for it is no more a sin to understand what I see and hear, and in many cases cannot help seeing, hearing, and understanding, than it is to have eyes and ears. "But if the Devil interjects wandering thoughts, are not those thoughts evil?" They are troublesome, and in that sense evil; but they are not sinful. I do not know that he spoke to our Lord with an audible voice; perhaps he spoke to his heart only when he said, "All these things will I give you, if you will fall down and worship me." But whether he spoke inwardly or outwardly, our Lord doubtless understood what he said. He had therefore a thought correspondent to those words. But was it a sinful thought? We know it was not. In him there was no sin, either in action or word or thought. Nor is there any sin in a thousand thoughts of the same kind which Satan may interject into any of our Lord's followers.

7. It follows that none of these wandering thoughts (whatever unwary persons may have affirmed, thus grieving those whom the Lord had not grieved) are inconsistent with perfect love. Indeed, if they were, then not only sharp pain but sleep itself would be inconsistent with it. For whenever this supervenes, whatever we were thinking of before, it will interrupt our thinking, and of course draw our

thoughts into another channel and even sleep itself; as it is a state of insensibility and stupidity; and as such is generally mixed with thoughts wandering over the earth, loose, wild, and incoherent. Yet certainly these are consistent with perfect love: so then are all wandering thoughts of this kind.

IV. 1. From what has been observed, it is easy to give a clear answer to the last question: What kind of wandering thoughts may we expect and pray to be delivered from?

From the former sort of wandering thoughts—those in which the heart wanders from God; from all that are contrary to his will, or that leave us without God in the world; everyone who is perfected in love is unquestionably delivered. This deliverance, therefore, we may expect; this we may, we ought to pray for. Wandering thoughts of this kind imply unbelief, if not enmity against God; but both of these he will destroy, will bring utterly to an end. And indeed, from all sinful wandering thoughts we shall be absolutely delivered. All that are perfected in love are delivered from these; or else they were not saved from sin. Men and devils will tempt them in all manner of ways, but they cannot prevail over them.

2. With regard to the latter sort of wandering thoughts, the case is widely different. Until the cause is removed, we cannot in reason expect that the effect should cease. But the causes or occasions of these will remain as long as we remain in the body. So long, therefore, we have all reason to believe the effects will remain also.

3. To be more particular: suppose a soul, however holy, should dwell in a distempered body; suppose the brain should be so thoroughly disordered that raging madness results; will not all the thoughts be wild and unconnected as long as that disorder continues? Suppose a fever causes that temporary madness which we term delirium; can there be any orderly connection of thought before that delirium is removed? Yes, even suppose what is called a nervous disorder to rise to so high a degree as to occasion at least a partial madness; will there not be a thousand wandering thoughts? And must not these irregular thoughts last as long as the disorder which occasions them?

4. Will not the case be the same with regard to those thoughts that necessarily arise from violent pain? They will more or less continue

while that pain continues, by the inviolable order of nature. This order, likewise, will obtain where the thoughts are disturbed, broken, or interrupted, by any defect of the apprehension, judgment, or imagination, flowing from the natural constitution of the body. And how many interruptions may spring from the unaccountable and involuntary association of our ideas! Now, all these are directly or indirectly caused by the corruptible body pressing down the mind. Nor, therefore, can we expect them to be removed until "this corruptible shall put on incorruption."

5. And then only, when we lie down in the dust, shall we be delivered from those wandering thoughts which are occasioned by what we see and hear, among those by whom we are now surrounded. To avoid these, we must go out of the world: for as long as we remain there, as long as there are men and women round about us, and we have eyes to see and ears to hear, the things which we daily see and hear will certainly affect our mind, and will more or less break in upon and interrupt our previous thoughts.

6. And as long as evil spirits roam to and fro in a miserable, disordered world, so long will they assault (whether they can prevail or not) every inhabitant of flesh and blood. They will trouble even those whom they cannot destroy: They will attack, if they cannot conquer. And from these attacks of our restless, unwearied enemies, we must not look for an entire deliverance till we are lodged "where the wicked cease from troubling, and where the weary are at rest."

7. To sum up the whole: to expect deliverance from those wandering thoughts which are occasioned by evil spirits is to expect that the Devil should die or fall asleep, or, at least, should no more go about as a roaring lion. To expect deliverance from those which are occasioned by other men is to expect either that men should cease from the earth, or that we should be absolutely secluded from them, and have no interactions with them; or that having eyes we should not see, neither hear with our ears, but be as senseless as stocks or stones. And to pray for deliverance from those which are occasioned by the body is, in effect, to pray that we may leave the body: otherwise it is praying for impossibilities and absurdities; praying that God would reconcile contradictions by continuing our union with a corruptible body without the natural, necessary

SERMON 36

consequences of that union. It is as if we should pray to be angels and men, mortal and immortal, at the same time. No!—but when that which is immortal has come, mortality shall be done away.

8. Rather let us pray, both with the spirit and with the understanding, that all these things may work together for our good; that we may suffer all the infirmities of our nature, all the interruptions of men, all the assaults and suggestions of evil spirits, and in all be "more than conquerors." Let us pray, that we may be delivered from all sin; that both the root and branch may be destroyed; that we may be "cleansed from all pollution of flesh and spirit," from every evil temper, and word, and work; that we may "love the Lord our God with all our heart, with all our mind, with all our soul, and with all our strength"; that all the fruit of the Spirit may be found in us—not only love, joy, peace, but also "patience, gentleness, goodness, fidelity, meekness, temperance." Pray that all these things may flourish and abound, may increase in you more and more, until an abundant entrance be ministered unto you, into the everlasting kingdom of our Lord Jesus Christ!

For Readers

Questions

1. Why should we zero in on wandering thoughts in dealing with the challenges of becoming more like Christ?
2. Why do we continue to lose direction in our thinking after we become Christians as contrasted with life before we are Christians?
3. What wandering thoughts are utterly unavoidable and therefore not a source of self-censure or false guilt?
4. How does an analysis of wandering thoughts support the idea that the Christian life is primarily one of progress and growth?
5. How might we better deal with the inevitable impact of other people in dragging us into sin?

Helpful Information

Having dealt in more general terms with our resistance to a higher Christian life in the previous sermon, Wesley here tackles a question that clearly became a hot topic in early Methodism and elsewhere. We might call this the problem of cognitive distraction.

This problem arises if we think of the Christian life as marked by the single intention to follow God in all that we do. Intention seems to imply that we should be thinking of God all the time, or at least of making an effort to have a single eye to the glory of God in all that we do. However, this is clearly impossible. So, we need to find a way to deal with this acute dilemma.

It would have helped if Wesley had noted the important distinction between intention and disposition. Much of what we do is intentional without our actions being governed by a very particular intention in the moment when we act; we form dispositions in which our intentionality becomes natural to us. So, we give to the poor intentionally as a matter of course simply because we have the disposition to do so; we do not need every time we do so to work ourselves up into forming conscious intentions. However, Wesley does not go down this road.

The heart of Wesley's response is to have us once again recalibrate our expectations. There are multiple causes of wandering thoughts; some of these causes need attention, and others are perfectly natural and unavoidable. Once we begin to make this distinction we can act with prudence and wisdom. We need to avoid silly forms of spiritual scrupulosity and get a grip on life as it really is. We need to grow up and make good judgments about what is and is not avoidable, what we can and cannot tackle morally.

There is a neat move close to the beginning of this sermon. By noting how human agents in their current, natural state are not in the least interested in God, Wesley indirectly reminds his readers that if they care about God at all, they have crossed the threshold of the Christian life and should relax and not beat up on themselves. They need to exercise good sense as they tackle this very particular obstacle to their growth in grace. In the next sermon, Wesley makes use of this move in a very clever way when he tackles the problem of spiritual failure and even spiritual envy.

SERMON 37

Satan's Devices

"We are not ignorant of his devices" (2 Cor. 2:11).

1. The devices by which the subtle god of this world labours to destroy the children of God—or at least to torment whom he cannot destroy, to perplex and hinder them in running the race which is set before them—are as numberless as the stars of heaven or the sand upon the seashore. But it is of one of them only that I now propose to speak, although exerted in various ways, by which he endeavours to divide the gospel against itself, and by one part of it to overthrow the other.

2. The inward kingdom of heaven, which is set up in the heart of all that repent and believe the gospel, is none other than "righteousness and peace and joy in the Holy Spirit." Every babe in Christ knows we are made partakers of these the very hour that we believe in Jesus. But these are only the first-fruits of his Spirit; the harvest is not yet. Although these blessings are inconceivably great, yet we trust to see greater than these. We trust to love the Lord our God, not only as we do now, with a weak though sincere affection, but "with all our heart, with all our mind, with all our soul, and with all our strength." We look for power to "rejoice always, to pray without ceasing, and in everything to give thanks"; knowing, "this is the will of God in Christ Jesus concerning us."

3. We expect to be "made perfect in love"; in that love which casts out all painful fear, and all desire but that of glorifying him we love, and of loving and serving him more and more. We look for such an increase in the experimental knowledge and love of God our Saviour as will enable us always "to walk in the light as he is in the light." We believe the whole mind will be in us, "which was also in Christ Jesus"; that we shall so love every man as to be ready to lay down our life for his sake; so as, by this love, to be freed from anger, and pride, and from every unkind affection. We expect to be "cleansed from all our idols," "from all filthiness," whether "of flesh or spirit"; to be "saved from all our uncleanness," inward or outward; to be "purified as He is pure."

SERMON 37

4. We trust in his promise who cannot lie, that the time will surely come when, in every word and work, we shall do his blessed will on earth as it is done in heaven; when all our conversation shall be seasoned with salt, all fit to minister grace to the hearers; when, whether we eat or drink or whatever we do, it shall be done to the glory of God; when all our words and deeds shall be "in the name of the Lord Jesus, giving thanks to God, even the Father, through him."

5. Now this is the grand device of Satan, to destroy the first work of God in the soul, or at least to hinder its increase, by our expectation of that greater work. It is therefore my present design, first, to point out the various ways by which he endeavours this; and, secondly, to observe how we may turn back these fiery darts of the wicked one, how we may rise the higher by what he intends for an occasion of our falling.

I. 1. I am, first, to point out the several ways whereby Satan endeavours to destroy the first work of God in the soul, or at least to hinder its increase by our expectation of that greater work. And, 1. He endeavours to dampen our joy in the Lord by the consideration of our own vileness, sinfulness, unworthiness; added to this, that there must be a far greater change than is yet, or we cannot see the Lord. If we knew we must remain as we are even to the day of our death, we might possibly draw a kind of comfort, poor as it was, from that necessity. But as we know we need not remain in this state, as we are assured there is a greater change to come, and that unless sin be all done away in this life we cannot see God in glory. That subtle adversary often damps the joy we should otherwise feel in what we have already attained, by a perverse representation of what we have not attained, and the absolute necessity of attaining it. So we cannot rejoice in what we have, because there is more which we have not. We cannot rightly taste the goodness of God, who has done such great things for us, because there are so much greater things which as yet he has not done. Likewise, the deeper conviction God works in us of our present unholiness, and the more vehement desire we feel in our heart of the entire holiness he has promised, the more are we tempted to think lightly of the present gifts of God, and to undervalue what we have already received because of what we have not received.

2. If he can prevail thus far, if he can damp our joy, he will soon attack our peace also. He will suggest, "Are you worthy to see God? He is of purer eyes than to behold iniquity. How then can you flatter yourself so as to imagine he looks at you with approval? God is holy: you are unholy. What fellowship has light with darkness? How is it possible that you, unclean as you are, should be in a state of acceptance with God? You see indeed the mark, the prize of your high calling; but do you not see it is far off? How can you presume then to think that all your sins are already blotted out? How can this be, until you are brought nearer to God, until you bear more resemblance to him?" Thus will he endeavour not only to shake your peace, but even to overturn the very foundation of it; to bring you back, by insensible degrees, to the point from which you first set out, even to seek for justification by works, or by your own righteousness—to make something in you the reason for your acceptance, or at least necessarily previous to it.

3. Or, if we hold fast, "Other foundation can no man lay than that which is laid, even Jesus Christ"; and, "I am justified freely by God's grace, through the redemption which is in Jesus"; yet he will not cease to urge, "But the tree is known by its fruits: and do you have the fruits of justification? Is that mind in you which was in Christ Jesus? Are you dead to sin and alive to righteousness? Are you made conformable to the death of Christ, and do you know the power of his resurrection?" And then, comparing the small fruits we feel in our souls with the fullness of the promises, we shall be ready to conclude: "Surely God has not said that my sins are forgiven me! Surely I have not received the remission of my sins; for what place have I among them that are sanctified?"

4. More especially in the time of sickness and pain he will press this with all his might: "Is it not the word of Him who cannot lie, 'Without holiness no man shall see the Lord'? But you are not holy. You know it well; you know holiness is the full image of God; and how far is this above, out of your sight? You cannot attain unto it. Therefore, all your labour has been in vain. All these things you have suffered in vain. You have spent your strength for nothing. You are still in your sins and must therefore perish in the end." And thus, if your eye is not steadily fixed on Him who has borne

SERMON 37

all your sins, he will bring you again under that "fear of death," by which you were so long "subject to bondage," and by this means impair, if not wholly destroy, your peace as well as your joy in the Lord.

5. But his masterpiece of subtlety is still behind. Not content to strike at your peace and joy, he will carry his attempts farther still: he will level his assault against your righteousness also. He will endeavour to shake, yes, if it be possible, even to destroy the holiness you have already received by your very expectation of receiving more, of attaining all the image of God.

6. The manner in which he attempts this may partly appear from what has been already observed. For first, by striking at our joy in the Lord, he strikes likewise at our holiness. Since joy in the Holy Spirit is a precious means of promoting every holy temper; a choice instrument of God by which he carries on much of his work in a believing soul. And it is a considerable help not only to inward but also to outward holiness. It strengthens our hands to go on in the work of faith, and in the labour of love; manfully to "fight the good fight of faith, and to lay hold of eternal life." It is especially designed by God to be a balance both against inward and outward sufferings; to "lift up the hands that hang down and confirm the feeble knees." Consequently, whatever damps our joy in the Lord proportionately obstructs our holiness. And therefore, as far as Satan shakes our joy he hinders our holiness also.

7. The same effect will ensue if he can, by any means, either destroy or shake our peace. For the peace of God is another precious means of advancing the image of God in us. There is scarcely any greater help to holiness than this, a continual tranquility of spirit, the evenness of a mind settled upon God, a calm repose in the blood of Jesus. And without this, it is scarcely possible to "grow in grace," and in the vital "knowledge of our Lord Jesus Christ." For all fear (except the tender, filial fear) freezes and benumbs the soul. It binds up all the springs of spiritual life and stops all motion of the heart toward God. And doubt, as it were, bemires the soul, so that it sticks fast in the deep clay. Therefore, in the same proportion as either of these prevail, our growth in holiness is hindered.

8. At the same time that our wise adversary endeavours to make our conviction of the necessity of perfect love an occasion of shaking our peace by doubts and fears, he endeavours to weaken, if not destroy, our faith. Indeed these are inseparably connected, so that they must stand or fall together. As long as faith subsists we remain in peace; our heart stands fast while it believes in the Lord. But if we let go of our faith, our filial confidence in a loving, pardoning God, our peace is at an end, the very foundation on which it stood being overthrown. And this is the only foundation of holiness as well as of peace; consequently whatever strikes at this, strikes at the very root of all holiness: for without this faith, without an abiding sense that Christ loved me, and gave himself for me, without a continuing conviction that God for Christ's sake is merciful to me a sinner, it is impossible that I should love God. "We love him because he first loved us"; and in proportion to the strength and clearness of our conviction that he has loved us and accepted us in his Son. And unless we love God, it is not possible that we should love our neighbour as ourselves; nor, consequently, that we should have any right affections, either toward God or toward man. It evidently follows that whatever weakens our faith must, in the same degree, obstruct our holiness: and this is not only the most effective but also the most comprehensive way of destroying all holiness; since it does not affect any one Christian temper, any single grace or fruit of the Spirit, but, so far as it succeeds, tears up the very root of the whole work of God.

9. No wonder, therefore, that the ruler of the darkness of this world should here put forth all his strength. And so we find by experience. For it is far easier to conceive than it is to express the unspeakable violence with which this temptation is frequently urged on those who hunger and thirst after righteousness. When they see, in a strong and clear light, on the one hand, the desperate wickedness of their own hearts—on the other hand, the unspotted holiness to which they are called in Christ Jesus; on the one hand, the depth of their own corruption, of their total alienation from God—on the other, the height of the glory of God, that image of the Holy One in which they are to be renewed; there is, many times, no spirit left in them; they could almost cry out, "With God this is impossible!"

They are ready to give up both faith and hope; to cast away that very confidence by which they are to overcome all things, and do all things, through Christ strengthening them; by which after they have done the will of God, they are to "receive the promise."

10. And if they "hold fast the beginning of their confidence steadfastly to the end," they shall undoubtedly receive the promise of God, reaching through both time and eternity. But here is another snare laid for our feet: while we earnestly pant for that part of the promise which is to be accomplished here, "for the glorious liberty of the children of God," we may be led unawares from the consideration of the glory which shall hereafter be revealed. Our eye may be insensibly turned aside from that crown which the righteous Judge has promised to give at that day "to all that love his appearing"; and we may be drawn away from the view of that incorruptible inheritance which is reserved in heaven for us. But this also would be a loss to our souls and an obstruction to our holiness. For to walk in the continual sight of our goal is a necessary aid to our running the race that is set before us. Thus it was the having "looked ahead to the promise of reward," which of old encouraged Moses "to suffer affliction with the people of God rather than enjoy the pleasures of sin for a season; considering the reproach of Christ greater riches than the treasures of Egypt." No, it is even explicitly said of one greater than he, that "for the joy that was set before him he endured the cross, and despised the shame," until he "sat down at the right hand of the throne of God." From this we may easily infer how much more needful for us is the view of that joy set before us, that we may endure whatever cross the wisdom of God lays upon us, and press on through holiness to glory.

11. But while we are reaching to this, as well as to that glorious liberty which is preparatory to it, we may be in danger of falling into another snare of the Devil, by which he labours to entangle the children of God. We may take too much thought for tomorrow, so as to neglect the improvement of today. We may so expect perfect love as not to use that which is already shed abroad in our hearts. There is no shortage of examples of those who have greatly suffered here. They were so taken up with what they were to receive hereafter as utterly to neglect what they had already received. In expectation of

having five talents more, they buried their one talent in the earth. At least, they did not improve it as they might have done, to the glory of God and the good of their own souls.

12. Thus does the subtle adversary of God and man endeavour to make void the counsel of God, by dividing the gospel against itself and making one part of it overthrow the other; while the first work of God in the soul is destroyed by the expectation of his perfect work. We have seen several of the ways in which he attempts this by cutting off, as it were, the springs of holiness. But this he likewise does more directly by making that blessed hope an occasion of unholy tempers.

13. Thus, whenever our heart is eagerly athirst for all the great and precious promises; when we pant after the fullness of God, as the deer after the water-brook; when our soul breaks out in fervent desire, "Why are his chariot-wheels so long a-coming?"—he will not neglect the opportunity of tempting us to murmur against God. He will use all his wisdom and all his strength if perhaps, in an unguarded hour, we may be influenced to complain at our Lord for thus delaying his coming. At least, he will labour to excite some degree of fretfulness or impatience; and perhaps of envy at those whom we believe to have already attained the prize of our high calling. He well knows that, by giving way to any of these tempers, we are pulling down the very thing we would build up. By thus following after perfect holiness, we become more unholy than before. Indeed, there is great danger that our last state should be worse than the first; like those of whom the Apostle speaks in those dreadful words, "It had been better they had never known the way of righteousness, than, after they had known it, to turn back from the holy commandment delivered to them."

14. And from hence he hopes to reap another advantage, even to bring up an evil report of the good way. He is aware of how few are able to distinguish (and too many are not willing so to do) between the accidental abuse and the natural tendency of a doctrine. These, therefore, he will continually blend together with regard to the doctrine of Christian perfection; in order to prejudice the minds of unwary men against the glorious promises of God. And how frequently, how generally—I had almost said, how universally—has

SERMON 37

he prevailed here! For who is there that observes any of these accidental ill effects of this doctrine and does not immediately conclude that this is its natural tendency; and does not readily cry out, "See, these are the fruits (meaning the natural, necessary fruits) of such doctrine"? Not so: they are fruits which may accidentally spring from the abuse of a great and precious truth. But the abuse of this, or any other scriptural doctrine, does by no means destroy its use. Neither can the unfaithfulness of man perverting his right way make the promise of God of no effect. No! Let God be true, and every man a liar. The word of the Lord, it shall stand. "Faithful is he that has promised; he also will do it." Let not us then be "removed from the hope of the gospel." Rather let us observe, which was the second thing proposed, how we may turn back these fiery darts of the wicked one: how we may rise the higher by what he intends as an occasion of our falling.

II. 1. And, first, does Satan endeavour to damp your joy in the Lord, by the consideration of your sinfulness; added to this, that without entire, universal holiness no man can see the Lord? You may cast back this dart upon his own head while through the grace of God, the more you feel of your own vileness, the more you rejoice in confident hope, that all this shall be done away. While you hold fast this hope, every evil temper you feel, though you hate it with a perfect hatred, may be a means, not of lessening your humble joy, but rather of increasing it. "This and this," may you say, "shall likewise perish from the presence of the Lord. Just as the wax melts at the fire, so shall this melt away before his face." By this means, the greater that change is which remains to be wrought in your soul, the more may you triumph in the Lord and rejoice in the God of your salvation, who has done so great things for you already, and will do so much greater things than these.

2. Secondly, the more vehemently he assaults your peace with that suggestion, "God is holy; you are unholy; you are immensely distant from that holiness without which you cannot see God: how then can you be in the favour of God? How can you fancy you are justified?"—take the more earnest heed to hold fast that, "Not by works of righteousness which I have done I am found in him; I am accepted among the Beloved; not having my own righteousness

(as the cause, either in whole or in part, of our justification before God) but that which is by faith in Christ, the righteousness which is of God by faith." O bind this about your neck: write it upon the tablet of your heart. Wear it as a bracelet upon your arm, as frontlets between your eyes: "I am 'justified freely' by his grace, through the redemption that is in Jesus Christ." Value and esteem, more and more, that precious truth, "By grace we are saved through faith." Admire more and more the free grace of God in so loving the world as to give "his only Son, that whoever believes on him might not perish but have everlasting life." So shall the sense of the sinfulness you feel, on the one hand, and of the holiness you expect, on the other, both contribute to establish your peace, and to make it flow as a river. So shall that peace flow on with an even stream, in spite of all those mountains of ungodliness, which shall become a plain in the day when the Lord comes to take full possession of your heart. Neither will sickness, or pain, or the approach of death occasion any doubt or fear. You know a day, an hour, a moment with God, is as a thousand years. He cannot be pressed for time in which to work whatever remains to be done in your soul. And God's time is always the best time. Therefore do not be concerned for anything; only make your request known to Him, and that not with doubt or fear, but with thanksgiving; as being previously assured that He cannot withhold from you any manner of thing that is good.

3. Thirdly: the more you are tempted to give up your shield, to cast away your faith, your confidence in his love, so much the more take heed that you hold fast to that which you have attained; so much the more labour to stir up the gift of God which is in you. Never let that slip, "I have 'an Advocate with the Father, Jesus Christ the righteous'"; and, "The life I now live, I live by faith in the Son of God, who loved me and gave himself for me." Be this your glory and crown of rejoicing. And see that no one takes your crown. Hold that fast: "I know that my Redeemer lives and shall stand at the latter day upon the earth"; and, "I now 'have redemption in his blood, even the forgiveness of sins.'" Thus, being filled with all peace and joy in believing, press on, in the peace and joy of faith to the renewal of your whole soul in the image of him that created you! Meanwhile, cry continually to God that you may see that prize

of your high calling, not as Satan represents it, in a horrid dreadful shape, but in its genuine natural beauty; not as something that must be or you will go to hell, but as what may be, to lead you to heaven. Look upon it as the most desirable gift which is in all the stores of the rich mercies of God. Beholding it in this true point of light, you will hunger after it more and more; your whole soul will be athirst for God and for this glorious conformity to his likeness; and having received a good hope of this, and strong consolation through grace, you will no more be weary or faint in your mind, but will follow on till you attain it.

4. In the same power of faith, press on to glory. Indeed this is the same prospect still. God has joined from the beginning pardon, holiness, heaven. And why should man put them asunder? O beware of this! Let not one link of the golden chain be broken. "God, for Christ's sake has forgiven me. He is now renewing me in his own image. Shortly he will make me worthy of himself and take me to stand before his face. I, whom he has justified through the blood of his Son, being thoroughly sanctified by his Spirit, shall quickly ascend to the 'New Jerusalem, the city of the living God.' Just a little while, and I shall 'come to the general assembly and church of the first-born, and to God the Judge of all, and to Jesus the Mediator of the New Covenant.' How soon will these shadows flee away, and the day of eternity dawn upon me! How soon shall I drink of 'the river of the water of life, going out of the throne of God and of the Lamb! There all his servants shall praise him, and shall see his face, and his name shall be upon their foreheads. And no night shall be there; and they have no need of a candle or the light of the sun. For the Lord God is their light, and they shall reign for ever and ever.'"

5. And if you thus "taste of the good word and of the powers of the world to come," you will not murmur against God, because you are not yet "ready for the inheritance of the saints in light." Instead of complaining at your not being wholly delivered, you will praise God for delivering you thus far. You will magnify God for what he has done and take it as a guarantee of what he will do. You will not fret against him because you are not yet renewed but bless him because you shall be; and because "now your salvation" from all sin "is nearer than when you" first "believed." Instead of uselessly

tormenting yourself because the time has not fully come, you will calmly and quietly wait for it, knowing that it "will come, and will not delay." You may, therefore, the more cheerfully endure, as yet, the burden of sin that still remains in you because it will not always remain. Yet a little while, and it shall be clean gone. Only "wait for the Lord's leisure": be strong, and "he shall comfort your heart"; and put you your trust in the Lord!

6. And if you see any who appear (as far as man can judge, though God alone searches the hearts) to be already partakers of their hope, already "made perfect in love"; far from envying the grace of God in them, let it rejoice and comfort your heart. Glorify God for their sake! "If one member is honoured," shall not "all the members rejoice with it"? Instead of jealousy or evil surmising concerning them, praise God for the consolation! Rejoice in having a fresh proof of the faithfulness of God in fulfilling all his promises; and stir yourself up the more, to "apprehend that for which you also are apprehended of Christ Jesus"!

7. To this end, redeem the time. Improve the present moment. Buy up every opportunity of growing in grace, or of doing good. Let not the thought of receiving more grace tomorrow make you negligent of today. You have one talent now: if you expect five more, so much the rather improve what you have. And the more you expect to receive hereafter, the more labour for God here. Sufficient for the day is the grace thereof. God is now pouring his benefits upon you: now show yourself to be a faithful steward of the present grace of God. Whatever may be tomorrow, give all diligence today to "add to your faith courage, temperance, patience, brotherly-kindness," and the fear of God, until you attain that pure and perfect love! Let these things be now "in you and abound"! Be not now slothful or unfruitful: "so shall an entrance be ministered into the everlasting kingdom of our Lord Jesus Christ"!

8. Lastly: if in times past you have abused this blessed hope of being holy as he is holy, do not therefore cast it away. Let the abuse cease, the use remain. Use it now to the more abundant glory of God, and profit of your own soul. In steadfast faith, in calm tranquility of spirit, in full assurance of hope, rejoicing evermore for what God has done, press on to perfection! Daily growing in the knowledge

of our Lord Jesus Christ, and going on from strength to strength, in resignation, in patience, in humble thankfulness for what you have attained and for what you shall, run the race set before you, "looking to Jesus" until, through perfect love, you enter into his glory!

For Readers

Questions

1. What is the problem that is identified and addressed here?
2. What kind of Christian is especially prone to the problem identified and why?
3. How is the problem broken down into manageable elements that can then be tackled one at a time?
4. How might we see the solution as a clever case of making a virtue out of necessity?
5. How is a vision of the ultimate future brought to bear on the quest for holiness? What earthly analogies can illuminate the principle involved?

Helpful Information

Wesley cleverly surprises us in this sermon by radically undermining our initial expectations given the title and the content of the biblical text. We are prepared for a treatise on the work of the devil but are given a fascinating analysis of how our spiritual aspirations can become the occasion for spiritual depression, if not spiritual disaster. As Wesley neatly puts the point: the gospel comes across as divided against itself.

We should not be distracted by the very general way in which Wesley depicts the action of Satan. We already know that he sees the world as enemy-occupied territory. The ingenuity shows up in the way he provides a thoroughly human analysis of the problem at issue. This ingenuity is also visible in the careful way in which he breaks the basic problem into smaller, manageable components. So, he shows psychologically how lack of joy, peace, and assurance derived from faith undercut the quest for holiness.

To know what is going on in our minds is to have half the solution. We can refuse to accept the inferences we naturally draw from lack of joy and peace and thus stop the downward spiral into doubt, denial, darkness, and even to complete loss of faith. The other half of the solution is to go back again and take heart from our earlier experiences of joy, peace, and assurance. By doing this we ward off spiritual lethargy and murmuring against God. We should also ward off the siren calls of critics who make fun of the whole drive to live a life in conformity with the will of God, or who have made shipwreck of the faith by adopting dysfunctional visions of holiness and thereby given holiness a bad name in the public arena.

Notice that while Wesley never tires of insisting that progress in holiness is due to the power of God, ample space exists for taking ourselves in hand and for playing our part. We are to stir up the gift within us and redeem the time. There is a real place for genuine human action. Our first steps in faith are a platform for moving forward rather than an occasion for allowing our positive expectations to drive us into failure.

Editor's Introduction to Sermon 38

At first glance, Sermons 38 and 39 stick out like sore thumbs; they do not seem to fit the general pattern in which Wesley deals with characteristic challenges facing the believer and that are apt to threaten their survival as healthy Christians. Initially, I thought that they might fit as a kind of refresher course that dealt with two crucial foundational themes in need of reiteration. However, this reading was dispelled by a careful reading of the introduction to Sermon 38. In the opening paragraph, it is clear that he is responding to a serious intellectual attack on a critical element of Christian teaching, namely, its doctrine of sin. And in the final paragraph, he warns the believer in typically blunt terms to beware of teachers of lies.

Hence, we need to see this sermon as mandating the crucial need for apologetics in securing the health of the Christian convert. By apologetics I do not mean here offering an apology for one's beliefs. I mean dealing head-on with an intellectual challenge that, if not rebutted, will undermine the intellectual confidence of the believer.

Wesley lived at a time in the beginning of the modern era when the Christian faith was attacked on the grounds that it had a much too nasty and negative vision of human nature. In time, the whole content of Christianity would come under concerted attack, so much so that it is now common not just to argue that Christianity is false or irrational, but that it is poisonous and a sure and certain pathway to human misery.

The attack on the Christian vision of human nature that Wesley takes up here is focused on its doctrine of sin, commonly identified as the doctrine of original sin. In response, Wesley is not content to appeal to Scripture, although he begins there in no uncertain terms. He mounts a powerful case based on general human experience for the truth of the Christian position on human nature. As part of this he begins to show why the doctrine of sin is often rejected. It is not because it is false, but because it calls into question the origins of that rejection in our moral and spiritual nature.

Wesley's brief treatment more generally of atheism is fascinating.

EDITOR'S INTRODUCTION TO SERMON 38

Those who take this sermon seriously will find fascinating hints on how that challenge might best be pursued. However, those hints are just that; his primary concern is to get believers to think through the intellectual challenge of the doctrine of sin and not be intimidated by the hosts of people who disagree with them.

SERMON 38

Original Sin

"And God saw that the wickedness of man was great on the earth, and that every imagination of the thoughts of his heart was only evil continually" (Gen. 6:5).

1. How widely different is this from the fair pictures of human nature which men have drawn in all ages! The writings of many of the ancients abound with pleasant descriptions of the dignity of man; whom some of them paint as having all virtue and happiness in his composition, or, at least, entirely in his power, without being beholden to any other being; indeed, as self-sufficient, able to live on his own stock and little inferior to God himself.

2. Nor have Heathens alone, men who are guided in their search by little more than the dim light of reason, but many likewise of those that bear the name of Christ, and to whom are entrusted the oracles of God, have spoken as magnificently concerning the nature of man, as if it were all innocence and perfection. Accounts of this kind have particularly abounded in the present century; and perhaps in no part of the world more than in our own country. Here, not a few persons of strong understanding as well as extensive learning have employed their utmost abilities to show what they termed "the fair side of human nature." And it must be acknowledged that, if their accounts of him be just, man is still only "a little lower than the angels"; or, as the words may be more literally rendered, "a little less than God."

3. Is it any wonder that these accounts are very readily received by the generality of men? For who is not easily persuaded to think favourably of himself? Accordingly, writers of this kind are most universally read, admired, applauded. And innumerable are the converts they have made, not only in the frivolous, but the learned world. So it is now quite unfashionable to talk otherwise, to say anything to the disparagement of human nature; which is generally allowed, notwithstanding a few infirmities, to be very innocent, and wise, and virtuous!

4. But in the meantime, what must we do with our Bibles? For they will never agree with this. These accounts, however pleasing to flesh and

blood, are utterly irreconcilable with the scriptural. The Scripture avers that "by one man's disobedience all men were constituted sinners"; that "in Adam all died"; spiritually died, lost the life and the image of God; that fallen, sinful Adam then "fathered a son in his own likeness" (nor was it possible he should beget him in any other, for "who can bring a clean thing out of an unclean?") that consequently we, as well as other men, were by nature "dead in trespasses and sins," "without hope, without God in the world," and therefore "children of wrath," so that every man may say, "I was shaped in wickedness, and in sin my mother conceived me"; "there is no difference," for "all have sinned and come short of the glory of God," of that glorious image of God wherein man was originally created. And hence, when "the Lord looked down from heaven upon the children of men, he saw they had all gone out of the way; they were completely abominable, there was none righteous, no, not one," none who truly sought after God. This exactly agrees with what is declared by the Holy Spirit in the words above recited, "God saw," when he looked down from heaven before, "that the wickedness of man was great on the earth"; so great that "every imagination of the thoughts of his heart was only evil continually."

This is God's account of man. From which I shall take occasion, first, to show what men were before the flood; secondly, to inquire whether they are not the same now; and, thirdly, to add some inferences.

I. 1. I am, first, by opening the words of the text, to show what men were before the flood. And we may fully depend on the account here given: for God saw it, and he cannot be deceived. He "saw that the wickedness of man was great"—Not of this or that man; not of a few men only; not merely of the greater part, but of man in general; of men universally. The word includes the whole human race, every partaker of human nature. And it is not easy for us to calculate their numbers, to tell how many thousands and millions they were. The earth then retained much of its primeval beauty and original fruitfulness. The face of the globe was not rent and torn as it is now; and spring and summer went hand in hand. It is therefore probable that it afforded sustenance for far more inhabitants than it is now capable of sustaining; and these must be immensely multiplied, while men begat sons and daughters for seven or eight hundred years together. Yet among all this inconceivable number, only "Noah found favour with God." He alone (perhaps including part of his household) was an exception from the universal wickedness, which, by the just judgment of God, in a short time after brought on universal destruction. All the rest were partakers in the same guilt, as they were in the same punishment.

2. "God saw all the imaginations of the thoughts of his heart"—of his soul, his inward man, the spirit within him, the principle of all his inward and outward motions. He "saw all the imaginations." It is not possible to find a word of a more extensive signification. It includes whatever is formed, made, fabricated within; all that is or passes in the soul; every inclination, affection, passion, appetite; every temper, intention, thought. It must of consequence include every word and action, as naturally flowing from these fountains, and being either good or evil according to the fountain from which they flow.

3. Now God saw that all this, the whole of it, was evil—contrary to moral rectitude; contrary to the nature of God, which necessarily includes all good; contrary to the divine will, the eternal standard of good and evil; contrary to the pure, holy image of God, in which man was originally created, and in which he stood when God, surveying the works of his hands, saw them all to be very good; contrary to justice, mercy, and truth, and to the essential relations which each man bore to his Creator and his fellow-creatures.

4. But was there not good mingled with the evil? Was there not light intermixed with the darkness? No; none at all: "God saw that the whole imagination of the heart of man was only evil." It cannot indeed be denied but that many of them, perhaps all, had good motions put into their hearts, for the Spirit of God did then also "strive with man," if perhaps he might repent, more especially during that gracious reprieve, the hundred and twenty years while the ark was being built. But still "in his flesh dwelt no good thing"; all his nature was purely evil: it was wholly consistent with itself and unmixed with anything of an opposite nature.

5. However, it may still be matter of inquiry, "Was there no intermission of this evil? Were there no lucid intervals in which something good

might be found in the heart of man?" We are not here to consider what the grace of God might occasionally work in his soul; and, abstracted from this, we have no reason to believe that there was any intermission of that evil. For God, who "saw the whole imagination of the thoughts of his heart to be only evil," saw likewise that it was always the same, that it "was only evil continually"; every year, every day, every hour, every moment. He never deviated into good.

II. Such is the authentic account of the whole race of mankind which He who knows what is in man, who searches the heart and tries the reins, has left upon record for our instruction. Such were all men before God brought the flood upon the earth. We are, secondly, to inquire whether they are the same now.

1. And this is certain, the Scripture gives us no reason to think any otherwise of them. On the contrary, all the above cited passages of Scripture refer to those who lived after the flood. It was more than a thousand years afterward that God declared by David concerning the children of men, "They have all gone out of the way, of truth and holiness; "there is none righteous, no, not one." And to this all the Prophets bear witness in their various generations. So Isaiah, concerning God's peculiar people (and certainly the Heathens were in no better condition), "The whole head is sick, and the whole heart faint. From the sole of the foot up to the head there is no soundness, but wounds, and bruises, and putrefying sores." The same account is given by all the Apostles; indeed, by the whole tenor of the oracles of God. From all these we learn, concerning man in his natural state, unassisted by the grace of God, that "every imagination of the thoughts of his heart is" still "evil, only evil," and that "continually."

2. And this account of the present state of man is confirmed by daily experience. It is true that the natural man discerns it not, and this is not to be wondered at. As long as a man born blind continues so, he is scarcely aware of his deficiency. Much less could we suppose that in a place where all were born without sight, they would be aware of the lack of it. In like manner, as long as men remain in their natural blindness of understanding, they are not aware of their spiritual needs, and of this in particular. But as soon as God

opens the eyes of their understanding, they see the state they were in before; they are then deeply convinced that "every man living," themselves especially, are, by nature, "utter vanity"; that is, folly and ignorance, sin and wickedness.

3. We see, when God opens our eyes, that we were before ἄθεοι ἐν τῷ κόσμῳ, "without God," or rather "atheists, in the world." We had, by nature, no knowledge of God, no acquaintance with him. It is true, as soon as we came to the use of reason we learned "the invisible things of God, even his eternal power and Godhead, from the things that are made." From the things that are seen we inferred the existence of an eternal, powerful Being that is not seen. But still, although we acknowledged his being we had no acquaintance with him. As we know there is an Emperor of China, whom yet we do not know; so we knew there was a King of all the earth, yet we knew him not. Indeed we could not by any of our natural faculties. By none of these could we attain the knowledge of God. We could no more perceive him by our natural understanding than we could see him with our eyes. For "no one knows the Father but the Son, and he to whom the Son wills to reveal him. And no one knows the Son but the Father, and he to whom the Father reveals him."

4. We read of an ancient king, who, being desirous to know what was the "natural language of men," in order to bring the matter to a certain issue, made the following experiment: He ordered two infants, as soon as they were born, to be conveyed to a place prepared for them, where they were brought up without any instruction at all, and without ever hearing a human voice. And what was the result? Why, that when they were at last brought out of their confinement, they spoke no language at all; they uttered only inarticulate sounds, like those of other animals. Were two infants in a similar manner to be brought up from the womb without being instructed in any religion, there is little room to doubt but (unless the grace of God interposed) the result would be just the same. They would have no religion at all: they would have no more knowledge of God than the beasts of the field, than the wild ass's colt. Such is natural religion, abstracted from the traditional and from the influences of God's Spirit!

SERMON 38

5. And having no knowledge, we can have no love of God: we cannot love him we do not know. Most men talk indeed of loving God, and perhaps imagine they do; at least, few will acknowledge they do not love him. But the fact is too plain to be denied. No man loves God by nature, any more than he does a stone, or the earth he treads upon. What we love we delight in: but no man naturally has any delight in God. In our natural state we cannot conceive how any one should delight in him. We take no pleasure in him at all; he is utterly tasteless to us. To love God! it is far above, out of our sight. We cannot naturally attain unto it.

6. We have by nature not only no love, but no fear of God. It is allowed, indeed, that most men have, sooner or later, a kind of senseless, irrational fear, properly called superstition; though the blundering Epicureans gave it the name of religion. Yet even this is not natural but acquired; chiefly by conversation or from example. By nature "God is not in all our thoughts." We leave him to manage his own affairs, to sit quietly, as we imagine, in heaven, and leave us on earth to manage ours; so that we have no more of the fear of God before our eyes than of the love of God in our hearts.

7. Thus are all men "atheists in the world." But Atheism itself does not screen us from idolatry. In his natural state, every man born into the world is a rank idolater. Perhaps, indeed, we may not be such in the vulgar sense of the word. We do not, like the idolatrous Heathens, worship molten or graven images. We do not bow down to the stock of a tree, to the work of our own hands. We do not pray to the angels or saints in heaven any more than to the saints that are upon the earth. But what then? We have set up our idols in our hearts; and to these we bow down and worship them. We worship ourselves when we pay that honour to ourselves which is due to God only. Therefore all pride is idolatry; it is ascribing to ourselves what is due to God alone. And although pride was not made for man, yet where is the man who is born without it? But by this we rob God of his inalienable right and idolatrously usurp his glory.

8. But pride is not the only sort of idolatry of which we are all by nature guilty. Satan has stamped his own image on our heart also in self-will. "I will," he said before he was cast out of heaven, "I will sit upon the sides of the north." I will do my own will and

pleasure, independently of that of my Creator. Every man born into the world says the same, and that in a thousand instances; nay, and avow it too, without ever blushing upon the account, without either fear or shame. Ask the man, "Why did you do this?" He answers, "Because I had a mind to it." What is this but, "Because it was my will," that is, in effect, because the Devil and I agreed; because Satan and I govern our actions by one and the same principle. The will of God, meanwhile, is not in his thoughts, is not considered in the least degree; although it is the supreme rule of every intelligent creature, whether in heaven or earth, resulting from the essential, unalterable relation which all creatures bear to their Creator.

9. This far we bear the image of the Devil and tread in his steps. But at the next step we leave Satan behind; we run into an idolatry of which he is not guilty: I mean love of the world; which is as natural now to every man as to love his own will. What is more natural to us than to seek happiness in the creature instead of the Creator?—to seek that satisfaction in the works of his hands which can be found in God only? What more natural than "the desire of the flesh"?—that is, of the pleasure of sense in every kind? Men indeed talk magnificently of despising these low pleasures, particularly men of learning and education. They pretend to sit loose to the gratification of these appetites on which they stand on a level with the beasts that perish. But it is mere pretension; for every man is conscious to himself that in this respect he is, by nature, a very beast. Sensual appetites, even those of the lowest kind, have more or less the dominion over him. They lead him captive; they drag him to and fro in spite of his boasted reason. The man, with all his good breeding, and other accomplishments, has no pre-eminence over the goat: Indeed, it is much to be doubted whether the beast has not the pre-eminence over him. Certainly he has, if we may hearken to one of their modern oracles, who very decently tells us,

> Once in a season beasts too taste of love;
> Only the beast of reason is its slave,
> And in that folly drudges all the year.

A considerable difference indeed, it must be allowed, there is between man and man, arising (beside that wrought by preventing grace) from difference of constitution and of education. But, notwithstanding this, who, that is not utterly ignorant of himself, can here cast the first stone at another? Who can abide the test of our blessed Lord's comment on the Seventh Commandment: "He who gazes upon a woman with lust has committed adultery with her already in his heart"? So that one knows not which to wonder at more, the ignorance or the insolence of those men who speak with such disdain of those who are overcome by desires which every man has felt in his own breast; the desire of every pleasure of sense, innocent or not, being natural to every child of man.

10. And so is "the desire of the eye," the desire of the pleasures of the imagination. These arise from great, or beautiful, or uncommon objects—if the two former do not coincide with the latter; for perhaps it would appear, upon a diligent inquiry, that neither grand nor beautiful objects please any longer than they are new; that when the novelty of them is over, the greatest part, at least, of the pleasure they give is over; and in the same proportion as they become familiar they become flat and insipid. But let us experience this ever so often, the same desire will remain still. The inbred thirst continues fixed in the soul; nay, the more it is indulged, the more it increases, and incites us to follow after another and yet another object; although we leave every one with an abortive hope, and a deluded expectation. Yes,

> The hoary fool, who many days
>   Has struggled with continued sorrow,
> Renews his hope, and fondly lays
>   The desperate bet upon tomorrow!

> Tomorrow comes! 'Tis noon! 'Tis night!
>   This day, like all the former, flies:
> Yet on he goes, to seek delight
>   Tomorrow, till tonight he dies!

11. A third symptom of this fatal disease, the love of the world, which is so deeply rooted in our nature, is "the pride of life"; the desire of praise, of the honour which comes from men. This the greatest admirers of human nature allow to be strictly natural; as natural as sight, or hearing, or any other of the external senses. And are they ashamed of it, even men of letters, men of refined and improved

understanding? So far from it that they glory in it! They applaud themselves for their love of applause! Yes, even eminent Christians, so called, make no difficulty of adopting the saying of the old, vain Heathen, *Animi dissoluti est et nequam negligere quid de se homines sentient*, "To disregard what men think of us is the mark of a wicked and abandoned mind." So to go calm and unmoved through honour and dishonour, through evil report and good report, is with them a sign of one that is, indeed, not fit to live: "Away with such a fellow from the earth!" But would one imagine that these men had ever heard of Jesus Christ or his Apostles; or that they knew who it was that said, "How can you believe who receive honour from one another, and do not seek the honour which comes from God alone?" But if this is really so, if it be impossible to believe, and consequently to please God, as long as we receive or seek honour from one another, and do not seek the honour which comes from God alone; then in what a condition are all mankind—the Christians as well as Heathens—since they all seek honour from one another since it is as natural for them so to do, themselves being the judges, as it is to see the light which strikes upon their eye, or to hear the sound which enters their ear; yes, since they even count it a sign of a virtuous mind to seek the praise of men, and of a vicious one to be content with the honour that comes from God alone!

III. 1. I proceed to draw a few inferences from what has been said. And, first, from this we may learn one grand fundamental difference between Christianity, considered as a system of doctrines, and the most refined Heathenism. Many of the ancient Heathens have largely described the vices of particular men. They have spoken much against their covetousness, or cruelty; their luxury, or prodigality. Some have dared to say that "no man is born without vices of one kind or another." But still as none of them were taught about the fall of man, none of them knew of his total corruption. They knew not that all men were empty of all good and filled with all manner of evil. They were wholly ignorant of the entire depravation of the whole human nature, of every man born into the world, in every faculty of his soul, not so much by those particular vices which reign in particular persons, as by the general flood of Atheism and idolatry, of pride, self-will, and love of the world. This, therefore, is the first grand distinguishing point between Heathenism and Christianity. The one acknowledges that many men are infected with many vices, and even born with a proneness to them; but supposes notwithstanding that in some the natural good much overbalances the evil; the other declares that all men are conceived in sin, and "shaped in wickedness" and that hence there is in every man a "carnal mind, which is enmity against God, which is not, cannot be, subject to" his "law"; and which so infects the whole soul that "there dwells in" him, "in his flesh," in his natural state, "no good thing"; but "every imagination of the thoughts of his heart is evil," only evil, and that "continually."

2. Hence we may learn, secondly, that all who deny this, call it original sin or by any other title, are Heathens still on the fundamental point which distinguishes Heathenism from Christianity. They may indeed allow that men have many vices; that some are born with us; and that, consequently, we are not born altogether so wise or so virtuous as we should be; there being few that will roundly affirm, "We are born with as much propensity to good as to evil, and every man is, by nature, as virtuous and wise as Adam was at his creation." But here is the shibboleth: is man by nature filled with all manner of evil? Is he void of all good? Is he wholly fallen? Is his soul totally corrupted? Or, to come back to the text, is "every imagination of the thoughts of his heart only evil continually"? Allow this, and you are so far a Christian. Deny it, and you are but a Heathen still.

3. We may learn from this, in the third place, what is the proper nature of religion, of the religion of Jesus Christ. It is θεραπεία ψυχῆς, God's method of "healing a soul" which is thus diseased. By this the great Physician of souls applies medicines to heal this sickness; to restore human nature, totally corrupted in all its faculties. God heals all our Atheism by the knowledge of Himself and of Jesus Christ whom he has sent; by giving us faith, a divine evidence and conviction of God, and of the things of God—in particular, of this important truth: "Christ loved me and gave himself for me." By repentance and lowliness of heart, the deadly disease of pride is healed; that of self-will by resignation, a meek and thankful submission to the will of God; and for the love of the world in all its branches, the love of God is the sovereign remedy. Now, this is properly religion,

"faith" thus "working by love"; working the genuine meek humility, entire deadness to the world, with a loving, thankful acquiescence in, and conformity to, the whole will and word of God.

4. Indeed, if man were not thus fallen, there would be no need of all this. There would be no occasion for this work in the heart, this renewal in the spirit of our mind. The superfluity of godliness would then be a more proper expression than the "superfluity of naughtiness." For an external religion, without any godliness at all, would suffice to all rational intents and purposes. It does, accordingly, suffice in the judgment of those who deny this corruption of our nature. They make very little more of religion than the famous Mr. Hobbes did of reason. According to him, reason is only "a well-ordered train of words." According to them, religion is only a well-ordered train of words and actions. And they speak consistently with themselves; for if the inside is not full of wickedness, if this is clean already, what remains but to "clean the outside of the cup"? Outward reformation, if their supposition is valid, is indeed the only thing necessary.

5. But you have not so learned the oracles of God. You know that He who sees what is in man gives a far different account both of nature and grace, of our fall and our recovery. You know that the great purpose of religion is to renew our hearts in the image of God, to repair that total loss of righteousness and true holiness which we sustained by the sin of our first parents. You know that all religion which does not answer this end, all that stops short of this, the renewal of our soul in the image of God after the likeness of Him that created it, is no other than a poor farce, and a mere mockery of God, to the destruction of our own soul. O beware of all those teachers of lies who would palm this upon you for Christianity! Regard them not, though they should come to you with all the deceptiveness of unrighteousness; with all smoothness of language, all decency; yes, even beauty and elegance of expression, all professions of earnest good-will to you, and reverence for the Holy Scriptures. Keep to the plain, old faith "once delivered to the saints," and delivered by the Spirit of God to our hearts. Know your disease! Know your cure! You were born in sin; therefore "you must be born again," born of God. By nature you are wholly

SERMON 38

corrupted. By grace you shall be wholly renewed. In Adam you all died: in the second Adam, in Christ, you all are made alive. "You who were dead in sins he has quickened": He has already given you a principle of life, even faith in him who loved you and gave himself for you! Now "go on from faith to faith," until your whole sickness is healed; and all that "mind be in you which was also in Christ Jesus"!

For Readers

Questions

1. Why does this sermon tackle the topic of original sin as revealed in the opening paragraph?
2. What are the crucial elements in the description of sin that are developed here?
3. Why are atheism and idolatry the default positions as far as human nature is concerned?
4. How does this sermon argue for the claim that the doctrine of sin is essential to the very meaning of Christianity?
5. How helpful is it to think of salvation in terms of healing, and how might that help us deal with objections to the doctrine of sin today?

Helpful Information

It is very clear that Wesley is going deep in his treatment of the doctrine of original sin. Thus, he notes how unpopular the doctrine is, why any optimistic vision of human nature is inescapably superficial, and why it is not just a minor element in the intellectual content of Christianity. On the latter score, the doctrine of sin is a critical distinguishing feature of Christianity properly understood.

Wesley is not wedded to the language of original sin; he is interested in providing a deep analysis of its crucial elements rather than sticking to a form of words. Moreover, his choice of text is amazing. He works off a verse in Genesis 6 rather than rehearsing the standard interpretation of Genesis 3. He does this with good reason: it allows him to argue that optimistic views of human nature do not fit with people as we know them all too well across space and time.

Wesley works off a fascinating account of atheism here. He does not fasten on potential arguments for and against Christianity, but looks to the underlying causes of atheism in spiritual blindness. So, atheism is a matter of cognitive malfunction; it is not just a matter of following inferential arguments for and against God.

Wesley includes a lovely touch toward the end when he turns to medicine and the idea of healing as a fresh way to think of the nature of salvation. This does not rule out other ways of thinking of salvation, say, in juridical or legal terms. These analogies can be complementary rather than disjunctive. Here the analogy with healing helps those who defend the faith to offer a more attractive image for thinking of Christianity.

Editor's Introduction to Sermon 39

It was very tempting to link this sermon with Sermon 38. Both of them clearly begin to take the believer into deep theological waters, and both deal with serious objections to Wesley's vision of Christianity. So, both could be taken as inviting believers to engage in the task of apologetics. My main reason for separating them is that this sermon does more than engage in what we might call positive as opposed to negative apologetics; it invites believers to begin thinking through a whole new level a critical theological theme that is central to Christianity. In short, it is a brilliant little charter for taking up the tasks of theology.

The arguments for this distinct endeavor are these: First, the sermon provides a very rich account of why new birth is needed, what it is, and the goals new birth serves. Wesley even provides a very clean definition of new birth that will encourage clear and precise thinking. Second, the sermon introduces ancient and contemporary source material that will encourage readers to begin the task of mining the history of reflection on new birth; it draws on ancient Jewish practice and on the teachings of the Anglican tradition. Third, it engages in very careful conceptual analysis, working out the distinction between sanctification and new birth as far as temporal features are concerned. Finally, the sermon takes up the very thorny problem of the relation between new birth and baptism. Wesley's word is not the last word, but it provides exceptionally important food for thought.

As ever, at the end, Wesley cannot avoid drifting into his vocation as an evangelist. However, this is no throwaway observation; it tells us something very important about the task of theology, especially in a time when we need to develop an intimate connection between theology and evangelism.

SERMON 39

The New Birth

"You must be born again" (John 3:7).

1. If any doctrines within the whole compass of Christianity may be properly termed fundamental, they are doubtless these two—the doctrine of justification, and that of the new birth. The former relates to that great work which God does for us, in forgiving our sins; the latter to the great work which God does in us, in renewing our fallen nature. In order of time, neither of these is before the other: in the moment we are justified by the grace of God, through the redemption that is in Jesus, we are also "born of the Spirit"; but in order of thinking, as it is termed, justification precedes the new birth. We first conceive his wrath to be turned away, and then his Spirit to work in our hearts.

2. How very important it must it be, then, for every child of man to thoroughly understand these fundamental doctrines! From a full conviction of this, many excellent men have written at great length concerning justification, explaining every point relating to it, and opening the Scriptures which treat upon it. Many likewise have written on the new birth, and some of them largely enough; but still not so clearly as might have been desired, nor so deeply and accurately, having either given a dark, abstruse account of it or a slight and superficial one. Therefore a full, and at the same time a clear, account of the new birth, seems to be wanting still; such as may enable us to give a satisfactory answer to these three questions: First, why must we be born again? What is the foundation of this doctrine of the new birth? Secondly, how must we be born again? What is the nature of the new birth? And, thirdly, why must we be born again? To what end is it necessary? These questions, by the assistance of God, I shall briefly and plainly answer; and then subjoin a few inferences which will naturally follow.

I. 1. And first, why must we be born again? What is the foundation of this doctrine? The foundation of it lies nearly as deep as the creation of the world; in the scriptural account in which we read, "And God," the three-one God, "said, 'Let us make man in our image, according to our likeness.' So God created man in his own image,

SERMON 39

in the image of God he created him" (Gen. 1:26–27), not merely in his natural image, a picture of his own immortality; a spiritual being, endued with understanding, freedom of will, and various affections—nor merely in his political image, the governor of this lower world, having "dominion over the fishes of the sea, and over all the earth"—but chiefly in his moral image; which, according to the Apostle, is "righteousness and true holiness" (Eph. 4:24). In this image of God was humanity made. "God is love"; accordingly, man at his creation was full of love, which was the sole principle of all his tempers, thoughts, words, and actions. God is full of justice, mercy, and truth; so was man as he came from the hands of his Creator. God is spotless purity; and so man was in the beginning pure from every sinful blot, otherwise God could not have pronounced him, as well as all the other works of his hands, "very good" (Gen. 1:31). This he could not have been, had he not been pure from sin and filled with righteousness and true holiness. For there is no medium or middle way: if we suppose an intelligent creature not to love God, not to be righteous and holy, we necessarily suppose him not to be good at all, much less to be "very good."

2. But although man was made in the image of God, he was not made immutable. This would have been inconsistent with the state of trial in which God was pleased to place him. He was therefore created able to stand and yet liable to fall. And this God himself apprised him of and gave him a solemn warning against it. Nevertheless, man did not abide in honour: he fell from his high estate. He "ate of the tree of which the Lord had commanded him, 'You shall not eat of this.'" By this willful act of disobedience to his Creator, this flat rebellion against his Sovereign, he openly declared that he would no longer have God to rule over him; that he would be governed by his own will and not the will of Him that created him; and that he would not seek his happiness in God but in the world, in the works of his hands. Now God had told him before, "In the day that you eat" of that fruit, "you shall surely die." And the word of the Lord cannot be broken. Accordingly, in that day he did die: he died to God—the most dreadful of all deaths. He lost the life of God: he was separated from Him, in union with whom his spiritual life consisted. The body dies when it is separated from the soul;

the soul, when it is separated from God. But this separation from God, Adam sustained in the day, the hour, he ate of the forbidden fruit. And of this he gave immediate proof; quickly showing by his behaviour that the love of God was extinguished in his soul, which was now "alienated from the life of God." Instead of this, he was now under the power of servile fear, so that he fled from the presence of the Lord. Indeed, so little did he retain even of the knowledge of Him who fills heaven and earth that he endeavoured to "hide himself from the Lord God among the trees of the garden" (Gen. 3:8). Thus had he lost both the knowledge and the love of God without which the image of God could not subsist. Of this, therefore, he was deprived at the same time, and became unholy as well as unhappy. Instead, he had sunk into pride and self-will, the very image of the Devil; and into sensual appetites and desires, the image of the beasts that perish.

3. If it is said, "No, that warning, 'In the day that you eat from it, you shall surely die,' refers to temporal death and that alone, to the death of the body only," the answer is plain: to affirm this is flatly and palpably to make God a liar; to declare that the God of truth positively affirmed a thing contrary to truth. For it is evident Adam did not die in this sense, "in the day that he ate from it." He lived, in the sense opposite to this death, more than nine hundred years after. So this cannot possibly be understood as the death of the body without impeaching the veracity of God. It must therefore be understood as spiritual death, the loss of the life and image of God.

4. And in Adam all died, all humankind, all the children of men who were then in Adam's loins. The natural consequence of this is that everyone descended from him comes into the world spiritually dead, dead to God, wholly dead in sin; entirely void of the life of God; void of the image of God, of all that righteousness and holiness in which Adam was created. Instead of this, every man born into the world now bears the image of the Devil in pride and self-will; the image of the beast, in sensual appetites and desires. This, then, is the foundation of the new birth—the entire corruption of our nature. Hence it is that, being born in sin, we must be "born again." Hence everyone who is born of a woman must be born of the Spirit of God.

II. 1. But how must a man be born again? What is the nature of the new birth? This is the second question. And it is a question of the highest conceivable importance. We ought not therefore, in so weighty a concern, to be content with a short inquiry; but to examine it with all possible care and to ponder it in our hearts, until we fully understand this important point, and clearly see how we are to be born again.

2. Not that we are to expect any detailed, philosophical account of the manner how this is done. Our Lord sufficiently guards us against any such expectation by the words immediately following the text; in which he reminds Nicodemus of as indisputable a fact as any in the whole compass of nature, which, notwithstanding, the wisest man under the sun is not able fully to explain. "The wind blows where it pleases"—not by your power or wisdom; "and you hear its sound"—you are absolutely assured, beyond all doubt, that it does blow; "but you cannot tell from where it comes, nor where it is going"—the precise manner how it begins and ends, rises and falls, no man can tell. "So it is with everyone who is born of the Spirit"—you may be as absolutely assured of the fact as of the blowing of the wind; but the precise manner how it is done, how the Holy Spirit works this in the soul, neither you nor the wisest of the children of men is able to explain.

3. However, it suffices for every rational and Christian purpose that, without descending into curious, critical inquiries, we can give a plain scriptural account of the nature of the new birth. This will satisfy every reasonable man who desires only the salvation of his soul. The expression, "being born again," was not first used by our Lord in his conversation with Nicodemus: it was well known before that time and was in common use among the Jews when our Saviour appeared among them. When an adult Gentile was convinced that the Jewish religion was of God and desired to join it, it was the custom to baptize him first, before he was admitted to circumcision. And when he was baptized, he was said to be born again, by which they meant that he who was before a child of the Devil was now adopted into the family of God and accounted one of his children. This expression, therefore, which Nicodemus, being "a Teacher in Israel," ought to have understood well, our Lord

uses in conversing with him; only in a stronger sense than he was accustomed to. And this might be the reason of his asking, "How can these things be?" They cannot be literally—a man cannot "enter a second time into his mother's womb, and be born"—but they may spiritually: a man may be born from above, born of God, born of the Spirit, in a manner which bears a very near analogy to the natural birth.

4. Before a child is born into the world, he has eyes but sees not; he has ears but does not hear. He has a very imperfect use of any other sense. He has no knowledge of any of the things of the world, or any natural understanding. We do not even give the name of life to that manner of existence which he then has. It is only when a man is born that we say he begins to live. For as soon as he is born, be begins to see the light, and the various objects with which he is encompassed. His ears are then opened, and he hears the sounds which successively strike upon them. At the same time, all the other organs of sense begin to be exercised upon their proper objects. He likewise breathes, and lives in a manner wholly different from what he did before. How exactly does the parallel hold in all these instances! While a man is in a mere natural state, before he is born of God, he has, in a spiritual sense, eyes and sees not; a thick impenetrable veil lies upon them; he has ears, but hears not; he is utterly deaf to what he is most of all concerned to hear. His other spiritual senses are all locked up: he is in the same condition as if he did not have them. Hence he has no knowledge of God; no intercourse with him; he is not at all acquainted with him. He has no true knowledge of the things of God, either of spiritual or eternal things; therefore, though he is a living man, he is a dead Christian. But as soon as he is born of God, there is a total change in all these particulars. The "eyes of his understanding are opened"; (such is the language of the great Apostle); and, He who of old "commanded light to shine out of darkness shining on his heart, he sees the light of the glory of God," his glorious love, "in the face of Jesus Christ." His ears being opened, he is now capable of hearing the inward voice of God, saying, "Be of good cheer; your sins are forgiven"; "go and sin no more." This is the thrust of what God speaks to his heart; although perhaps not in these very words. He

is now ready to hear whatever "He who teaches man knowledge" is pleased, from time to time, to reveal to him. He "feels in his heart," to use the language of our Church, "the mighty working of the Spirit of God," not in a gross, carnal sense as the men of the world stupidly and willfully misunderstand the expression; though they have been told again and again, we mean by it neither more nor less than this: he feels, is inwardly aware of, the graces which the Spirit of God works in his heart. He feels, he is conscious of, a "peace which passes all understanding." He many times feels such a joy in God as is "unspeakable, and full of glory." He feels "the love of God shed abroad in his heart by the Holy Spirit which is given unto him"; and all his spiritual senses are then exercised to discern spiritual good and evil. By the use of these, he is daily increasing in the knowledge of God, of Jesus Christ whom he has sent and to all the things pertaining to his inward kingdom. And now he may be properly said to live: God having quickened him by his Spirit, he is alive to God through Jesus Christ. He lives a life which the world does not know, a "life which is hidden with Christ in God." God is continually breathing, as it were, upon the soul; and his soul is breathing unto God. Grace is descending into his heart; and prayer and praise ascending to heaven. And by this intercourse between God and man, this fellowship with the Father and the Son, as by a kind of spiritual respiration, the life of God in the soul is sustained; and the child of God grows up, until he comes to the "full measure of the stature of Christ."

5. From this it manifestly appears what the nature of the new birth is. It is that great change which God works in the soul when he brings it into life; when he raises it from the death of sin to the life of righteousness. It is the change wrought in the whole soul by the almighty Spirit of God when it is "created anew in Christ Jesus"; when it is "renewed after the image of God in righteousness and true holiness"; when the love of the world is changed into the love of God; pride into humility; passion into meekness; hatred, envy, malice, into a sincere, tender, disinterested love for all mankind. In a word, it is that change by which the earthly, sensual, devilish mind is turned into the "mind which was in Christ Jesus." This is the nature of the new birth: "thus is every one that is born of the Spirit."

III. 1. It is not difficult for any who has considered these things to see the necessity of the new birth, and to answer the third question, "Why, for what reason, is it necessary that we should be born again?" It is very easily discerned that this is necessary, first, in order to holiness. For what is holiness according to the oracles of God? Not a mere external religion, a round of outward duties, however many there be, and however exactly performed. No: gospel holiness is nothing less than the image of God stamped upon the heart; it is nothing other than the whole mind which was in Christ Jesus; it consists of all heavenly affections and tempers mingled together in one. It implies such a continual, thankful love to Him who has not withheld from us his Son, his only son, as makes it natural, and in a manner necessary to us, to love every child of man; as fills us "with bowels of mercies, kindness, gentleness, long-suffering." It is such a love of God as teaches us to be blameless in all manner of conversation; as enables us to present our souls and bodies, all we are and all we have, all our thoughts, words, and actions, a continual sacrifice to God, acceptable through Christ Jesus. Now, this holiness can have no existence until we are renewed in the image of our mind. It cannot commence in the soul until that change be wrought; until, by the power of the Highest overshadowing us, we are "brought from darkness to light, from the power of Satan unto God"; that is, until we are born again; which, therefore, is absolutely necessary in order to holiness.

2. But "without holiness no man shall see the Lord," shall see the face of God in glory. Of consequence, the new birth is absolutely necessary in order to eternal salvation. Men may indeed flatter themselves (so desperately wicked and so deceitful is the heart of man!) that they may live in their sins till they come to the last gasp and yet afterwards live with God; and thousands do really believe that they have found a broad way which does not lead to destruction. "What danger," say they, "can a woman be in who is so harmless and so virtuous? What fear is there that so honest a man, one of such strict morality, should miss of heaven; especially if, over and above all this, they constantly attend on church and sacrament?" One of these will ask with all assurance, "What! Shall not I do as well as my neighbours?" Yes, as well as your unholy neighbours; as

well as your neighbours that die in their sins! For you will all drop into the pit together, into the lowest hell! You will all lie together in the lake of fire; "the lake of fire burning with brimstone." Then, at length, you will see (but God grant you may see it before!) the necessity of holiness in order to glory; and, consequently, of the new birth, since none can be holy unless he is born again.

3. For the same reason, unless he is born again, no one can be happy even in this world. For it is not possible, in the nature of things, that a man should be happy who is not holy. Even the poor, ungodly poet (Juvenal) could tell us, *Nemo malus felix,* "no wicked man is happy." The reason is plain: all unholy tempers are uneasy tempers. Not only do malice, hatred, envy, jealousy, revenge, create a present hell in the breast; but even the softer passions, if not kept within due bounds, give a thousand times more pain than pleasure. Even "hope," when "deferred" (and how often must this be the case!) "makes the heart sick"; and every desire which is not according to the will of God is liable to "pierce" us "through with many sorrows." And all those general sources of sin—pride, self-will, and idolatry—are, in the same proportion as they prevail, general sources of misery. Therefore, as long as these reign in any soul, happiness has no place there. But they must reign until the bent of our nature is changed, that is, until we are born again. Consequently, the new birth is absolutely necessary in order to happiness in this world, as well as in the world to come.

IV. I proposed in the last place to subjoin a few inferences which naturally follow from the preceding observations.

1. And, first, it follows that baptism is not the new birth: They are not one and the same thing. Many indeed seem to imagine that they are just the same; at least, they speak as if they thought so; but I do not know that this opinion is publicly avowed by any denomination of Christians whatever. Certainly it is not by any within these kingdoms, whether of the established Church, or dissenting from it. The judgment of the latter is clearly declared in the large Catechism.

> Question: What are the parts of a sacrament?
> Answer: The parts of a sacrament are two: The one an outward

THE NEW BIRTH

and sensible sign; the other, an inward and spiritual grace, thereby signified.

Question: What is baptism?

Answer: Baptism is a sacrament, wherein Christ has ordained the washing with water, to be a sign and seal of regeneration by his Spirit.

Here it is manifest: baptism, the sign, is spoken of as distinct from regeneration, the thing signified. In the Church Catechism likewise, the judgment of our Church is declared with the utmost clearness.

Question: What does the word "sacrament" mean?

Answer: It means an outward and visible sign of an inward and spiritual grace.

Question: What is the outward part or form in baptism?

Answer: Water, in which the person is baptized in the name of the Father, Son, and Holy Spirit.

Question: What is the inward part; the thing signified?

Answer: A death unto sin and a new birth unto righteousness.

Nothing, therefore, is plainer than that; according to the Church of England, baptism is not the new birth.

But indeed the reason of the thing is so clear and evident as not to need any other authority. For what can be more plain than that the one is an external, the other an internal work?—that the one is a visible, the other an invisible thing, and therefore wholly different from each other?—the one being an act of man, purifying the body; the other a change wrought by God in the soul. So the former is just as distinguishable from the latter as the soul from the body, or water from the Holy Spirit.

2. From the preceding reflections we may, secondly, observe that, as the new birth is not the same thing as baptism, so it does not always accompany baptism: they do not constantly go together. A man may possibly be "born of water" and yet not be "born of the Spirit." There may sometimes be the outward sign where there is not the inward grace. I do not now speak with regard to infants: it is certain our Church supposes that all who are baptized in their infancy are at the same time born again; and it is allowed that

the whole Office for the Baptism of Infants proceeds upon this supposition. Nor is it an objection of any weight against this that we cannot comprehend how this work can be wrought in infants; for neither can we comprehend how it is wrought in a person of riper years. But whatever be the case with infants, it is sure that not all of riper years who are baptized are at the same time born again. "The tree is known by its fruit," and in this it appears, too plain to be denied, that many of those who were children of the Devil before they were baptized continue the same after baptism, "for they do works of their father." They continue as servants of sin without any pretence either to inward or outward holiness.

3. A third inference which we may draw from what has been observed is that the new birth is not the same as sanctification. This is indeed taken for granted by many; particularly by an eminent writer in his late treatise on "The Nature and Grounds of Christian Regeneration." To waive several other weighty objections which might be made to that tract, this is a palpable one: it all along speaks of regeneration as a progressive work, carried on in the soul by slow degrees, from the time of our first turning to God. This is undeniably true of sanctification; but of regeneration, the new birth, it is not true. This is a part of sanctification, not the whole; it is the gate to it, the entrance into it. When we are born again, then our sanctification, our inward and outward holiness, begins; and thenceforward we are gradually to "grow up in Him who is our Head." This expression of the Apostle admirably illustrates the difference between one and the other, and further points out the exact analogy there is between natural and spiritual things. A child is born of a woman in a moment, or at least in a very short time: afterward he gradually and slowly grows until he attains to the stature of a man. In like manner, a child is born of God in a short time, if not in a moment. But it is by slow degrees that he afterward grows up to the measure of the full stature of Christ. The same relation, therefore, which there is between our natural birth and our growth, there is also between our new birth and our sanctification.

4. One point more we may learn from the preceding observations. But it is a point of so great importance as may excuse the considering it the more carefully and prosecuting it at some length. What must one

who loves the souls of men, and is grieved that any of them should perish, say to one whom he sees living in sabbath-breaking, drunkenness, or any other willful sin? What can he say, if the foregoing observations are true, but "You must be born again"? "No," says a zealous man, "that cannot be. How can you talk so uncharitably to the man? Has he not been baptized already? He cannot be born again now." Can he not be born again? Do you affirm this? Then he cannot be saved. Though he be as old as Nicodemus was, yet "unless he is born again, he cannot see the kingdom of God." Therefore in saying, "He cannot be born again," you in effect deliver him over to damnation. And who is uncharitable now—me or you? I say he may be born again and so become an heir of salvation. You say, "He cannot be born again": and if so, he must inevitably perish! So you utterly block up his way to salvation and send him to hell, out of charity!

But perhaps the sinner himself, to whom in real charity we say "You must be born again," has been taught to say, "I defy your new doctrine. I need not be born again: I was born again when I was baptized. Would you have me deny my baptism?" I answer, first, There is nothing under heaven which can excuse a lie; otherwise I should say to an open sinner, "If you have been baptized, do not claim it." For how highly does this aggravate your guilt! How will it increase your damnation! Were you devoted to God at eight days old, and have you been all these years devoting yourself to the Devil? Were you, even before you had the use of reason, consecrated to God the Father, the Son, and the Holy Spirit? And have you, ever since you had the use of it, been flying in the face of God and consecrating yourself to Satan? Does the abomination of desolation—the love of the world, pride, anger, lust, foolish desire, and a whole train of vile affections—stand where it ought not? Have you set up all the accursed things in that soul which was once a temple of the Holy Spirit; set apart for a "habitation of God through the Spirit"; indeed, solemnly consecrated to him? And do you glory in this, that you once belonged to God? O be ashamed! Blush! Hide yourself in the earth! Never boast again of what ought to fill you with confusion, to make you ashamed before God and man!

I answer, secondly, you have already denied your baptism; and that in the most effectual manner. You have denied it a thousand

and a thousand times; and you do so still, day by day. For in your baptism you renounced the Devil and all his works. Whenever, therefore, you give place to him again, whenever you do any of the works of the Devil, you then deny your baptism. Therefore you deny it by every voluntary sin; by every act of uncleanness, drunkenness, or revenge; by every obscene or profane word; by every oath that comes out of your mouth. Every time you profane the day of the Lord, you thus deny your baptism; indeed, every time you do anything to another which you would not he should do to you.

I answer, thirdly, Whether you are baptized or unbaptized, "you must be born again"; otherwise it is not possible you should be inwardly holy; and without inward as well as outward holiness you cannot be happy even in this world, much less in the world to come. Do you say, "No, I do no harm to any man; I am honest and just in all my dealings; I do not curse, or take the Lord's name in vain; I do not profane the Lord's day; I am no drunkard; I do not slander my neighbour, nor live in any knowing sin"? If this be so, it were much to be wished that all men went as far as you do. But you must go further still or you cannot be saved: "You must be born again." Do you add, "I do go further still, for I not only do no harm but do all the good I can"? I doubt that fact; I fear you have had a thousand opportunities of doing good which you have allowed to pass by unimproved, and for which therefore you are accountable to God. But if you had improved them all, if you really had done all the good you possibly could to all men, yet this does not at all alter the case; still, "you must be born again." Without this nothing will do any good to your poor, sinful, polluted soul. "No, I constantly attend all the ordinances of God: I keep to my church and sacrament." It is well you do: But all this will not keep you from hell, unless you are born again. Go to church twice a day; go to the Lord's table every week; say ever so many prayers in private; hear ever so many good sermons; read ever so many good books; still, "you must be born again." None of these things will stand in the place of the new birth; no, nor anything under heaven.

Let this therefore, if you have not already experienced this inward work of God, be your continual prayer: "Lord, add this to all your blessings. Let me be born again! Deny whatever you please, but do not deny me this; let me be 'born from above'! Take away whatever seems good to you—my reputation, my fortune, my friends, my health—only give me this, to be born of the Spirit, to be received among the children of God! Let me be born, 'not of corruptible seed, but incorruptible, by the word of God, which lives and abides forever'; and then let me daily 'grow in grace, and in the knowledge of our Lord and Saviour Jesus Christ'!"

For Readers

Questions

1. Why are justification and new birth not just important but foundational doctrines?
2. How does this sermon lay out the broad Christian narrative of creation, freedom, fall, and salvation?
3. What would a minute philosophical account of new birth look like, and why is it not available?
4. How does the analogy with physical birth throw light on the nature of spiritual new birth?
5. How should we handle the connection between new birth and baptism?

Helpful Information

Read as an exercise in theology for beginners, this is a brilliant sermon. It takes a difficult concept (new birth) and starts by providing motivation for thinking it through with care. Then, it provides the deeper theological horizon in which the doctrine of new birth finds its natural home. Beyond that, it provides a splendid example of analogical thinking, a vital skill to learn in explaining theological concepts and ideas. Next, it makes sure we have a precise, warranted definition that we can then continue to walk around and interrogate. Finally, it tackles the difficult problem of the relation between a central theological concept (new birth) and church practice (baptism).

In rejecting the quest for a detailed philosophical explanation of new birth, Wesley is setting limits to the extent we can identify the mechanism of divine action in new birth. This does not mean we throw up our hands and proclaim mystery. We can insist that new birth is a work of the Spirit, and we can develop illuminating analogies.

Notice that here, as elsewhere in these canonical sermons, Wesley insists on sanctification as a process. The implicit message is that we need to be careful about dealing with experiences of crisis and dedication; these are important human elements, but they are secondary in the end.

Notice also that Wesley is not intimidated by serious objections to his claims about the potential relation between new birth and baptism. Indeed, he cleverly turns the tables by noting that if we believe we were born again in baptism, then, if we are not living up to what new birth signifies, we are in deep spiritual trouble. So, we should develop objections to our theological claims in order to arrive at a deeper understanding of the faith. All this will then strengthen us as we seek to stay the course in the journey of faith.

Editor's Introduction to Sermons 40–41

These two sermons were clearly intended by Wesley to be read together. He says so expressly at the beginning—he uses material in the first to act as a contrast for the material in the second—and in both sermons he is at pains to reject certain teaching that he attributes to various writers on Christian mysticism. They also share a further feature: they show Wesley both as an astute observer of the spiritual life and as a sensitive spiritual director.

Sermon 40 deals with the problem of backsliding, of beginning well in the Christian life and then veering off course. We might say that the early Methodists did not just believe in backsliding, they practiced it. Even so, Wesley begins the sermon obliquely by casting the problem as the problem of the wilderness state. In this he was drawing on a common way of thinking about the spiritual life in his day. However, his soft touch suggests that he is easing us into a very unhappy subject.

The problem of backsliding is, of course, a perennial one. Folks begin well and then drift into unbelief, even to the point where they abandon the faith for good. Wesley took the latter possibility with radical seriousness. He was not happy to solve the problem by arguing that those who lost their faith were not Christians in the first place. He takes the problem of loss of faith as real and seeks to provide a clear account of its etiology and cure.

Sermon 41 deals with the very different problem of what we might call spiritual depression. Perhaps he was thinking of those who had developed false expectations about the results of serious Christian commitment. They somehow think that their faith will act as a shield against the crises and demands of human existence. They develop a fantasy faith that cannot cope with life as it really is. They then experience dangerous forms of disappointment.

The problem of spiritual depression is also a perennial problem. We hear the good news of the gospel and build sandcastles in the air. There is no going back, to be sure, but going forward has turned out to be beset with all kinds of difficulties that cause us to lose heart or to become spiritually depressed. Wesley's realism is shown in his treatment of grief at the loss of a child and in his searing analysis of the human and spiritual impact of poverty. These passages are astonishing in their sensitivity and precision.

If we think of Sermon 39 as an invitation to start doing theology for ourselves, we can surely begin to develop our theological muscles by thinking through his response to some of the claims of the theologians of Christian mysticism as articulated and rebutted by Wesley.

SERMON 40

The Wilderness State

"You now have sorrow: but I will see you again, and your heart shall rejoice, and no one shall take away your joy" (John 16:22).

1. After God had wrought a great deliverance for Israel by bringing them out of the house of bondage, they did not immediately enter into the land which he had promised to their fathers; but "wandered out of the way in the wilderness," and were variously tempted and distressed. In like manner, after God has delivered those who fear him from the bondage of sin and Satan; after they are "justified freely by his grace, through the redemption that is in Jesus," yet not many of them immediately enter into "the rest which remains for the people of God." The greater part of them wander, more or less, out of the good way into which he has brought them. They come, as it were, into a "wasteland and a howling desert," where they are variously tempted and tormented; and some have termed this, in allusion to the case of the Israelites, "a wilderness state."

2. It is certain that those who are in this condition have a right to the gentlest compassion. They labour under an evil and sore disease; though one that is not commonly understood; and for this very reason it is the more difficult for them to find a remedy. Being in darkness themselves, they cannot be supposed to understand the nature of their own disorder; and few of their brethren—nor, perhaps, of their teachers—know either what their sickness is or how to heal it. So much the more need there is to inquire, first, "What is the nature of this disease?" secondly, "What is the cause?" and, thirdly, "What is the cure of it?"

I. 1. And, first, what is the nature of this disease, into which so many fall after they have believed? In what does it properly consist; and what are the genuine symptoms of it? It properly consists in the loss of that faith which God once wrought in their heart. They that are in the wilderness, have not now that divine "evidence," that satisfactory conviction "of things not seen," which they once enjoyed. They have not

SERMON 40

now that inward demonstration of the Spirit which before enabled each of them to say, "The life I live, I live by faith in the Son of God, who loved me, and gave himself for me." The light of heaven does not now "shine in their hearts," neither do they "see him who is invisible"; but darkness is again on the face of their souls, and blindness on the eyes of their understanding. The Spirit no longer "witnesses with their spirits, that they are the children of God"; neither does he continue as the Spirit of adoption, "crying" in their hearts, "Abba, Father." They have not now a sure trust in his love, and a liberty of approaching him with holy boldness. "Even if he slay me, I will trust in him," is no more the language of their heart; but they are shorn of their strength, and become weak and feeble-minded, even as other men.

2. Hence, secondly, proceeds the loss of love; which cannot but rise or fall, at the same time, and in the same proportion, with true, living faith. Accordingly, they who are deprived of their faith are deprived of the love of God also. They cannot now say, "Lord, you know all things, you know that I love you." They are not now happy in God as everyone is that truly loves him. They do not delight in him as in time past, and "smell the fragrance of his ointments." Once, all their "desire was for him, and for the remembrance of his name"; but now even their desires are cold and dead, if not utterly extinguished. And as their love of God has grown cold, so also has their love of their neighbour. They have not now that zeal for the souls of men, that longing after their welfare, that fervent, restless, active desire of being reconciled to God. They do not feel those "bowels of mercies" for the sheep that are lost—that tender "compassion for the ignorant and those who are out of the way." Once they were "gentle toward all men," meekly instructing such as opposed the truth; and, "if any were overtaken in a fault, restoring such a one in the spirit of meekness." But after a suspension, perhaps of many days, anger begins to regain its power; indeed, peevishness and impatience thrust fiercely at them that they may fall, and it is well if

THE WILDERNESS STATE

they are not sometimes driven even to "render evil for evil and cursing for cursing."

3. In consequence of the loss of faith and love follows, thirdly, loss of joy in the Holy Spirit. For if the loving consciousness of pardon is no more, the joy resulting from it cannot remain. If the Spirit does not witness with our spirit that we are the children of God, the joy that flowed from that inward witness must also end. And in like manner, they who once "rejoiced with joy unspeakable," "in hope of the glory of God," now that they are deprived of that "hope full of immortality," are deprived of the joy it occasioned; as also of that which resulted from a consciousness of "the love of God" then "shed abroad in their hearts." For the cause is removed, so is the effect: the fountain being dammed up, those living waters spring no more to refresh the thirsty soul.

4. With loss of faith and love and joy there is also joined, fourthly, the loss of that peace which once passed all understanding. That sweet tranquility of mind, that composure of spirit, is gone. ==Painful doubt returns; doubt whether we ever did, and perhaps whether we ever shall, believe==. We begin to doubt whether we ever did find in our hearts the real testimony of the Spirit; whether we did not rather deceive our own souls and mistake the voice of nature for the voice of God. And perhaps even whether we shall ever hear his voice and find favour in his sight. And these doubts are again joined with servile fear, with that fear which brings torment. We fear the wrath of God even as we did before we believed: we fear lest we should be cast out of his presence; and from there sink again into that fear of death from which we were before entirely delivered.

5. But even this is not all; for loss of peace is accompanied by loss of power. We know that everyone who has peace with God through Jesus Christ has power over all sin. But whenever he loses the peace of God, he also loses the power over sin. While that peace remained, power also remained, even over the besetting sin, whether it were the sin of his nature, his constitution, of his education, or that

of his profession; yes, and even over those evil tempers and desires which, until then, he could not conquer. Sin then had no more dominion over him; but now he has no more dominion over sin. He may struggle, indeed, but he cannot overcome; the crown has been knocked from his head. His enemies again prevail over him and, more or less, bring him into bondage. The glory has departed from him, even the kingdom of God which was in his heart. He is dispossessed of righteousness as well as of peace and joy in the Holy Spirit.

II. 1. Such is the nature of what many have termed, and not improperly, "the wilderness state." But the nature of it may be more fully understood by inquiring, secondly, What are the causes of it? These indeed are various. But I dare not rank among these the bare, arbitrary, sovereign will of God. He "rejoices in the prosperity of his servants: He does not delight in afflicting or grieving the children of men." His invariable will is our sanctification, attended with "peace and joy in the Holy Spirit." These are his own free gifts; and we are assured that "the gifts of God are," on his part, "without repentance." He never repents of what he has given, or desires to withdraw them from us. Therefore he never deserts us, as some speak; it is only we that desert him.

(I). 2. The most usual cause of inward darkness is sin, of one kind or another. This it is which generally occasions what is often a complication of sin and misery. First, sin of commission. This may frequently be observed to darken the soul in a moment; especially if it is a known, a willful, or presumptuous sin. If, for instance, a person who is now walking in the clear light of God's countenance should be any way prevailed upon to commit a single act of drunkenness, or uncleanness, it would be no wonder if, in that very hour, he fell into utter darkness. It is true, there have been some very rare cases, in which God has prevented this, by an extraordinary display of his pardoning mercy, almost in the very instant. But in general, such an abuse of the goodness of God, so gross an insult to his love, occasions an immediate estrangement from God and a "darkness that may be felt."

3. But it may be hoped this case is not very frequent; that there are not many who so despise the riches of his goodness as, while they walk in his light, so grossly and presumptuously to rebel against him. That light is much more frequently lost by giving way to sins of omission. This, indeed, does not immediately quench the Spirit, but gradually and slowly. The former may be compared to pouring water upon a fire; the latter to withdrawing the fuel from it. And many times will that loving Spirit reprove our neglect before he departs from us. Many are the inward checks, the secret notices he gives, before his influences are withdrawn. So only a train of omissions, willfully persisted in, can bring us into utter darkness.

4. Perhaps no sin of omission more frequently occasions this than the neglect of private prayer; the lack of which cannot be supplied by any other ordinance whatever. Nothing can be more plain than that the life of God in the soul does not continue, much less increase, unless we use all opportunities of communing with God and pouring out our hearts before him. If therefore we are negligent of this, if we suffer business, company, or any avocation whatever, to prevent these secret exercises of the soul (or, which comes to the same thing, to make us hurry them over in a slight and careless manner), that life will surely decay. And if we long or frequently intermit them, it will gradually die away.

5. Another sin of omission which frequently brings the soul of a believer into darkness, is the neglect of what was so strongly enjoined, even under the Jewish dispensation: "Rebuke your neighbour frankly, and do not allow sin to remain upon him: do not hate your brother in your heart." Now, if we do hate our brother in our heart, if we do not rebuke him when we see him in a fault, but allow sin to remain upon him, this will soon bring leanness to our own soul; since in this we become partakers of his sin. By neglecting to reprove our neighbour, we make his sin our own: we become accountable for it to

SERMON 40

God. We saw his danger and gave him no warning: so, "if he should perish in his iniquity," God may justly require "his blood at our hands." No wonder then, if by thus grieving the Spirit, we lose the light of his countenance.

6. A third cause of our losing this is giving way to some kind of inward sin. For example, we know everyone who is "proud in heart is an abomination to the Lord"; even though this pride of heart should not appear in the outward conversation. Now, how easily may a soul filled with peace and joy fall into this snare of the Devil! How natural is it for him to imagine that he has more grace, more wisdom or strength, than he really has to "think more highly of himself than he ought to think"! How natural to glory in something he has received, as if he had not been given it! But since God continually "opposes the proud, and gives grace" only "to the humble," this must certainly obscure, if not wholly destroy, the light which before shone on his heart.

7. The same effect may be produced by giving place to anger, whatever the provocation or occasion be; yes, even though it were coloured over with the name of zeal for the truth, or for the glory of God. Indeed all zeal which is any other than the flame of love is "earthly, animal, devilish." It is the flame of wrath: it is flat, sinful anger, neither better nor worse. And nothing is a greater enemy to the mild, gentle love of God than this. They never did, they never can, subsist together in one heart. In the same proportion as this prevails, love and joy in the Holy Spirit decrease. This is particularly observable in the case of offence; by which I mean anger at any of our brethren, at any of those who are united with us either by civil or religious ties. If we give way to the spirit of offence even one hour, we lose the sweet influences of the Holy Spirit; so that, instead of amending them, we destroy ourselves and become an easy prey to any enemy that assaults us.

8. But suppose we are aware of this snare of the Devil; we may be attacked from another quarter. When fierceness and anger are asleep, and love alone is waking, we may

be no less endangered by desire, which equally tends to darken the soul. This is the sure effect of any foolish desire, any vain or inordinate affection. If we set our affection on things of the earth, on any person or thing under the sun; if we desire anything but God and what leads to God; if we seek happiness in any creature; the jealous God will surely contend with us, for he can admit of no rival. And if we will not hear his warning voice and return to him with our whole soul, we continue to grieve him with our idols; and running after other gods, we shall soon be cold, barren, and dry; and the god of this world will blind and darken our hearts.

9. But this he frequently does, even when we do not give way to any positive sin. It is enough, it gives him sufficient advantage, if we do not "stir up the gift of God which is in us"; if we do not struggle continually "to enter in at the narrow gate"; if we do not earnestly "strive for the mastery" and "take the kingdom of heaven by force." There needs nothing more than not to fight, and we are sure to be conquered. Let us only be careless or "faint in our mind," let us be easy and indolent, and our natural darkness will soon return and overspread our soul. It is enough, therefore, if we give way to spiritual sloth; this will effectively darken the soul. It will as surely destroy the light of God, if not as swiftly, as murder or adultery.

10. But it is well to be observed that the cause of our darkness (whatever it be, whether omission or commission, whether inward or outward sin) is not always nigh at hand. Sometimes the sin which occasioned the present distress may lie at a considerable distance. It might be committed days, or weeks, or months before. And that God now withdraws his light and peace on account of what was done so long ago is not (as one might at first imagine) an instance of his severity, but rather a proof of his forbearance and tender mercy. He waited all this time if perhaps we would see, acknowledge, and correct what was amiss. And in default of this he at length shows his displeasure, if thus, at last, he may bring us to repentance.

(II). 1. Another general cause of this darkness is ignorance; which is likewise of various kinds. If men know not the Scriptures, if they imagine there are passages either in the Old or New Testament which assert that all believers, without exception, must sometimes be in darkness; this ignorance will naturally bring upon them the darkness which they expect. And how common a case has this been among us! How few are there that do not expect it! And no wonder, since they are taught to expect it; since their guides lead them into this way. Not only the mystic writers of the Romish Church, but many of the most spiritual and experimental in our own (very few of the last century excepted) lay it down with all assurance as a plain, unquestionable Scripture doctrine, and cite many texts to prove it.

2. Ignorance also of the work of God in the soul frequently occasions this darkness. Men imagine (because so they have been taught, particularly by writers of the Romish communion, whose plausible assertions too many Protestants have received without due examination) that they are not always to walk in luminous faith; that this is only a lower dispensation; that as they rise higher they are to leave those sensible comforts, and to live by naked faith (naked indeed, if it be stripped both of love, and peace, and joy in the Holy Spirit!) that a state of light and joy is good but a state of darkness and dryness is better; that it is by these alone we can be purified from pride, love of the world, and inordinate self-love; and that, therefore, we ought neither to expect nor desire to walk in the light always. Hence it is (though other reasons may concur) that the main body of pious men in the Romish Church generally walk in a dark uncomfortable way, and if they ever receive, soon lose, the light of God.

(III). 1. A third general cause of this darkness is temptation. When the candle of the Lord first shines on our head, temptation frequently flees away and totally disappears. All is calm within; perhaps without too, while God makes our enemies to be at peace with us. It is then very natural to suppose that we shall not see war any more. And there are instances in which this calm has continued, not only for weeks, but for months or years. But typically it is otherwise. In a short time "the winds blow, the rains descend, and the floods arise" anew. They who know not either the Son or the Father, and consequently hate his children, when God eases the bit which is in their mouth, will show that hatred in various instances. As of old, "he that was born after the flesh persecuted him that was born after the Spirit, even so it is now"; the same cause still producing the same effect. The evil which yet remains in the heart will then also move afresh; anger and many other roots of bitterness will endeavour to spring up. At the same time, Satan will not fail to cast his fiery darts; and the soul will have to wrestle not only with the world, not only "with flesh and blood, but with principalities and powers, with the rulers of the darkness of this world, with wicked spirits in high places." Now, when so various assaults are made at once, and perhaps with the utmost violence, it is not strange if it should occasion not only heaviness, but even darkness in a weak believer—more especially if he were not watching; if these assaults were made in an hour when he was not looking for them; if he expected nothing less but had fondly told himself that the day of evil would return no more.

2. The force of those temptations which arise from within will be exceedingly heightened if we before thought too highly of ourselves, as if we had been cleansed from all sin. And how naturally do we imagine this during the warmth of our first love! How ready we are to believe that God has "fulfilled in us the" whole "work of faith with power," that because we feel no sin, we have none in us; but the soul is all love! And well may a sharp attack from an enemy, whom we supposed to be not only conquered but slain, throw us into much heaviness of soul; yes, sometimes even into utter darkness: particularly when we reason with this enemy instead of instantly calling upon God, and casting ourselves upon Him by simple faith, who "alone knows how to deliver" his "out of temptation."

SERMON 40

III. These are the usual causes of this second darkness. Inquire we, thirdly, What is the cure of it?

1. To suppose that this is one and the same in all cases is a fatal mistake; yet extremely common, even among many who pass for experienced Christians, indeed, perhaps even those who take it upon themselves to be teachers in Israel, to be the guides of other souls. Accordingly, they know and use but one medicine, whatever the cause of the distemper. They begin immediately to apply the promises; to preach the gospel, as they call it. To give comfort is the single point at which they aim; in order to which they say many soft and tender things concerning the love of God to poor helpless sinners, and the efficacy of the blood of Christ. Now this is quackery indeed, and that of the worse sort, as it tends, if not to kill men's bodies, yet without the peculiar mercy of God, "to destroy both their bodies and souls in hell." It is hard to speak of these "daubers with untempered mortar," these promise-mongers, as they deserve. They well deserve the title which has been ignorantly given to others: they are spiritual mountebanks. They do, in effect, make "the blood of the covenant an unholy thing." They vilely prostitute the promises of God by thus applying them to all without distinction. Whereas, indeed, the cure of spiritual, as of bodily diseases, must be as various as are the causes of them. The first thing, therefore, is to find out the cause; and this will naturally point out the cure.

2. For instance: Is it sin which occasions darkness? What sin? Is it outward sin of any kind? Does your conscience accuse you of committing any sin, whereby you grieve the Holy Spirit of God? Is it on this account that he is departed from you, and that joy and peace are departed with him? And how can you expect they should return until you put away the accursed thing? "Let the wicked forsake his way"; "cleanse your hands, you sinners"; "put away the evil of your doings"; so shall your "light break out of darkness"; the Lord will return and "abundantly pardon."

3. If, upon the closest search, you can find no sin of commission which causes the cloud upon your soul, inquire next if there be not some sin of omission which separates God and you. Do you "not allow your brother to remain in his sin"? Do you reprove those who sin in your sight? Do you walk in all the ordinances of God? in public, family, private prayer? If not, if you habitually neglect any one of these known duties, how can you expect that the light of his countenance should continue to shine upon you? Make haste to "strengthen the things that remain"; then your soul shall live. "Today, if you will hear his voice," by his grace supply what is lacking. When you hear a voice behind you saying, "This is the way, walk in it," do not harden your heart; do not be "disobedient to the heavenly calling" any more. Until the sin, whether of omission or commission, is removed, all comfort is false and deceitful. It is only skinning the wound over, which still festers and rankles beneath. Look for no peace within until you are at peace with God; which cannot be without "fruits meet for repentance."

4. But perhaps you are not conscious of even any sin of omission which impairs your peace and joy in the Holy Spirit. Is there not then some inward sin, which as a root of bitterness, springs up in your heart to trouble you? Is not your dryness and barrenness of soul occasioned by your heart's "departing from the living God"? Has not "the foot of pride come against" you? Have you not thought of yourself "more highly than you ought to think"? Have you not, in any respect, "sacrificed to your own net and burned incense to your own dragnet"? Have you not ascribed your success in any undertaking to your own courage, or strength, or wisdom? Have you not boasted of something "you have received, as though you had not been given it"? Have you not gloried in anything "except the cross of our Lord Jesus Christ"? Have you not sought after or desired the praise of men? Have you not taken pleasure in it? If so, you see the way you are to take. If you have fallen by pride, "humble yourself under the mighty hand of God, and he will exalt

SERMON 40

you in due time." Have you not forced him to depart from you by giving place to anger? Have you not "fretted yourself because of the ungodly" or "been envious against the evil-doers"? Have you not been offended at any of your brethren, looking at their (real or imagined) sin, so as to sin yourself against the great law of love by estranging your heart from them? Then look unto the Lord, that you may renew your strength; that all this sharpness and coldness may be done away; that love and peace and joy may return together and you may be invariably kind to each other, and "tender-hearted, forgiving one another even as God for Christ's sake has forgiven you." Have not you given way to any foolish desire? To any kind or degree of inordinate affection? How then can the love of God have place in your heart till you put away your idols? "Be not deceived: God is not mocked." He will not dwell in a divided heart. As long, therefore, as you cherish Delilah in your bosom he has no place there. It is vain to hope for a recovery of his light until you pluck out your right eye and cast it from you. O let there be no longer delay! Cry to Him, that he may enable you to do so! Bewail your own impotence and helplessness and, the Lord being your helper, enter in at the strait gate; take the kingdom of heaven by force! Cast out every idol from his sanctuary, and the glory of the Lord shall soon appear.

5. Perhaps it is this very thing, the lack of striving, spiritual sloth, which keeps your soul in darkness. You dwell at ease in the land; there is no war on your coasts and so you are quiet and unconcerned. You go on in the same even track of outward duties and are content there to abide. And do you wonder, meanwhile, that your soul is dead? O stir yourself up before the Lord! Arise, and shake yourself from the dust; wrestle with God for the mighty blessing; pour out your soul unto God in prayer and continue there with all perseverance! Watch! Wake out of sleep; and stay awake! Otherwise there is nothing to be expected but that you will be alienated more and more from the light and life of God.

6. If, upon the fullest and most impartial examination of yourself, you cannot discern that you at present give way either to spiritual sloth or any other inward or outward sin, then call to mind the time that is past. Consider your former tempers, words, and actions. Have these been right before the Lord? "Commune with him in your chamber and be still"; and desire of him to try the ground of your heart and bring to your remembrance whatever has at any time offended the eyes of his glory. If the guilt of any unrepented sin remains on our soul, it cannot be but you will remain in darkness till, having been renewed by repentance, you are again washed by faith in the "fountain opened for sin and uncleanness."

7. Entirely different will be the manner of the cure, if the cause of the disease is not sin but ignorance. It may be ignorance of the meaning of Scripture; perhaps occasioned by ignorant commentators; ignorant, at least, in this respect, however knowing and learned they may be in other particulars. And in this case that ignorance must be removed before we can remove the darkness arising from it. We must show the true meaning of those texts which have been misunderstood. My design does not permit me to consider all the passages of Scripture which have been pressed into this service. I shall just mention two or three, which are frequently brought to prove that all believers must, sooner or later, "walk in darkness."

8. One of these is Isaiah 50:10: "Who is among you who fears the Lord, and obeys the voice of his servant, who walks in darkness and has no light? Let him trust in the name of the Lord and wait upon his God." But how does it appear, either from the text or context, that the person here spoken of ever had light? One who is convinced of sin, "fears the Lord, and obeys the voice of his servant." And him we should advise, though he was still dark of soul, and had never seen the light of God's countenance, still to "trust in the name of the Lord and wait upon his God." This text, therefore, proves nothing less than that believer in Christ "must sometimes walk in darkness."

SERMON 40

9. Another text which has been supposed to speak the same doctrine is Hosea 2:14: "I will allure her and bring her into the wilderness, and speak comfortably unto her." Hence it has been inferred that God will bring every believer into the wilderness, into a state of deadness and darkness. But it is certain the text speaks no such thing; for it does not appear that it speaks of particular believers at all: it plainly refers to the Jewish nation; and perhaps to that only. But if it is applicable to particular persons, the plain meaning of it is this: I will draw him by love; I will next convince him of sin; and then comfort him by pardoning mercy.

10. A third Scripture from whence the same inference has been drawn is that above recited, "You now have sorrow: but I will see you again, and your heart shall rejoice, and no one shall take away your joy." This has been supposed to imply that God would after a time withdraw himself from all believers; and that they could not, until after they had thus sorrowed, have the joy which no man could take from them. But the whole context shows that our Lord is here speaking personally to the Apostles and no others; and that he is speaking concerning those particular events, his own death and resurrection. "A little while," he says, "and you shall not see me"; that is, while I am in the grave. "And again, a little while and you shall see me"; when I am risen from the dead. You will weep and lament, and the world will rejoice: but your sorrow shall be turned into joy." "You now have sorrow," because I am about to be taken from your head; "but I will see you again," after my resurrection, "and your heart shall rejoice; and your joy," which I will then give you, "no one shall take away from you." All this we know was literally fulfilled in the particular case of the Apostles. But no inference can be drawn from here with regard to God's dealings with believers in general.

11. A fourth text (to mention no more) which has been frequently cited in proof of the same doctrine is 1 Peter 4:12: "Beloved, do not think it strange concerning the fiery trial which is to try you." But this is equally as foreign to the point as the

preceding. The text, literally rendered, runs thus: "Beloved, wonder not at the burning which is among you, which is for your trial." Now, however, this may be accommodated to inward trials in a secondary sense; yet primarily it doubtless refers to martyrdom, and the sufferings connected with it. Neither, therefore, is this text anything at all to the purpose for which it is cited. And we may challenge all men to bring one text, either from the Old or New Testament, which is any more to the purpose than this.

12. "But is not darkness much more profitable for the soul than light? Is not the work of God in the heart most swiftly and effectually carried on during a state of inward suffering? Is not a believer more swiftly and thoroughly purified by sorrow than by joy? By anguish, and pain, and distress, and spiritual martyrdom, than by continual peace?" So the mystics teach; so it is written in their books, but not in the oracles of God. The Scripture nowhere says that the absence of God best perfects his work in the heart! Rather his presence and a clear communion with the Father and the Son (a strong consciousness of this) will do more in an hour than his absence in an age. Joy in the Holy Spirit will far more effectually purify the soul than the absence of that joy; and the peace of God is the best means of refining the soul from the dross of earthly affections. Away then with the idle conceit that the kingdom of God is divided against itself; that the peace of God and joy in the Holy Spirit are obstructive of righteousness; and that we are saved, not by faith, but by unbelief; not by hope, but by despair!

13. So long as men dream thus, they may well "walk in darkness." Nor can the effect cease before the cause is removed. Yet we must not imagine it will immediately cease, even when the cause is no more. When either ignorance or sin has caused darkness, one or the other may be removed, and yet the light which was obstructed thereby may not immediately return. As it is the free gift of God, he may restore it sooner or later, as it pleases him. In the case of sin, we cannot reasonably expect that it should immediately return. The sin began

before the punishment, which may, therefore, justly remain after the sin is at an end. And even in the natural course of things, though a wound cannot be healed while the dart is sticking in the flesh, yet neither is it healed as soon as that is drawn out, but soreness and pain may remain long after.

14. Lastly, if darkness be occasioned by many heavy and unexpected temptations, the best way of removing and preventing this is to teach believers always to expect temptation, since they dwell in an evil world, among wicked, subtle, malicious spirits, and have a heart capable of all evil. Convince them that the whole work of sanctification is not, as they imagined, wrought at once; that when they first believe they are only like newborn babes, who are gradually to grow up, and may expect many storms before they come to the full stature of Christ. Above all, let them be instructed, when the storm is upon them, not to reason with the Devil but to pray; to pour out their souls before God, and show him their trouble. And these are the persons to whom, chiefly, we are to apply the great and precious promises; not to the ignorant before the ignorance is removed, much less to the impenitent sinner. To these we may largely and affectionately declare the loving-kindness of God our Saviour, expound upon his tender mercies, which have been ever of old. Here we may dwell upon the faithfulness of God, whose "word is tried to the uttermost"; and upon the virtue of that blood which was shed for us, to "cleanse us from all sin." And God will then bear witness to his word, and bring their souls out of trouble. He will say, "Arise, shine; for your light has come, and the glory of the Lord has risen upon you." Indeed, that light, if you walk humbly and closely with God, will "shine more and more unto the perfect day."

For Readers

Questions

1. How widespread is the problem of backsliding, that is, the problem of beginning well and then losing our way?

2. What are the spiritual states that are involved in backsliding?
3. Of the causes mentioned here, which are the most important?
4. Refusal to rebuke a neighbor sounds silly as a cause, but can it be restated more sensitively?
5. Do you think God might ever cause darkness directly? Why or why not?

Helpful Information

In Wesley's treatment of loss of faith, he spends more time on the causes than on its nature and cure. In this he is surely inviting us to think long and hard about why some folks begin well and then either drift away or leave the faith with a bang. That so many begin well and then fail is surely a scandal whose causes need all the attention we can muster.

One particular cause comes across as harsh and insensitive. In listing failure to rebuke our neighbors as a cause, it looks as if Christians should become moral and spiritual busybodies. Yet, we can also see what may be rescued as an important insight in the neighborhood. Think of the relevant cause as our reluctance to tackle evil when we find it in our neighbors or in our societies. We become morally complacent, or we become afraid of intimidation or opposition. The salt begins to lose its cleansing savor.

Wesley's exposition of loss of faith begins with loss of assurance of the love of God for us, and this in turn begins a downward spiral of loss of love, joy, hope, and peace. This ends with a sense of fear. It is surprising that Wesley does not suggest that we should take seriously this falling back into fear as a serious warning light that should cause us to deal with the danger we are facing.

However, he is surely on target when he notes that the recovery involved may mean that we have to deal over time with the pain involved in losing our way. He implicitly suggests that serious repentance and healing may take time. He is also prescient to note that new believers may get ahead of themselves and not allow the whole process of sanctification to take its proper course.

SERMON 41

Heaviness through Manifold Temptations

"Now for a season, if need be, you are in heaviness through manifold temptations" (1 Pet. 1:6).

1. In the preceding discourse I have particularly spoken of that darkness of mind into which those are often observed to fall who once walked in the light of God's countenance. Nearly related to this is the heaviness of soul, which is still more common, even among believers. Indeed, almost all the children of God experience this, in a higher or lower degree. And so great is the resemblance between one and the other that they are frequently confounded together; and we are apt to say, indifferently, "Such a one is in darkness," or "Such a one is in heaviness"—as if they were equivalent terms, one of which implied no more than the other. But they are far, very far from it. Darkness is one thing; heaviness is another. There is a difference, indeed, a wide and essential difference between the former and the latter. And such a difference it is as all the children of God are deeply concerned to understand: otherwise nothing will be easier than for them to slide out of heaviness into darkness. In order to prevent this, I will endeavour to show,

   I. What manner of persons those were to whom the Apostle says, "You are in heaviness."
   II. What kind of heaviness they were in.
   III. What were the causes; and,
   IV. What were the results of it. I shall conclude with some inferences.

I. 1. I am, in the first place, to show what manner of persons those were to whom the Apostle says, "You are in heaviness." And first, it is beyond all dispute that they were believers at the time the Apostle thus addressed them; for so he expressly says (1 Pet. 1:5), "You who are kept through the power of God by faith unto salvation." Again (1 Pet. 1:7), he mentions "the trial of their faith, much more precious than that of gold which perishes." Yet again (1 Pet. 1:9), he speaks of their "receiving the end of their faith, the salvation of their souls." At the same time, therefore, that they were "in heaviness," they were possessed of living faith. Their heaviness did not destroy their faith: they still "endured, as seeing him that is invisible."

2. Neither did their heaviness destroy their peace; the "peace that passes all understanding"; which is inseparable from true, living faith. This we may easily gather from the second verse, in which the Apostle prays, not that grace and peace may be given them, but only that it may "be multiplied to them"; that the blessing which they already enjoyed might be more abundantly bestowed upon them.

3. The persons to whom the Apostle here speaks were also full of a living hope. For thus he speaks (1 Pet. 1:3), "Blessed be the God and Father of our Lord Jesus Christ, who according to his abundant mercy has begotten us again," me and you, all of us, who are "sanctified by the Spirit" and enjoy the "sprinkling of the blood of Jesus Christ" "to a living hope, to an inheritance," that is, to a living hope of an inheritance, "incorruptible, undefiled, and that does not pass away." So, notwithstanding their heaviness, they still retained a hope full of immortality.

4. And they still "rejoiced in hope of the glory of God." They were filled with joy in the Holy Spirit. So (1 Pet. 1:8), the Apostle having just mentioned the final "revelation of Jesus Christ" (namely, when he comes to judge the world) immediately adds, "In whom, though now you see him not," not with your physical eyes, "yet believing, you rejoice with joy unspeakable and full of glory." Their heaviness, therefore, was not only consistent with living hope but also with joy unspeakable: at the same time they were thus heavy, they nevertheless rejoiced with joy full of glory.

5. In the midst of their heaviness they likewise still enjoyed the love of God, which had been shed abroad in their hearts—"whom," says the Apostle, "having not seen, you love." Though you have not yet seen him face to face; yet, knowing him by faith, you have obeyed his word, "My son, give me your heart." He is your God, and your love, the desire of your eyes and your "exceedingly great reward." You have sought and found happiness in Him; you "delight in the Lord," and he has given you your heart's desire.

6. Once more: though they were heavy, yet they were holy; they retained the same power over sin. They were still "kept" from this

"by the power of God"; they were "obedient children, not shaped according to their former desires" but, "as He that had called them is holy," so were they "holy in all manner of conversation." Knowing they were "redeemed by the precious blood of Christ, as a Lamb without spot and without blemish," they had, through the faith and hope which they had in God, "purified their souls by the Spirit." So, upon the whole, their heaviness easily consisted with faith, with hope, with love of God and man, with the peace of God, with joy in the Holy Spirit, with inward and outward holiness. It did no way impair, much less destroy, any part of the work of God in their hearts. It did not at all interfere with that "sanctification of the Spirit" which is the root of all true obedience; neither with the happiness which must needs result from grace and peace reigning in the heart.

II. 1. Hence we may easily learn what kind of heaviness they were in, the second thing which I shall endeavour to show. The word in the original is λυπηθέντες, "made sorrowful, grieved"; from λύπη, "grief" or "sorrow." This is the constant, literal meaning of the word. And, this being observed, there is no ambiguity in the expression, nor any difficulty in understanding it. The persons spoken of here were grieved. The heaviness they were in was neither more nor less than sorrow or grief—a passion with which every child of man is well acquainted.

2. It is probable our translators rendered it "heaviness" (though a less common word) to denote two things: first, the degree, and next, the continuance, of it. It does indeed seem that it is not a slight or inconsiderable degree of grief which is here spoken of; but such as makes a strong impression upon, and sinks deep into, the soul. Neither does this appear to be a transient sorrow, such as passes away in an hour; but rather such as, having taken fast hold of the heart, is not quickly shaken off but continues for some time as a settled temper, rather than a passion—even in those who have living faith in Christ and the genuine love of God in their hearts.

3. Even in these, this heaviness may sometimes be so deep as to overshadow the whole soul; to give a colour, as it were, to all the affections; such as will appear in the whole behaviour. It may likewise have an influence over the body, particularly in those who are either of a naturally weak constitution or weakened by some

accidental disorder, especially of the nervous kind. In many cases, we find "the corruptible body presses down the soul." In this, the soul rather presses down the body and weakens it more and more. I will not say that deep and lasting sorrow of heart may not sometimes even weaken a strong constitution and lay the foundation of such bodily disorders as are not easily removed: yet all this may consist with a measure of that faith which still works by love.

4. This may well be termed a "fiery trial." And though it is not the same with that the Apostle speaks of in the fourth chapter (1 Pet. 4), yet many of the expressions there used concerning outward sufferings may be accommodated to this inward affliction. They cannot, indeed, with any propriety be applied to those who are in darkness: These do not, cannot rejoice; neither is it true, that "the Spirit of glory and of God rests upon" them. But he frequently does on those who are in heaviness, so that, though sorrowful, yet they are always rejoicing.

III. 1. But to proceed to the third point: What are the causes of such sorrow or heaviness in a true believer? The Apostle tells us clearly: "You are in heaviness," he says, "through manifold temptations," ποικίλοις—"manifold," not only many in number but of many kinds. They may be varied and diversified a thousand ways by the change or addition of numberless circumstances. And this very diversity and variety makes it more difficult to guard against them. Among these we may rank all bodily disorders; particularly acute diseases and violent pain of every kind, whether affecting the whole body or the smallest part of it. It is true, some who have enjoyed uninterrupted health and have felt none of these may make light of them, and wonder that sickness or pain of body, should bring heaviness upon the mind. And perhaps one in a thousand is of so special a constitution as not to feel pain like other men. So has it pleased God to show his almighty power by producing some of these prodigies of nature, who have seemed not to regard pain at all, though of the severest kind; if that contempt of pain was not owing partly to the force of education, partly to a preternatural cause—to the power either of good or evil spirits who raised those men above the state of mere nature. But, abstracting from these particular cases, it is in general a just observation that

> Pain is perfect misery, and extreme.
> Quite overturns all patience.

And even where this is prevented by the grace of God, where men do "possess their souls in patience," it may nevertheless occasion much inward heaviness; the soul sympathizing with the body.

2. All diseases of long continuance, though less painful, are apt to produce the same effect. When God appoints over us consumption, or the chilling and burning ague, if it is not speedily removed it will not only "consume the eyes," but "cause sorrow of heart." This is eminently the case with regard to all those which are termed nervous disorders. And faith does not overturn the course of nature: natural causes still produce natural effects. Faith no more hinders the sinking of the spirits (as it is called) in a hysterical illness than the rising of the pulse in a fever.

3. Again: when "calamity comes like a whirlwind, and poverty like an armed man," is this a little temptation? Is it strange if it occasions sorrow and heaviness? Although this also may appear but a small thing to those who stand at a distance, or who look and "pass by on the other side," yet it is otherwise to those who feel it. "Having food and raiment" (indeed, the latter word, σκεπάσματα, implies lodging as well as apparel), we may, if the love of God is in our hearts, "be content with that." But what shall they do who have none of these? who, as it were, "embrace the rock for a shelter"? who have only the earth to lie upon, and only the sky to cover them? who have not a dry or warm, much less clean, abode for themselves and their little ones: no, nor clothing to keep themselves or those they love next to themselves, from pinching cold, either by day or night? I laugh at the stupid Heathen, crying out, *Nil habet, inflex paupertas durius in se, Quam quod ridiculos homines facit!* Has poverty nothing worse in it than this, that it makes men liable to be laughed at? It is a sign this idle poet talked by rote of the things which he did not know. Is not lack of food something worse than this? God pronounced it as a curse upon man that he should earn his food "by the sweat of his brow." But how many are there in this Christian country that toil, and labour, and sweat, and have it not at the last, but struggle with weariness and hunger together? Is it not worse for one, after a hard day's labour, to come back to a poor, cold, dirty, uncomfortable

lodging, and to find there not even the food which is needful to repair his wasted strength? You who live at ease in the earth, who lack nothing but eyes to see, ears to hear, and hearts to understand how well God has dealt with you—is it not worse to seek bread day by day, and find none? Perhaps to find the comfort also of five or six children, crying for what he has not to give! Were it not that he is restrained by an unseen hand, would he not soon "curse God and die"? O want of bread! want of bread! Who can tell what this means unless he has felt it himself? I am astonished it occasions no more than heaviness even in them that believe!

4. Perhaps next to this we may place the death of those who were near and dear to us; of a tender parent, and one not much declined into the vale of years; of a beloved child, just rising into life, and clasping about our heart; of a friend who was as our own soul—next to the grace of God the last, best gift of Heaven. And a thousand circumstances may enhance the distress. Perhaps the child, the friend, died in our embrace!—perhaps was snatched away when we did not expect it! flourishing, cut down like a flower! In all these cases, we not only may, but ought, to be affected: it is the design of God that we should. He would not have us be sticks and stones. He would have our affections regulated, not extinguished. Therefore—"Nature unreproved may drop a tear." There may be sorrow without sin.

5. A still deeper sorrow we may feel for those who are dead while they live, on account of the unkindness, ingratitude, apostasy of those who were united to us in the closest ties. Who can express what a lover of souls may feel for a friend, a brother, dead to God? for a husband, a wife, a parent, a child rushing into sin as a horse to the battle; and, in spite of all arguments and persuasions, hastening to work out his own damnation? And this anguish of spirit may be heightened to an inconceivable degree by the consideration that he who is now rushing to destruction once ran well in the way of life. Whatever he was in time past serves now to no other purpose than to make our reflections on what he is more piercing and afflictive.

6. In all these circumstances, we may be assured our great adversary will be there, trying to improve his opportunity. He who is always "walking about, seeking whom he may devour," will then especially

use all his power, all his skill, if perhaps he may gain any advantage over the soul that is already cast down. He will not be sparing of his fiery darts such as are most likely to find an entrance, and to fix most deeply in the heart, by their suitableness to the temptation that assaults it. He will labour to interject unbelieving, or blasphemous, or dejected thoughts. He will suggest that God does not regard, does not govern, the earth; or, at least, that he does not govern it rightly, not by the rules of justice and mercy. He will endeavour to stir up the heart against God, to renew our natural enmity against him. And if we attempt to fight him with his own weapons, if we begin to reason with him, more and more heaviness will undoubtedly ensue, if not utter darkness.

7. It has been frequently supposed that there is another cause; if not of darkness, at least, of heaviness; namely, God's withdrawing himself from the soul because it is his sovereign will. Certainly he will do this if we grieve his Holy Spirit, either by outward or inward sin; either by doing evil or neglecting to do good; by giving way either to pride or anger, to spiritual sloth, to foolish desire, or inordinate affection. But that he ever withdraws himself because he feels like it, merely because it pleases him, I absolutely deny. There is no text in all the Bible which gives any colour for such a supposition. Nay, it is a supposition contrary not only to many particular texts, but to the whole tenor of Scripture. It is repugnant to the very nature of God: it is utterly beneath his majesty and wisdom (as an eminent writer strongly expresses it), "to play at bo-peep with his creatures." It is inconsistent both with his justice and mercy, and with the sound experience of all his children.

8 One more cause of heaviness is mentioned by many of those who are termed Mystic authors. And the notion has crept in, I know not how, even among plain people who have no acquaintance with them. I cannot better explain this than in the words of a late writer, who relates this as her own experience: "I continued so happy in my Beloved, that, although I should have been forced to live a vagabond in a desert, I should have found no difficulty in it. This state had not lasted long, when, in effect, I found myself led into a desert. I found myself in a forlorn condition, altogether poor, wretched, and miserable. The proper source of this grief is the

knowledge of ourselves; by which we find that there is an extreme unlikeness between God and us. We see ourselves most opposite to him; and that our inmost soul is entirely corrupted, depraved, and full of all kind of evil and malignity, of the world and the flesh, and all sorts of abominations." From hence it has been inferred that the knowledge of ourselves, without which we should perish everlastingly, must, even after we have attained justifying faith, occasion the deepest heaviness.

9. But upon this I would observe, (1) In the preceding paragraph, this writer says, "Hearing I had not a true faith in Christ, I offered myself up to God, and immediately felt his love." It may be so; and yet it does not appear that this was justification. It is more probable that it was no more than what are usually termed, the "drawings of the Father." And if so, the heaviness and darkness which followed was none other than conviction of sin; which in the nature of things must precede that faith whereby we are justified. (2) Suppose she was justified almost the same moment she was convinced of wanting faith, there was then no time for that gradually increasing self-knowledge which used to precede justification. In this case, therefore, it came after, and was probably the more severe the less it was expected. (3) It is allowed that there will be a far deeper, a far clearer and fuller knowledge of our inbred sin, of our total corruption by nature, after justification than ever there was before it. But this need not occasion darkness of soul: I will not say that it must bring us into heaviness. Were it so, the Apostle would not have used that expression, "if need be," for there would be an absolute, indispensable need of it for all that would know themselves; that is, in effect, for all that would know the perfect love of God and be thereby "made meet to be partakers of the inheritance of the saints in light." But this is by no means the case. On the contrary, God may increase the knowledge of ourselves to any degree and increase in the same proportion the knowledge of himself and the experience of his love. And in this case there would be no "desert, no misery, no forlorn condition"; but love, and peace, and joy, gradually springing up into everlasting life.

IV. 1. For what ends, then (which was the fourth thing to be considered), does God permit heaviness to befall so many of his children? The

Apostle gives us a plain and direct answer to this important question: "That the trial of their faith, which is much more precious than gold that perishes though it be tried by fire, may be found unto praise, and honour, and glory, at the revelation of Jesus Christ" (1 Pet. 1:7). There may be an allusion to this in that well-known passage of the fourth chapter (although it primarily relates to quite another thing, as has been already observed): "Think it not strange concerning the fiery trial which is to try you: but rejoice that you are partakers of the sufferings of Christ; that, when his glory shall be revealed, you may likewise rejoice with exceedingly great joy" (1 Pet. 4:12, etc.).

2. Hence we learn that the first and great end of God's permitting the temptations which bring heaviness on his children, is the trial of their faith, which is tried by these even as gold by the fire. Now we know, gold tried in the fire is purified thereby; is separated from its dross. And so is faith in the fire of temptation; the more it is tried, the more it is purified—indeed, and not only purified but also strengthened, confirmed, increased abundantly by so many more proofs of the wisdom and power, the love and faithfulness, of God. This, then—to increase our faith—is one gracious end of God's permitting those manifold temptations.

3. They serve to try, to purify, to confirm, and increase that living hope also, unto which "the God and Father of our Lord Jesus Christ has begotten us again of his abundant mercy." Indeed our hope cannot but increase in the same proportion with our faith. On this foundation it stands, believing in his name, living by faith in the Son of God, we hope for, we have a confident expectation of, the glory which shall be revealed. And consequently, whatever strengthens our faith increases our hope also. At the same time it increases our joy in the Lord, which cannot but attend a hope full of immortality. In this view the Apostle exhorts believers in the other chapter: "Rejoice that you are partakers of the sufferings of Christ." On this very account, "happy are you; for the Spirit of glory and of God rests upon you." And by this you are enabled, even in the midst of suffering, to "rejoice with joy unspeakable and full of glory."

4. They rejoice the more because the trials which increase their faith and hope increase their love also; both their gratitude to God for

all his mercies and their good-will to all mankind. Accordingly, the more deeply sensible they are of the loving-kindness of God their Saviour, the more their heart is inflamed with love to him who "first loved us." The clearer and stronger evidence they have of the glory that shall be revealed, the more do they love Him who has purchased it for them, and "given them the proof" of that "in their hearts." And this, the increase of their love, is another end of the temptations permitted to come upon them.

5. Yet another is their advance in holiness: holiness of heart and holiness of conversation; the latter naturally resulting from the former; for a good tree will bring forth good fruit. And all inward holiness is the immediate fruit of the faith that works by love. By this the blessed Spirit purifies the heart from pride, self-will, passion; from love of the world, from foolish and hurtful desires, from vile and vain affections. Besides that, sanctified afflictions have, through the grace of God, an immediate and direct tendency to holiness. Through the operation of his Spirit, they humble, more and more, and abase the soul before God. They calm our turbulent spirit and make it meek, tame the fierceness of our nature, soften our obstinacy and self-will, crucify us to the world, and bring us to expect all our strength from, and to seek all our happiness in, God.

6. And all these terminate in that great end, that our faith, hope, love, and holiness "may be found," if it does not yet appear "unto praise" from God himself, "and honour" from men and angels, "and glory" assigned by the great Judge to all that have endured to the end. And this will be assigned in that awful day to every man, "according to his works"; according to the work which God had wrought in his heart and the outward works which he has wrought for God; and likewise according to what he had suffered; so all these trials are unspeakable gain. So many ways do these "light afflictions, which are but for a moment, work out for us a far more exceeding and eternal weight of glory"!

7. Add to this the advantage which others may receive by seeing our behaviour under affliction. We find by experience that example frequently makes a deeper impression upon us than precept. And what examples have a stronger influence, not only on those who are partakers of like precious faith, but even on them who have not

known God, than that of a soul calm and serene in the midst of storms; sorrowful yet always rejoicing; meekly accepting whatever is the will of God, however grievous it may be to nature; saying in sickness and pain, "The cup which my Father has given me, shall I not drink it?"—in loss or want, "The Lord gave; the Lord has taken away; blessed be the name of the Lord!"

V. 1. I am to conclude with some inferences. First, how wide is the difference between darkness of soul and heaviness; which nevertheless are so generally confounded with each other, even by experienced Christians! Darkness, or the wilderness-state, implies a total loss of joy in the Holy Spirit: heaviness does not; in the midst of this we may "rejoice with joy unspeakable." They that are in darkness have lost the peace of God; they that are in heaviness have not; so far from it that at the very moment "peace," as well as "grace," may "be multiplied" unto them. In the former, the love of God has waxed cold, if it is not utterly extinguished; in the latter, it retains its full force or, rather, increases daily. In these, faith itself, if not totally lost, is grievously decayed: their evidence and conviction of things not seen, particularly of the pardoning love of God, is not so clear or strong as in times past: and their trust in him is proportionately weakened. Those, though they see him not, yet have a clear, unshaken confidence in God, and an abiding evidence of that love by which all their sins are blotted out. So as long as we can distinguish faith from unbelief, hope from despair, peace from war, the love of God from the love of the world, we may infallibly distinguish heaviness from darkness!

2. We may learn from hence, secondly, that there may be need of heaviness but there can be no need of darkness. There may be need of our being in "heaviness for a season" in order to the ends above recited; at least, in this sense, as it is a natural result of those "manifold temptations" which are needful to try and increase our faith, to confirm and enlarge our hope, to purify our heart from all unholy tempers, and to perfect us in love. And, consequently, they are needful in order to brighten our crown and add to our eternal weight of glory. But we cannot say that darkness is needful in order to any of these ends. It is no way conducive to them: the loss of faith, hope, or love is surely conducive neither to holiness nor to

the increase of that reward in heaven which will be in proportion to our holiness on earth.

3. From the Apostle's manner of speaking we may gather, thirdly, that even heaviness is not always needful. "Now, for a season, if need be"; so it is not needful for all persons; nor for any person at all times. God is able: he has both power and wisdom to work, when he pleases, the same work of grace in any soul by other means. And in some instances he does so; he causes those whom it pleases him to go on from strength to strength, even until they "perfect holiness in his fear," with scarcely any heaviness at all; as having an absolute power over the heart of man, and moving all the springs of it at his pleasure. But these cases are rare: God generally sees good to try "acceptable men in the furnace of affliction." So manifold temptations and heaviness, more or less, are usually the portion of his dearest children.

4. We ought, therefore, lastly, to watch and pray, and use our utmost endeavours to avoid falling into darkness. But we need not be solicitous how to avoid so much as how to improve by heaviness. Our great care should be how to behave ourselves under it, how to wait upon the Lord there, that it may fully answer all the design of his love in permitting it to come upon us; that it may be a means of increasing our faith, of confirming our hope, of perfecting us in all holiness. Whenever it comes, let us have an eye to these gracious ends for which it is permitted, and use all diligence that we may not make void the counsel of God against ourselves. Let us earnestly work together with him, by the grace which he is continually giving us, in "purifying ourselves from all pollution, both of flesh and spirit," and daily growing in the grace of our Lord Jesus Christ, until we are received into his everlasting kingdom!

For Readers

Questions

1. What is the difference between those who are backsliding and those who are going through a period of spiritual depression?

2. How might we add to the list of causes of spiritual depression given here?

3. How might clinical depression, the loss of a child, or experience of abject poverty cause us to be spiritually distraught and discouraged?

4. What is the difference between God causing darkness and God permitting darkness?

5. Why does God allow us to go through periods of spiritual depression?

Helpful Information

As in the previous sermon, Wesley gives extended attention to the causes of spiritual desolation and depression. And here too he is inviting us to think long and hard about why so many have to deal with this perennial spiritual problem. We cannot dismiss the problem as a passing fit of spiritual blues. We need to have an adequate set of diagnostic tools.

In the list provided, his treatment of the effects of abject poverty is a masterpiece of compassion and analytical skill. They deserve to be pondered with persistence because it is easy to allow our creature comforts to inoculate us to the dire straits involved. And he refuses to rest content with a humanitarian diagnosis that should spur us to effective action. He also picks up on the dramatic spiritual dimension of such suffering.

He mentions a revealing insight when he notes that deep knowledge of sin can be so devastating that we can only handle it if God also lets us know of the depths of his love for us. He also suggests that we do not know what sin really is until after we have become Christians. This too is an astute observation that should temper the standard practice to force people to come to a deeper knowledge of evil before they are ready to handle it.

As to the teaching that God directly causes darkness in order to make us more aware of our sin, he will have none of it. Perhaps this needs further attention as he is working off a rather superficial account of spiritual experience here. However, he is surely right to insist that any theory about the spiritual life that calls into question the love of God for us should be treated with skepticism. Yet God may take away all sorts of props of reason and experience precisely to enable us not so much to grow in knowledge of ourselves as to trust more fully in the Word of God's commitment to our welfare. Once again, we are called to deeper theological exploration.

Editor's Introduction to Sermons 42–44

It is far from clear whether we should take these three sermons as a unit or treat them as distinct challenges that deserve separate treatment in their own right. Everything hinges here on whether we can find a unifying thread. I propose we identify that thread as the cost of discipleship. In each case, we are dealing with exceptionally serious demands made upon us as believers, demands that we are systematically driven to resist either because of the corruption of our hearts or because of peer pressure.

The first challenge operates at a very general level. The central issue is the difficulty of bringing our wills into full alignment with the will of God. We might think of this as the fundamental challenge relative to the cost of discipleship. There is a battle of wills in which we are prone to set our own will against the will of God (phase one) and where we especially resist the will of God if it involves suffering (phase two). This choice, of course, is intensely personal. We stand alone before God and choose in a strictly either/or fashion, coming clean on the deepest orientation of our existence. Let's call this a metachoice for or against the will of God. It is a very general choice that then governs our more relative choices, say, as to what vocation to follow or where to live.

Sermons 43 and 44 help us sort out how that metachoice is played out in two important areas of our lives. Sermon 43 tackles the challenge of living with people who speak evil of us, and Sermon 44 tackles the challenge posed by the inescapable role of money in our lives.

Sermon 43 confines itself to one source of conflict that emerges again and again inside the church, namely, the toxic effects not just of backbiting and gossip, but of the deliberate attempt to do us harm by speaking evil of us. We all know the devastating effects this kind of behavior can have. If not dealt with in a timely manner, it poisons the life of the church from top to bottom. Yet, we are very reluctant to deal with it. It is extremely costly to us psychologically to face reality and take the steps needed to eradicate the network of vices involved. Refusing to take action is then a refusal to bear the cost of discipleship.

EDITOR'S INTRODUCTION TO SERMONS 42–44

Sermon 44 deals with an equally unpleasant challenge. How do we tackle the challenges related to money? It is a sign of the depth of the problem that many make money the root of all evil when it is not money but the love of money that is the problem. Refusing to deal with it is another instance of not facing up to the cost of discipleship.

There is no need to limit the particular challenges we face here to those discussed. We can readily extend the list to include the challenges related to sexual morality, public justice, racial prejudice, and the like. When we take these three sermons together we have in hand a pattern of advice. The first decision to be made is the decision to serve God alone even when that goes against our will and even though it will involve the suffering of bearing the cross. This, to be sure, has to be revisited again and again. With this in place we can then begin to drill down to the particular choices where this fundamental, framing choice hits the road in our lives. It can begin with how we handle evil speaking against us and with how we procure and use our money. The rest is a matter of thinking through the other challenges that crop up as we work through the cost of discipleship.

SERMON 42

Self-Denial

"And he said to them all, 'If any man will come after me, let him deny himself, and take up his cross daily, and follow me'" (Luke 9:23).

1. It has been frequently imagined that the direction here given related chiefly, if not wholly, to the Apostles; at least, to the Christians of the first age, or those in a state of persecution. But this is a grievous mistake. For although our blessed Lord is here directing his discourse more immediately to his Apostles and those other disciples who attended him in the days of his flesh; yet in them he speaks to us, and to all mankind, without any exception or limitation. The very reason of the thing puts it beyond dispute, that the duty which is here enjoined is not particular to them, or to the Christians of the early ages. It no more regards any particular order of men, or particular time, than any particular country. No: it is of the most universal nature, respecting all times, and all persons, yes, and even all things; not food and drink only, and things pertaining to the senses. The meaning is, "If any man," of whatever rank, station, circumstances, in any nation, in any age of the world, "will" effectually "come after me, let him deny himself" in all things; let him "take up his cross" of whatever kind; and that "daily; and follow me."

2. The denying ourselves and the taking up our cross, in the full extent of the expression, is not a thing of small concern: it is not merely useful, as are some of the nonessentials of religion, but it is absolutely, indispensably necessary, either to our becoming or continuing his disciples. It is absolutely necessary, in the very nature of the thing, to our coming after Him and following Him; insomuch that, as far as we do not practise it, we are not his disciples. If we do not continually deny ourselves, we do not learn of Him, but of other masters. If we do not take up our cross daily, we do not come after Him, but after the world, or the prince of the world, or our own fleshly mind. If we are not walking in the way of the cross, we are not following Him; we are not treading in his steps; but going back from, or at least wide of, Him.

3. It is for this reason that so many Ministers of Christ in almost every age and nation, particularly since the Reformation of the Church from

the innovations and corruptions gradually crept into it, have written and spoken so largely on this important duty, both in their public discourses and private exhortations. This induced them to disperse abroad many tracts upon the subject; and some in our own nation. They knew both from the oracles of God and from the testimony of their own experience, how impossible it was not to deny our Master unless we will deny ourselves; and how vainly we attempt to follow Him who was crucified unless we take up our cross daily.

4. But may not this very consideration make it reasonable to inquire, if much has already been said and written on the subject, what need is there to say or write more? I answer: There are no inconsiderable numbers, even of people fearing God, who have not had the opportunity either of hearing what has been spoken, or reading what has been written, upon it. And perhaps if they had read much of what has been written, they would not have been so much profited. Many who have written (some of them large volumes) do by no means appear to have understood the subject. Either they had imperfect views of the very nature of it (and then they could never explain it to others), or they were unacquainted with the due extent of it; they did not see how exceedingly broad this command is, or they were not aware of the absolute, the indispensable necessity of it. Others speak of it in so dark, so perplexed, so intricate, so mystical a manner as if they designed rather to conceal it from the vulgar than to explain it to common readers. Others speak admirably well, with great clearness and strength, on the necessity of self-denial; but then they deal in generals only, without coming to particular instances, and so are of little use to the bulk of mankind, to men of ordinary capacity and education. And if some of them do descend to particulars, it is only to those particulars which do not affect the generality of men, since they seldom, if ever, occur in common life—such as enduring imprisonment or torture; literally giving up their houses or lands, their husbands or wives, children, or life itself; to none of which we are called, nor are likely to be, unless God should permit times of public persecution to return. In the meantime, I know of no writer in the English tongue who has described the nature of self-denial in plain and intelligible terms, such as lie level with common understandings, and applied it to those little particulars which daily occur in common life. A discourse of this kind is wanted still; and it is wanted the more

because in every stage of the spiritual life, although there is a variety of particular hindrances of our attaining grace or growing therein, yet are all resolvable into these general ones: either we do not deny ourselves, or we do not take up our cross.

In order to supply this defect in some degree, I shall endeavour to show, first, what it is for a man to deny himself, and what to take up his cross; and, secondly, that if a man be not fully Christ's disciple, it is always owing to the want of this.

I. 1. I shall, first, endeavour to show what it is for a man to "deny himself and take up his cross daily." This is a point which is, of all others, most necessary to be considered and thoroughly understood, even on this account; that it is, of all others, most opposed by numerous and powerful enemies. All our nature must certainly rise up against this, even in its own defence; the world, consequently, the men who take nature, not grace, for their guide, abhor the very sound of it. And the great enemy of our souls, well knowing its importance, cannot but move every stone against it. But this is not all. Even those who have in some measure shaken off the yoke of the Devil, who have experienced, especially of late years, a real work of grace in their hearts, yet are no friends to this grand doctrine of Christianity, though it is so particularly insisted on by their Master. Some of them are as deeply and totally ignorant concerning it as if there were not one word about it in the Bible. Others are farther off still, having unawares imbibed strong prejudices against it. These they have received partly from outside Christians, men of a fair speech and behaviour who want nothing of godliness but the power, nothing of religion but the spirit—and partly from those who did once, if they do not now, "taste of the powers of the world to come." But are there any of these who do not both practise self-denial themselves, and recommend it to others? You are little acquainted with mankind if you doubt of this. There are whole bodies of men who only do not declare war against it. To go no farther than London: look upon the whole body of Predestinarians, who by the free mercy of God have lately been called out of the darkness of nature into the light of faith. Are they patterns of self-denial? How few of them even profess to practise it at all! How few of them recommend it themselves or are pleased with them that do! Rather, do they not continually represent it in the most odious colours, as if it were seeking "salvation by works," or seeking "to establish our own righteousness"? And how readily do Antinomians of all kinds, from the smooth Moravian to the boisterous, foul-mouthed Ranter, join the cry with their silly, senseless cant of legality and preaching the law! Therefore you are in constant danger of being wheedled, hectored, or ridiculed out of this important gospel-doctrine, either by false teachers or false brethren (more or less beguiled from the simplicity of the gospel), if you are not deeply grounded in it. Let fervent prayer, then, go before, accompany, and follow what you are now about to read, that it may be written in your heart by the finger of God, so as never to be erased.

2. But what is self-denial? In what are we to deny ourselves? And from where does the necessity of this arise? I answer, The will of God is the supreme, unalterable rule for every intelligent creature; equally binding every angel in heaven, and every man upon earth. Nor can it be otherwise: this is the natural, necessary result of the relation between creatures and their Creator. But if the will of God be our one rule of action in everything, great and small, it follows, by undeniable consequence, that we are not to do our own will in anything. Here, therefore, we see at once the nature, with the ground and reason, of self-denial. We see the nature of self-denial: it is the denying or refusing to follow our own will, from a conviction that the will of God is the only rule of action to us. And we see the grounds for it, because we are creatures; because "it is he that has made us, and not we ourselves."

3. This reason for self-denial must hold, even with regard to the angels of God in heaven, and with regard to man, innocent and holy, as he came out of the hands of his Creator. But a further reason for it arises from the condition in which all men are since the Fall. We are all now "shaped in wickedness, and in sin did our mothers conceive us." Our nature is altogether corrupt, in every power and faculty. And our will, depraved equally with the rest, is wholly bent to indulge our natural corruption. On the other hand, it is the will of God that we resist and counteract that corruption, not at some times, or in some things only, but at all times and in

all things. Here, therefore, is a further ground for constant and universal self-denial.

4. To illustrate this a little further: the will of God is a path leading straight to God. The will of man, which once ran parallel with it, is now another path, not only different from it but, in our present state, directly contrary to it. It leads from God. If, therefore, we walk in the one, we must necessarily quit the other. We cannot walk in both. Indeed, a man of "faint heart and feeble hands" may "go in two ways, one after the other." But he cannot walk in two ways at the same time: He cannot, at one and the same time, follow his own will and follow the will of God: he must choose the one or the other; denying God's will to follow his own; or denying himself to follow the will of God.

5. Now it is undoubtedly pleasing, for the time, to follow our own will, by indulging, in any instance that offers, the corruption of our nature. But by following it in anything, we so far strengthen the perverseness of our will; and by indulging it, we continually increase the corruption of our nature. So, by the food which is agreeable to the palate, we often increase a bodily disease: It gratifies the taste, but it inflames the disorder: it brings pleasure, but it also brings death.

6. On the whole, then, to deny ourselves is to deny our own will, where it does not fall in with the will of God; and that however pleasing it may be. It is to deny ourselves any pleasure which does not spring from, and lead to, God; that is, in effect, to refuse going out of our way, though into a pleasant, flowery path; to refuse what we know to be deadly poison, though agreeable to the taste.

7. And every one who would follow Christ, who would be his real disciple, must not only deny himself but take up his cross also. A cross is anything contrary to our will, anything displeasing to our nature. So that taking up our cross goes a little farther than denying ourselves; it rises a little higher and is a more difficult task for flesh and blood: it being easier to forego pleasure than to endure pain.

8. Now, in running "the race which is set before us," according to the will of God, there is often a cross lying in the way; that is, something which is not only not joyous, but grievous; something

which is contrary to our will, which is displeasing to our nature. What then is to be done? The choice is plain: either we must take up our cross, or we must turn aside from the way of God, "from the holy commandment delivered to us"; if we do not stop altogether or turn back to everlasting perdition!

9. In order to the healing of that corruption, that evil disease which every man brings with him into the world, it is often needful to pluck out, as it were, a right eye, to cut off a right hand—so painful is either the thing itself which must be done or the only means of doing it; the parting, suppose, with a foolish desire, with an inordinate affection; or a separation from the object of it, without which it can never be extinguished. In the former kind, tearing away such a desire or affection, when it is deeply rooted in the soul, is often like the piercing of a sword; yes, even like "the dividing asunder of the soul and spirit, the joints and marrow." The Lord then sits upon the soul as a refiner's fire, to burn all its dross. And this is a cross indeed; it is essentially painful; it must be so, in the very nature of the thing. The soul cannot be thus torn asunder, it cannot pass through the fire, without pain.

10. In the latter kind, the means to heal a sin-sick soul, to cure a foolish desire, an inordinate affection, are often painful, not in the nature of the thing but from the nature of the disease. So when our Lord said to the rich young man, "Go, sell that you have and give it to the poor" (as well knowing this was the only means of healing his covetousness), the very thought of it gave him so much pain that "he went away sorrowful"; choosing to part with his hope of heaven rather than his possessions on earth. This was a burden he could not consent to lift, a cross he would not take up. And in the one kind or the other, every follower of Christ will surely have need to "take up his cross daily."

11. The "taking up" differs a little from "bearing his cross." We are then properly said to "bear our cross" when we endure what is laid upon us without our choice, with meekness and resignation. Whereas we do not properly "take up our cross" except when we voluntarily suffer what it is in our power to avoid; when we willingly embrace the will of God, though contrary to our own; when we choose what is painful because it is the will of our wise and gracious Creator.

12. And thus it behooves every disciple of Christ to take up, as well as to bear, his cross. Indeed, in one sense, it is not his alone; it is common to him and many others; seeing there is no temptation that befalls any man εἰ μὴ ἀνθρώπινος—"but such as is common to humanity"; such as is incident and adapted to their common nature and situation in the present world. But in another sense, as it is considered with all its circumstances, it is his, peculiar to himself. It is prepared of God for him; it is given by God to him as a token of his love. And if he receives it as such, and, after using such means to remove the pressure as Christian wisdom directs, lies as clay in the potter's hand; it is disposed and ordered by God for his good, both with regard to the quality of it, and in respect to its quantity and degree, its duration, and every other circumstance.

13. In all this, we may easily conceive our blessed Lord to act as the Physician of our souls, not merely "for his own pleasure, but for our profit, that we may be partakers of his holiness." If, in searching our wounds, he puts us to pain, it is only in order to heal them. He cuts away what is putrefied or unsound in order to preserve the sound part. And if we freely choose the loss of a limb rather than the whole body should perish, how much more should we choose, figuratively, to cut off a right hand rather than the whole soul should be cast into hell!

14. We see plainly then both the nature and ground of taking up our cross. It does not imply disciplining ourselves (as some speak); literally tearing our own flesh, wearing hair-cloth, or iron girdles, or anything else that would impair our bodily health (although we know not what allowance God may make for those who act thus through involuntary ignorance); but embracing the will of God, though contrary to our own; choosing wholesome, though bitter medicines; freely accepting temporary pain, of whatever kind and in whatever degree, when it is either essentially or accidentally necessary to eternal pleasure.

II. 1. I am, secondly, to show that it is always owing to the want either of self-denial, or taking up his cross, that any man does not thoroughly follow Him, is not fully a disciple of Christ.

It is true this may be partly due, in some cases, to the lack of the means of grace; of hearing the true word of God spoken with power; of the sacraments, or of Christian fellowship. But where none of these is wanting, the great hindrance of our receiving or growing in the grace of God is always the want of denying ourselves or taking up our cross.

2. A few instances will make this plain. A man hears the word which is able to save his soul. He is well pleased with what he hears, acknowledges the truth, and is a little affected by it; yet he remains "dead in trespasses and sins," senseless and unaware. Why is this? Because he will not part with his pet sin, though he now knows it is an abomination to the Lord. He came to hear, full of lust and unholy desires, and he will not part with them. Therefore no deep impression is made upon him, but his foolish heart is still hardened. That is, he is still senseless and unaware because he will not deny himself.

3. Suppose he begins to awake out of sleep and his eyes are a little opened; why are they so quickly closed again? Why does he again sink into the sleep of death? Because he again yields to his pet sin; he drinks again of the pleasing poison. Therefore it is impossible that any lasting impression should be made upon his heart. That is, he relapses into his fatal insensibility because he will not deny himself.

4. But this is not the case with all. We have many instances of those who, when once awakened, sleep no more. The impressions once received do not wear away: they are not only deep but lasting. And yet, many of these have not found what they seek: They mourn and yet are not comforted. Now why is this? It is because they do not "bring forth fruits meet for repentance"; because they do not, according to the grace they have received, "cease from evil, and do good." They do not cease from the easily besetting sin, the sin of their constitution, of their education, or of their profession; or they omit doing the good they may, and know they ought to do, because of some disagreeable circumstance attending it. That is, they do not attain faith because they will not "deny themselves," or "take up their cross."

5. But this man did receive "the heavenly gift"; he did "taste of the powers of the world to come"; he saw "the light of the glory of

God in the face of Jesus Christ"; the "peace which passes all understanding" did "rule his heart and mind"; and "the love of God was shed abroad" there "by the Holy Spirit which was given unto him." Yet he is now weak as another man; he again relishes the things of earth, and has more taste for the things which are seen than for those which are not seen; the eye of his understanding is closed again, so that he cannot "see Him that is invisible"; his love has waxed cold, and the peace of God no longer rules in his heart. And no wonder, for he has again given place to the Devil and grieved the Holy Spirit of God. He has turned again to folly, to some pleasing sin; if not in outward act, yet in heart. He has given place to pride, or anger, or desire, to self-will, or stubbornness. Or he did not stir up the gift of God which was in him; he gave way to spiritual sloth and would not be at the pains of "praying always and being watchful with all perseverance." That is, he made a shipwreck of his faith for want of self-denial and taking up his cross daily.

6. But perhaps he has not made a shipwreck of his faith. He has still a measure of the Spirit of adoption which continues to witness with his spirit that he is a child of God. However, he is not "going on to perfection"; he is not, as once, hungering and thirsting after righteousness, panting after the whole image and full enjoyment of God as the deer for the water-brook. Rather he is weary and faint in his mind, and, as it were, hovering between life and death. And why is he thus but because he has forgotten the word of God? "By works is faith made perfect." He does not use all diligence in working the works of God. He does not "continue instant in prayer," private as well as public; in communicating, hearing, meditation, fasting, and religious conference. If he does not wholly neglect some of these means, at least he does not use them all with his might. Or he is not zealous of works of charity, as well as works of piety. He is not merciful after his power, with the full ability which God gives. He does not fervently serve the Lord by doing good to men, in every kind and in every degree he can, to their souls as well as their bodies. And why does he not continue in prayer? Because in time of dryness it is pain and grief unto him. He does not continue in hearing at all opportunities because sleep is sweet; or it is cold, or dark, or rainy. But why does he not continue in works of mercy?

Because he cannot feed the hungry, or clothe the naked, unless he retrench the expense of his own apparel, or use cheaper and less pleasing food. Beside which, visiting the sick or those that are in prison is attended with many disagreeable circumstances. And so are most works of spiritual mercy; reproof, in particular. He would reprove his neighbour; but sometimes shame, sometimes fear comes between: for he may expose himself not only to ridicule but to heavier inconveniences too. Upon these and the like considerations, he omits one or more, if not all, works of mercy and piety. Therefore, his faith is not made perfect, neither can he grow in grace; namely, because he will not deny himself, and take up his daily cross.

7. It manifestly follows that it is always owing to the want either of self-denial, or taking up his cross, that a man does not thoroughly follow his Lord, that he is not fully a disciple of Christ. It is owing to this that he who is dead in sin does not awake, though the trumpet be blown; that he who begins to awake out of sleep yet has no deep or lasting conviction; that he who is deeply and lastingly convinced of sin does not attain remission of sins; that some who have received this heavenly gift retain it not, but make shipwreck of the faith; and that others, if they do not draw back to perdition, yet are weary and faint in their mind, and do not reach the mark of the prize of the high calling of God in Christ Jesus.

III. 1. How easily may we learn from this that they know neither the Scripture nor the power of God who directly or indirectly, in public or in private, oppose the doctrine of self-denial and the daily cross! How totally ignorant are these men of an hundred particular texts, as well as of the general tenor of the whole oracles of God! And how entirely unacquainted must they be with true, genuine, Christian experience—of the manner in which the Holy Spirit ever did, and does at this day, work in the souls of men! They may talk, indeed, very loudly and confidently (a natural fruit of ignorance), as though they were the only men who understood either the word of God or the experience of his children, but their words are, in every sense, empty words; they are weighed in the balance, and found wanting.

2. We may learn from this, secondly, the real cause why not only many particular persons but even bodies of men, who were once burning and shining lights, have now lost both their light and heat.

If they did not hate and oppose, they at least lightly esteemed this precious gospel doctrine. If they did not boldly say, *Abnegationem omnem proculcamus, internecioni damus* ("We trample all self-denial under foot, we devote it to destruction"), yet they neither valued it according to its high importance nor took any pains in practising it. *Hanc mystici docent,* said that great, bad man: "The mystic writers teach self-denial." No, the inspired writers! And God teaches it to every soul who is willing to hear his voice!

3. We may learn from this, thirdly, that it is not enough for a Minister of the gospel not to oppose the doctrine of self-denial, to say nothing concerning it. Nay, he cannot satisfy his duty by saying a little in favour of it. If he would indeed be pure from the blood of all men, he must speak of it frequently and largely; he must inculcate the necessity of it in the clearest and strongest manner; he must press it with his might, on all persons, at all times, and in all places; laying "line upon line, line upon line, precept upon precept, precept upon precept": So shall he have a conscience clear of offence; so shall he save his own soul and those that hear him.

4. Lastly, see that you apply this, every one of you, to your own soul. Meditate upon it when you are in secret. Ponder it in your heart! Take care not only to understand it thoroughly but to remember it to your lives' end! Cry out to the Strong for strength, that you may no sooner understand than enter upon the practice of it. Delay not the time, but practise it immediately, from this very hour! Practise it universally, on every one of the thousand occasions which will occur in all circumstances of life! Practise it daily, without intermission, from the hour you first set your hand to the plough, and enduring therein to the end, till your spirit returns to God!

For Readers

Questions

1. How exactly should we define self-denial and cross-bearing in light of this sermon?
2. Is it possible and even likely that our will can be truly aligned with the will of God so that there is no need for self-denial in such cases?

3. Is it always wise to state the issue so starkly with a hard disjunction between doing our will and the will of God?

4. What examples best show that self-denial is person-relative, that is, appropriate to one person and not another?

5. Why is it important to place self-denial and cross-bearing within a vision of our Lord as the Great Physician of our souls?

Helpful Information

Wesley makes the startling claim at the outset that self-denial is constitutive of being fully a Christian. He refuses to be intimidated by charges that this means justification by works. And he drives home his proposal by working through stark disjunctions between following our own will and following the will of God. We can rightly look upon this sermon as Wesley's fundamental view on the cost of discipleship.

Initially, his stark disjunction can be seen as foolish because it seems to imply that there will always be a conflict between our will and the will of God. However, Wesley is very careful to rule out this inference even though he does not do so explicitly. Hence, the definition of self-denial that he offers is crucial: it is following our own will when it is contrary to the known will of God. Likewise, his definition of cross-bearing is very carefully stated; it involves voluntary suffering for the sake of doing the will of God.

Wesley is also keen to point out that some of our choices will be person-relative rather than general. Thus, the action of the rich young ruler is not to be taken as a general mandate; it applied specifically to him because of his love of money. In addition, Wesley totally rejects any idea that self-inflicted suffering is acceptable. Self-denial and suffering are inextricably linked to the healing of our lives by the Great Physician who clearly knows us better than we know ourselves. Hence, we need to bear in mind the overall goal, namely, becoming a Christian for whom the will of God is the central, overarching vision of their identity.

An interesting element in this sermon is the use Wesley makes of spiritual case studies, beginning with those who hear the Word of God and immediately reject it, and ending with those who have come to make shipwreck of their spiritual lives by ignoring the teaching on self-denial and cross-bearing. This is yet one more way to drive home the crucial importance of self-denial as essential to full Christian discipleship.

SERMON 43

The Cure of Evil-Speaking

"If your brother shall sin against you, go and tell him his fault between you and him alone: if he shall hear you, you have gained your brother. But if he will not hear, take with you one or two more, that in the mouth of two or three witnesses every word may be established. And if he will not hear them, tell it to the Church. But if he does not hear the church, let him be to you as a heathen man and a publican" (Matt. 18:15–17).

1. "Speak evil of no man," says the great Apostle—as plain a command as "You shall not murder." But who, even among Christians, regards this command? Indeed, how few are there that so much as understand it? What is evil-speaking? It is not, as some suppose, the same as lying or slandering. All a man says may be as true as the Bible; and yet the saying of it is evil-speaking. For evil-speaking is neither more nor less than speaking evil of an absent person; relating something evil which was really done or said by one that is not present when it is related. Suppose, having seen a man drunk, or heard him curse or swear, I tell this when he is absent; it is evil-speaking. In our language this is also, by an extremely proper name, termed backbiting. Nor is there any material difference between this and what we usually style tale-bearing. If the tale be delivered in a soft and quiet manner (perhaps with expressions of good-will to the person, and of hope that things may not be quite so bad), then we call it whispering. But in whatever manner it be done, the thing is the same, the same in substance, if not in circumstance. Still it is evil-speaking; still this command, "Speak evil of no man," is trampled underfoot; if we relate to another the fault of a third person when he is not present to answer for himself.

2. And how extremely common is this sin among all orders and degrees of men! How do high and low, rich and poor, wise and foolish, learned and unlearned, run into it continually! Persons who differ from each other in all other things nevertheless agree in this. How few are there that can testify before God, "I am clear in this matter; I have always set a watch before my mouth and guarded the door of my lips"! What conversation do you hear, of any considerable length, of which evil-speaking is not one ingredient? and that even among

persons who, in the general, have the fear of God before their eyes, and do really desire to have a conscience void of offence toward God and toward man.

3. And the very commonness of this sin makes it difficult to avoid. As we are encompassed with it on every side, so, if we are not deeply sensible of the danger and continually guarding against it, we are liable to be carried away by the torrent. In this instance, almost the whole of mankind is, as it were, in a conspiracy against us. And their example steals upon us we know not how, so that we unconsciously slide into the imitation of it. Besides, it is recommended from within as well as from without. There is scarcely any wrong temper in the mind of man which may not be occasionally gratified by it, and consequently incline us to it. It gratifies our pride to relate those faults of others of which we think ourselves not to be guilty. Anger, resentment, and all unkind tempers are indulged by speaking against those with whom we are displeased; and in many cases, by reciting the sins of their neighbours, men indulge their own foolish and hurtful desires.

4. Evil-speaking is more difficult to be avoided because it frequently attacks us in disguise. We speak thus out of a noble, generous (it is well if we do not say) holy indignation against these vile creatures! We commit sin from mere hatred of sin! We serve the devil out of pure zeal for God! It is merely in order to punish the wicked that we run into this wickedness. "So do the passions" (as one speaks) "all justify themselves," and palm sin upon us under the veil of holiness!

5. But is there no way to avoid the snare? Unquestionably there is. Our blessed Lord has marked out a plain way for His followers, in the words above recited. None who warily and steadily walk in this path will ever fall into evil-speaking. This rule is either an infallible preventive or a certain cure of it. In the preceding verses, our Lord had said, "Woe to the world, because of offences"—unspeakable misery will arise in the world from this baleful fountain. (Offences are all things by which anyone is turned out of, or hindered in, the ways of God.) "For it must be that offences come." Such is the nature of things; such is the wickedness, folly, and weakness of mankind. "But woe to that man"—miserable is that man—"by whom the offence comes." "For this reason, if your hand, your foot, your eye, causes you to offend"—if the most dear enjoyment, the most beloved and useful person, turn

you out of or hinder you in the way—"pluck it out"—cut them off and cast them from you. But how can we avoid giving offence to some and being offended at others? Especially, suppose they are quite in the wrong, and we see it with our own eyes? Our Lord here teaches us how. He lays down a sure method of avoiding offences and evil-speaking together. "If your brother sins against you, go and tell him of his fault, between you and him alone. If he will hear you, you have gained your brother. But if he will not hear you, take with you one or two more, that by the mouth of two or three witnesses every word may be established. And if he will not hear them, tell it to the church. But if he will not hear the Church, let him be to you as a heathen man and a publican."

I. 1. First, "if your brother sins against you, go and tell him of his fault, between you and him alone." The most literal way of following this first rule, where it is practical, is the best. Therefore, if you see with your own eyes a brother, a fellow Christian, commit undeniable sin, or if you hear it with your own ears, so that it is impossible for you to doubt the fact, then your part is plain. Take the very first opportunity of going to him; and, if you can have access, "tell him of his fault between you and him alone." Indeed, great care is to be taken that this is done in a right spirit and in a right manner. The success of a reproof greatly depends on the spirit in which it is given. Be not, therefore, wanting in earnest prayer to God, that it may be given in a lowly spirit; with a deep, piercing conviction, that it is God alone who makes you to differ; and that if any good be done by what is now spoken, God does it himself. Pray that he would guard your heart, enlighten your mind, and direct your tongue to such words as he may please to bless. See that you speak in a meek as well as a lowly spirit; "for the wrath of man works not the righteousness of God." If he is "overtaken in a fault," he can no otherwise be restored than "in the spirit of meekness." If he opposes the truth, he cannot be brought to the knowledge of it except by gentleness. Still speak in a spirit of tender love, "which many waters cannot quench." If love is not conquered, it conquers all things. Who can tell the force of love?

> Love can bow down the stubborn neck,
> The stone to flesh convert;

> Soften, and melt, and pierce and break
> An adamantine heart.

Confirm, then, your love toward him, and you will thus "heap coals of fire upon his head."

2. But see that the manner also wherein you speak be according to the Gospel of Christ. Avoid everything in look, gesture, word, and tone of voice that smells of pride or self-sufficiency. Studiously avoid everything magisterial or dogmatic, everything that looks like arrogance or assuming. Beware of the most distant approach to disdain, overbearing, or contempt. With equal care avoid all appearance of anger; and though you use great plainness of speech, yet let there be no reproach, no railing accusation, no token of any warmth but that of love. Above all, let there be no shadow of hate or ill-will, no bitterness or sourness of expression; but use the air and language of sweetness, as well as gentleness, that all may appear to flow from love in the heart. And yet this sweetness need not hinder your speaking in the most serious and solemn manner; as far as may be, in the very words of the oracles of God (for there are none like them) and as under the eyes of Him who is coming to judge the quick and dead.

3. If you have not an opportunity of speaking to him in person, or cannot have access, you may do it by a messenger; by a common friend in whose prudence, as well as uprightness, you can thoroughly confide. Such a person, speaking in your name, and in the spirit and manner above described, may answer the same end and, in a good degree, supply your lack of service. Only beware you do not feign the want of opportunity in order to shun the cross; nor take it for granted that you cannot have access without ever making the trial. Whenever you can speak in your own person, it is far better. But you should rather do it by another than not at all: this way is better than none.

4. But what if you can neither speak yourself nor find such a messenger as you can confide in? If this is really the case, it then only remains to write. And there may be some circumstances which make this the most advisable way of speaking. One of these circumstances is when the person with whom we have to do is of so warm and

impetuous a temper as does not easily bear reproof, especially from an equal or inferior. But it may be so introduced and softened in writing as to make it far more tolerable. Besides, many will read the very same words which they could not bear to hear. It does not give so violent a shock to their pride, nor so sensibly touch their honour. And suppose it makes little impression at first, they will, perhaps, give it a second reading, and upon farther consideration lay to heart what before they disregarded. If you add your name, this is nearly the same thing as going to him and speaking in person. And this should always be done, unless it is rendered improper by some very particular reason.

5. It should be well observed, not only that this is a step which our Lord absolutely commands us to take, but that he commands us to take this step first, before we attempt any other. No alternative is allowed, no choice of anything else: this is the way; walk you in it. It is true, he enjoins us if need require to take two other steps; but they are to be taken successively after this step, and neither of them before it: Much less are we to take any other step, either before or beside this. To do anything else, or not to do this, is, therefore, equally inexcusable.

6. Do not think to excuse yourself for taking an entirely different step by saying, "Why, I did not speak to anyone until I was so burdened that I could not refrain." You were burdened! It was no wonder you should, unless your conscience was seared; for you were under the guilt of sin, of disobeying a plain commandment of God! You ought immediately to have gone and told "your brother of his fault between you and him alone." If you did not, how should you be other than burdened (unless your heart were utterly hardened) while you were trampling the command of God underfoot and "hating your brother in your heart"? And what a way have you found to unburden yourself? God reproves you for a sin of omission, for not telling your brother of his fault; and you comfort yourself under His reproof by a sin of commission, by telling your brother's fault to another person! Ease bought by sin is a dear purchase! I trust in God, you will have no ease but will be burdened so much the more, until you "go to your brother and tell him," and no one else.

7. I know of only one exception to this rule: there may be a particular case in which it is necessary to accuse the guilty, though absent, in order to preserve the innocent. For instance: You are acquainted with the intention which a man has against the property or life of his neighbour. Now, the case may be so circumstanced that there is no other way of hindering that design from taking effect but by making it known, without delay, to him against whom it is laid. In this case, therefore, this rule is set aside, as is that of the Apostle, "Speak evil of no man," and it is lawful, truly, it is our bounden duty, to speak evil of an absent person in order to prevent his doing evil to others and himself at the same time. But remember, meanwhile, that all evil-speaking is, in its own nature, deadly poison. Therefore if you are sometimes constrained to use it as a medicine, use it with fear and trembling; since it is so dangerous a medicine that nothing but absolute necessity can excuse your using it at all. Accordingly, use it as seldom as possible; never except when there is such a necessity. And even then use as little of it as is possible; only so much as is necessary for the end proposed. At all other times, "go and tell him of his fault between you and him alone."

II. 1. But what "if he will not hear"? If he repay evil for good? If he is enraged rather than convinced? What, if he hears to no purpose, and goes on still in the evil of his way? We must expect this will frequently be the case; the mildest and most tender reproof will have no effect; but the blessing we wished for another will return into our own bosom. And what are we to do then? Our Lord has given us a clear and full direction. Then "take with you one or two more." This is the second step. Take one or two whom you know to be of a loving spirit, lovers of God and of their neighbour. See, likewise, that they be of a lowly spirit and "clothed with humility." Let them also be such as are meek and gentle, patient and long-suffering; not apt to "return evil for evil, or cursing for cursing, but contrariwise blessing." Let them be men of understanding, such as are endued with wisdom from above; and men unbiased, free from partiality, free from prejudice of any kind. Care should likewise be taken that both the persons and their characters be well known to him and let those that are acceptable to him be chosen preferable to any others.

2. Love will dictate the manner wherein they should proceed, according to the nature of the case. Nor can any one particular manner be prescribed for all cases. But perhaps, in general, one might advise, before they enter upon the thing itself, let them mildly and affectionately declare that they have no anger or prejudice toward him, and that it is merely from a principle of good-will that they now come, or at all concern themselves with his affairs. To make this the more apparent, they might then calmly attend to your repetition of your former conversation with him, and to what he said in his own defence, before they attempted to determine anything. After this they would be better able to judge in what manner to proceed, "that by the mouth of two or three witnesses, every word might be established"; that whatever you have said may have its full force by the additional weight of their authority.

3. In order to this, may they not (1) Briefly repeat what you said and what he answered? (2) Enlarge upon, open, and confirm the reasons which you had given? (3) Give weight to your reproof, showing how just, how kind, and how seasonable it was? And, lastly, enforce the advices and persuasions which you had annexed to it? And these may likewise hereafter, if need should require, bear witness to what was spoken.

4. With regard to this, as well as the preceding rule, we may observe that our Lord gives us no choice, leaves us no alternative, but expressly commands us to do this and nothing else in the place of it. He likewise directs us when to do this; neither sooner nor later; namely, after we have taken the first, and before we have taken the third step. It is then only that we are authorized to relate the evil another has done to those whom we desire to bear a part with us in this great instance of brotherly love. But let us have a care how we relate it to any other person, until both these steps have been taken. If we neglect to take these, or if we take any others, what wonder if we are burdened still? For we are sinners against God and against our neighbour; and however fairly we may colour it, yet if we have any conscience, our sin will find us out and bring a burden upon our soul.

III. 1. That we may be thoroughly instructed in this weighty affair, our Lord has given us a still further direction. "If he will not hear them," then, and not before then, "tell it to the church." This is the third step. The only question is how this word "church" is here to be understood. But the very nature of the thing will determine this beyond all reasonable doubt. You cannot tell it to the national Church, the whole body of men termed "the Church of England." Neither would it answer any Christian end if you could; this, therefore, is not the meaning of the word. Neither can you tell it to that whole body of people in England with whom you have a more immediate connection. Nor, indeed, would this answer any good end. The word, therefore, is not to be understood thus. It would not answer any valuable end to tell the faults of every particular member to the church (if you would so term it), the congregation or society, united together in London. It remains that you tell it to the elder or elders of the church, to those who are overseers of that flock of Christ to which you both belong, who watch over your and his soul, "as those who must give account." And this should be done, if it conveniently can, in the presence of the person concerned, and, though plainly, yet with all the tenderness and love which the nature of the thing will admit. It properly belongs to their office to determine concerning the behaviour of those under their care, and to rebuke, according to the demerit of the offence, "with all authority." When, therefore, you have done this, you have done all which the Word of God, or the law of love, requires of you: you are not now partaker of his sin; but if he perish, his blood is on his own head.

2. Here also let it be observed that this, and no other, is the third step which we are to take; and that we are to take it in its order after the other two; not before the second, much less the first, unless in some very particular circumstance. Indeed, in one case, the second step may coincide with this: they may be, in a manner, one and the same. The elder or elders of the church may be so connected with the offending brother that they may set aside the necessity, and supply the place, of the one or two witnesses; so that it may suffice to tell it to them after you have told it to your brother, "between you and him alone."

3. When you have done this, you have delivered your own soul. "If he will not hear the church," if he persists in his sin, "let him

be to you as a heathen man and a publican." You are under no obligation to think of him any more; only when you commend him to God in prayer. You need not speak of him any more, but leave him to his own Master. Indeed, you still owe to him, as to all other heathens, earnest, tender good-will. You owe him courtesy, and, as occasion offers, all the offices of humanity. But have no friendship, no familiarity with him; no other intercourse than with an open Heathen.

4. But if this be the rule by which Christians walk, which is the land where Christians live? A few you may possibly find scattered up and down who make a conscience of observing it. But how very few! How thinly scattered upon the face of the earth! And where is there any body of men that universally live by this? Can we find them in Europe? Or, to go no farther, in Great Britain or Ireland? I fear not: I fear we may search these kingdoms throughout and yet search in vain. Alas for the Christian world! Alas for Protestants, for Reformed Christians! O, "who will rise up with me against the wicked"? "Who will take God's part" against the evil-speakers? Are you the man? By the grace of God, will you be one who is not carried away by the torrent? Are you fully determined, God being your helper, from this very hour to set a watch, a continual "watch before your mouth, and keep the door of your lips"? From this hour will you walk by this rule, "speaking evil of no man"? If you see your brother do evil, will you "tell him of his fault between you and him alone"? Afterwards, "take one or two witnesses," and then only "tell it to the church"? If this be the full purpose of your heart, then learn one lesson well, "Hear evil of no man." If there were no hearers, there would be no speakers, of evil. And is not (according to the vulgar proverb) the receiver as bad as the thief? If, then, any begin to speak evil in your hearing, stop him immediately. Refuse to hear the voice of the charmer, charm he never so sweetly; let him use ever so soft a manner, so mild an accent, ever so many professions of good-will for him whom he is stabbing in the dark, whom he smites under the fifth rib! Resolutely refuse to hear, though the whisperer complain of being "burdened till he speak." Burdened! You fool! Do you labour under your cursed secret as a woman labours with child? Go, then, and be delivered

of your burden in the way the Lord has ordained! First, "go and tell your brother of his fault between you and him alone"; next, "take with you one or two" common friends, and tell him in their presence: If neither of these steps takes effect, then "tell it to the church." But, at the peril of your soul, tell it to no one else, either before or after, unless in that one exempt case, when it is absolutely needful to preserve the innocent! Why should you burden another as well as yourself by making him partaker of your sin?

5. O that all you who bear the reproach of Christ, who are in derision called Methodists, would set an example to the Christian world, so called, at least in this one instance! Put away evil-speaking, talebearing, whispering: Let none of them proceed out of your mouth! See that you "speak evil of no man"; of the absent, nothing but good. If you must be distinguished, whether you will or no, let this be the distinguishing mark of a Methodist. "He censures no man behind his back: by this fruit you may know him." What a blessed effect of this self-denial should we quickly feel in our hearts! How would our "peace flow as a river," when we thus "followed peace with all men"! How would the love of God abound in our own souls, while we thus confirmed our love to our brethren! And what an effect would it have on all that were united together in the name of the Lord Jesus! How would brotherly love continually increase, when this grand hindrance of it was removed! All the members of Christ's mystical body would then naturally care for each other. "If one member suffered, all would suffer with it; if one was honoured, all would rejoice with it"; and everyone would love his brother "with a pure heart fervently." Nor is this all: but what an effect might this have even on the wild unthinking world! How soon would they observe in us what they could not find among all the thousands of their brethren, and cry (as Julian the Apostate to his heathen courtiers), "See how these Christians love one another!" By this chiefly would God convince the world, and prepare them also for His kingdom; as we may easily learn from those remarkable words in our Lord's last, solemn prayer: "I pray for those who will believe in me, that they all may be one as you, Father, are in me, and I in you; that the world may believe that you Have sent me!" (John 17:21). The Lord hasten the day! The

Lord enable us thus to love one another, not only "in word and in tongue, but in deed and in truth," even as Christ has loved us.

For Readers

Questions

1. How might we distinguish between gossip and the problem addressed in this sermon?
2. How does this sermon help in dealing with the problem of conflict arising from evil speaking in our communities?
3. What is the wisdom, if any, in following the order of the rules proposed here?
4. What pressures inhibit us from tackling deep conflict in the church?
5. What do you think of the nuclear strike option given at the end, where we end friendships with those who refuse to deal with the underlying problem?

Helpful Information

This is yet another sermon where we can read it in a shallow or a deeper way. Read in a shallow fashion, it proposes that we become busybodies, constantly taking action against those who speak evil of us. Read in a deep fashion, it invites us to deal with a perennial problem in any group, that is, the appalling effects of gossip, false witness, slander, and other evils related to speaking evil of others. One does not have to turn to the diatribes we find on social media to recognize that this is indeed a serious issue.

Notice that Wesley does not invite us to turn the other cheek, to pretend nothing has happened, or to take impulsive action. We are asked to think through the problem and to put into practice not Wesley's teaching, but the teaching of our Lord. The clear assumption here is that we are dealing with serious offenses that are disruptive not just of our own lives, but of the community of believers. There is no doubt that the advice given here will prevent the problem from becoming a running sore in a community.

The exposition of the second rule includes a nice touch, where Wesley insists that the person confronted should be present when we are not acting alone. We are to adhere to a principle of fairness so that the person in question is fully involved in the process.

Wesley leaves open the details of what we are to do when the attempt at reconciliation fails. He is clearly a hard-headed realist: the time for niceness is over, and even the link of friendship should be severed. However, this still leaves us with plenty of options. For example, if the case is serious enough, should we have recourse to criminal or civil law? Surely, Wesley would allow if not mandate this option. In general, he is happy for us to work this out according to our good sense in each case that presents itself.

SERMON 44

The Use of Money

"I say to you, make friends for yourselves with the mammon of unrighteousness; so that, when you fail, they may receive you into the everlasting habitations" (Luke 16:9).

1. Our Lord, having finished the beautiful parable of the Prodigal Son, which he had particularly addressed to those who murmured at his receiving publicans and sinners, adds another relation of a different kind, addressed rather to the children of God. "He said to his disciples," not so much to the scribes and Pharisees to whom he had been speaking before—"There was a certain rich man, who had a steward, and he was accused to him of wasting his goods. And calling him, he said, 'Give an account of your stewardship, for you can no longer be steward'" (Luke 16:1–2). After reciting the method which the bad steward used to provide against the day of necessity, our Saviour adds, "His lord commended the unjust steward"; namely, in this respect, that he used timely precaution; and subjoins this weighty reflection, "The children of this world are wiser in their generation than the children of light" (Luke 16:8). Those who seek no other portion than this world "are wiser" (not absolutely; for they are one and all certain fools, the most egregious madmen under heaven; but, "in their generation," in their own way; they are more consistent with themselves; they are truer to their acknowledged principles; they more steadily pursue their end) "than the children of light"—than they who see "the light of the glory of God in the face of Jesus Christ." Then follow the words above recited: "And I"—the only-begotten Son of God, the Creator, Lord, and Possessor of heaven and earth and all that is in them; the Judge of all, to whom you are to "give an account of your stewardship," when you "can no longer be stewards"; "I say to you"—learn in this respect, even of the unjust steward—"make friends for yourselves," by wise, timely precaution, "with the mammon of unrighteousness." "Mammon" means riches or money. It is termed "the mammon of unrighteousness" because of the unrighteous manner in which it is frequently procured, and in which even that which was honestly procured is generally employed. "Make friends for yourselves" with this by doing all possible good, particularly

to the children of God; "so that, when you fail"—when you return to dust, when you have no more place under the sun—those of them who are gone before "may receive you," may welcome you, into the "everlasting habitations."

2. An excellent branch of Christian wisdom is here inculcated by our Lord on all his followers, namely, the right use of money—a subject largely spoken of, after their manner, by men of the world; but not sufficiently considered by those whom God has chosen out of the world. These generally do not consider, as the importance of the subject requires, the use of this excellent talent. Neither do they understand how to employ it to the greatest advantage; the introduction of which into the world is one admirable instance of the wise and gracious providence of God. It has, indeed, been the manner of poets, orators, and philosophers, in almost all ages and nations, to rail at this as the grand corrupter of the world, the bane of virtue, the pest of human society. Hence nothing so commonly heard, as:

Nocens ferrum, ferroque nocentius aurum: "And gold, more mischievous than keenest steel."

Hence the lamentable complaint, *Effodiuntur opes, irritamenta malorum*. ["Wealth is dug up, incentive to all ill."]

One celebrated writer even gravely exhorts his countrymen, in order to banish all vice at once, to "throw all their money into the sea." [*In mare proximum Summi materiem mali!*]

But is not all this mere empty rant? Is there any solid reason there? By no means. For, let the world be as corrupt as it will, is gold or silver to blame? "The love of money," we know, "is the root of all evil"; but not the thing itself. The fault does not lie in the money, but in them that use it. It may be used ill: and what may not? But it may likewise be used well: It is full as applicable to the best, as to the worst uses. It is of unspeakable service to all civilized nations, in all the common affairs of life: It is a most compendious instrument of transacting all manner of business, and (if we use it according to Christian wisdom) of doing all manner of good. It is true, were man in a state of innocence, or were all men "filled with the Holy Spirit" so that, like the infant Church at Jerusalem, "no man counted anything he had his own," but "distribution was made to everyone as he had need," the use of it would be superseded; as we cannot conceive there is anything of the kind among the inhabitants of heaven. But, in the present state of mankind, it is an excellent gift of God, answering the noblest ends. In the hands of his children, it is food for the hungry, drink for the thirsty, raiment for the naked: It gives to the traveller and the stranger a place to lay his head. By it we may supply the place of a husband to the widow, and of a father to the fatherless. We may be a defence for the oppressed, a means of health to the sick, of ease to them that are in pain; it may be as eyes to the blind, as feet to the lame; yes, even a lifter up from the gates of death!

3. It is therefore of the highest concern that all who fear God know how to employ this valuable talent; that they be instructed how it may answer these glorious ends, and in the highest degree. And, perhaps, all the instructions which are necessary for this may be reduced to three plain rules, by the exact observance of which we may prove ourselves faithful stewards of "the mammon of unrighteousness."

I. 1. The first of these (he that hears, let him understand!) is, "Gain all you can." Here we may speak like the children of the world: we meet them on their own ground. And it is our bounden duty to do this. We ought to gain all we can gain without buying gold too dear, without paying more for it than it is worth. But this it is certain we ought not to do; we ought not to gain money at the expense of life, nor (which is in effect the same thing) at the expense of our health. Therefore, no gain whatever should induce us to enter into, or to continue in, any employ which is of such a kind, or is attended with so hard or so long labour, as to impair our constitution. Neither should we begin or continue in any business which necessarily deprives us of proper seasons for food and sleep, in such a proportion as our nature requires. Indeed, there is a great difference here. Some employments are absolutely and totally unhealthy; as those which imply dealing much with arsenic or other equally hurtful minerals or breathing in air tainted with steams of melting lead, which must at length destroy the firmest constitution. Others may not be absolutely unhealthy, but only to persons of a weak constitution. Such are those which require many hours to be spent in writing; especially if a person write sitting, and lean upon his stomach, or remain long in an uneasy posture. But whatever it is which reason or experience shows to be destructive of health or strength, that we may not submit to; since "the life is more" valuable "than meat, and the body than raiment." And if we are already engaged in such an employ, we should exchange it as soon as possible for some which, if it lessen our gain, will however not lessen our health.

2. We are, secondly, to gain all we can without hurting our mind any more than our body. For neither may we hurt this. We must preserve, at all events, the spirit of a healthful mind. Therefore we may not engage or continue in any sinful trade, any that is contrary to the law of God or of our country. Such are all that necessarily imply our robbing or defrauding the king of his lawful customs. For it is at least as sinful to defraud the king of his right, as to rob our fellow subjects. And the king has full as much right, to his customs as we have to our houses and apparel. Other businesses there are which, however innocent in themselves, cannot be followed with innocence now; at least, not in England; such, for instance, as will not afford a competent maintenance without cheating or lying, or conformity to some custom which is not consistent with a good conscience. These likewise are sacredly to be avoided, whatever gain they may be attended with provided we follow the custom of the trade; for to gain money we must not lose our souls. There are yet others which many pursue with perfect innocence, without hurting either their body or mind, and yet perhaps you cannot: either they may entangle you in that company which would destroy your soul, and by repeated experiments it may appear that you cannot separate the one from the other; or there may be an idiosyncrasy—a peculiarity in your constitution of soul (as there is in the bodily constitution of many), by reason of which that employment is deadly to you which another may safely follow. So I am convinced, from many experiments, I could not study to any degree of perfection either mathematics, arithmetic, or algebra, without being a Deist, if not an Atheist. And yet others may study them all their lives without sustaining any inconvenience. None therefore can here determine for another; but every man must judge for himself and abstain from whatever he in particular finds to be hurtful to his soul.

3. We are, thirdly, to gain all we can without hurting our neighbour. But this we may not, cannot do, if we love our neighbour as ourselves. We cannot, if we love everyone as ourselves, hurt anyone in his substance. We cannot devour the increase of his lands, and perhaps the lands and houses themselves, by gaming, by overgrown bills (whether on account of physic, or law, or anything else), or by requiring or taking such interest as even the laws of our country forbid. In this all pawn-broking is excluded: since whatever good we might do by it, all unprejudiced men see with grief to be abundantly overbalanced by the evil. And if it were otherwise, yet we are not allowed to "do evil that good may come." We cannot, consistent with brotherly love, sell our goods below the market price; we cannot study to ruin our neighbour's trade in order to advance our own; much less can we entice away or receive any of his servants or workmen of whom he has need. None can gain by swallowing up his neighbour's substance without gaining the damnation of hell!

4. Neither may we gain by hurting our neighbour in his body. Therefore we may not sell anything which tends to impair health. Such is, eminently, all that liquid fire, commonly called drams or spirituous liquors. It is true, these may have a place in medicine; they may be of use in some bodily disorders; although there would rarely be occasion for them were it not for the unskillfulness of the practitioner. Therefore, those who prepare and sell them only for this end may keep their conscience clear. But who are they? Who prepare and sell them only for this end? Do you know ten such distillers in England? Then excuse these. But all who sell them in the common way, to any that will buy, are poisoners general. They murder His Majesty's subjects by wholesale, neither does their eye pity or spare. They drive them to hell like sheep. And what is their gain? Is it not the blood of these men? Who then would envy their large estates and sumptuous palaces? A curse is in the midst of them: the curse of God cleaves to the stones, the timber, the furniture of them. The curse of God is in their gardens, their walks, their groves; a fire that burns to the nethermost hell! Blood, blood is there: the foundation, the floor, the walls, the roof are stained with blood! And can you hope, O you person

of blood, though you are "clothed in scarlet and fine linen, and feast sumptuously every day," can you hope to deliver down your fields of blood to the third generation? Not so; for there is a God in heaven. Therefore your name shall soon be rooted out. Like those whom you have destroyed, body and soul, "your memorial shall perish with you"!

5. And are not they partakers of the same guilt, though in a lower degree, whether Surgeons, Apothecaries, or Physicians, who play with the lives or health of men to enlarge their own gain? Who purposely lengthen the pain or disease which they are able to remove speedily; who protract the cure of their patient's body in order to plunder his substance? Can any man be clear before God who does not shorten every disorder "as much as he can," and remove all sickness and pain "as soon as he can"? He cannot. For nothing can be more clear than that he does not "love his neighbour as himself"; than that he does not "do unto others as he would they should do unto himself."

6. This is dear-bought gain. And so is whatever is procured by hurting our neighbour in his soul; by ministering, suppose, either directly or indirectly, to his unchastity or intemperance, which certainly none can do who has any fear of God, or any real desire of pleasing Him. It nearly concerns all those to consider this, who have anything to do with taverns, victualling-houses, opera-houses, play-houses, or any other places of public, fashionable diversion. If these profit the souls of men, you are clear; your employment is good and your gain innocent; but if they are either sinful in themselves or natural inlets to sin of various kinds, then, it is to be feared, you have a sad account to make. O beware, lest God say in that day, "These have perished in their iniquity, but their blood do I require at your hands!"

7. These cautions and restrictions being observed, it is the bounden duty of all who are engaged in worldly business to observe that first and great rule of Christian wisdom with respect to money, "Gain all you can." Gain all you can by honest industry. Use all possible diligence in your calling. Lose no time. If you understand yourself and your relation to God and man, you know you have none to spare. If you understand your particular calling as you ought, you

will have no time that hangs upon your hands. Every business will afford some employment sufficient for every day and every hour. That in which you are placed, if you follow it in earnest, will leave you no leisure for silly, unprofitable diversions. You have always something better to do, something that will profit you, more or less. And "whatever your hand finds to do, do it with your might." Do it as soon as possible. No delay! No putting off from day to day, or from hour to hour! Never leave anything till tomorrow which you can do today. And do it as well as possible. Do not sleep or yawn over it. Put your whole strength to the work. Spare no pains. Let nothing be done by halves, or in a slight and careless manner. Let nothing in your business be left undone if it can be done by labour or patience.

8. Gain all you can, by common sense, by using in your business all the understanding which God has given you. It is amazing to observe how few do this; how men run on in the same dull track with their forefathers. But whatever they do who know not God, this is no rule for you. It is a shame for a Christian not to improve upon them, in whatever he takes in hand. You should be continually learning, from the experience of others or from your own experience, reading, and reflection, to do everything you have to do better today than you did yesterday. And see that you practise whatever you learn, that you may make the best of all that is in your hands.

II. 1. Having gained all you can, by honest wisdom and unwearied diligence, the second rule of Christian prudence is, "Save all you can." Do not throw the precious talent into the sea. Leave that folly to heathen philosophers. Do not throw it away in idle expenses, which is just the same as throwing it into the sea. Expend no part of it merely to gratify the desire of the flesh, the desire of the eye, or the pride of life.

2. Do not waste any part of so precious a talent merely in gratifying the desires of the flesh; in procuring the pleasures of sense of whatever kind; particularly in enlarging the pleasure of tasting. I do not mean avoid gluttony and drunkenness only; an honest heathen would condemn these. But there is a regular, reputable kind of sensuality, an elegant Epicureanism, which does not

immediately disorder the stomach nor (sensibly, at least) impair the understanding. And yet (to mention no other effects of it now) it cannot be maintained without considerable expense. Cut off all this expense! Despise delicacy and variety and be content with what plain nature requires.

3. Do not waste any part of so precious a talent merely in gratifying the desire of the eye by superfluous or expensive apparel, or by needless ornaments. Waste no part of it in curiously adorning your houses; in superfluous or expensive furniture; in costly pictures, painting, gilding, books; in elegant rather than useful gardens. Let your neighbours, who know nothing better, do this. "Let the dead bury their dead." But "what is that to you?" says our Lord: "Follow you me." Are you willing? Then you are able so to do.

4. Lay out nothing to gratify the pride of life, to gain the admiration or praise of men. This motive of expense is frequently interwoven with one or both of the former. Men are expensive in diet, or apparel, or furniture, not merely to please their appetite or to gratify their eye, their imagination, but their vanity too. "So long as you are doing well for yourself, men will speak well of you." So long as you are "clothed in purple and fine linen, and feast sumptuously" every day, no doubt many will applaud your elegance of taste, your generosity and hospitality. But do not buy their applause so dear. Rather be content with the honour that comes from God.

5. Who would expend anything in gratifying these desires if he considered that to gratify them is to increase them? Nothing can be more certain than this: daily experience shows, the more they are indulged, the more they increase. Whenever, therefore, you expend anything to please your taste or other senses, you pay so much for sensuality. When you lay out money to please your eye, you give so much for an increase of curiosity—for a stronger attachment to these pleasures which perish in the using. While you are purchasing anything which men use to applaud, you are purchasing more vanity. Had you not then enough of vanity, sensuality, curiosity before? Was there need of any addition? And would you pay for it too? What manner of wisdom is this? Would not literally throwing your money into the sea be a less mischievous folly?

6. And why should you throw away money upon your children any more than upon yourself, in delicate food, in gay or costly apparel, in superfluities of any kind? Why should you purchase for them more pride or lust, more vanity, or foolish and hurtful desires? They do not want any more; they have enough already; nature has made ample provision for them. Why should you be at farther expense to increase their temptations and snares, and to pierce them through with more sorrows?

7. Do not leave it to them to throw away. If you have good reason to believe that they would waste what is now in your possession in gratifying and thus increasing the desire of the flesh, the desire of the eye, or the pride of life at the peril of theirs and your own soul, do not set these traps in their way. Do not offer your sons or your daughters to Belial any more than to Moloch. Have pity upon them and remove out of their way what you may easily foresee would increase their sins and consequently plunge them deeper into everlasting perdition! How amazing then is the infatuation of those parents who think they can never leave their children enough! What! can you not leave them enough of arrows, firebrands, and death? Not enough of foolish and hurtful desires? Not enough of pride, lust, ambition, vanity? not enough of everlasting burnings? Poor wretch! you fear where no fear is. Surely both you and they, when you are lifting up your eyes in hell, will have enough both of the "worm that never dies" and of "the fire that never shall be quenched"!

8. "What then would you do, if you were in my case? If you had a considerable fortune to leave?" Whether I would do it or no, I know what I ought to do. This will admit of no reasonable question. If I had one child, elder or younger, who knew the value of money, one who I believed would put it to the true use, I should think it my absolute, indispensable duty to leave that child the bulk of my fortune; and to the rest just so much as would enable them to live in the manner they had been accustomed to do. "But what, if all your children were equally ignorant of the true use of money?" I ought then (hard saying! who can hear it?) to give each what would keep him above want, and to bestow all the rest in such a manner as I judged would be most for the glory of God.

III. 1. But let not any man imagine that he has done anything simply by going thus far, by "gaining and saving all he can," if he were to stop here. All this is nothing if a man go no further, if he does not point all this at a farther end. Nor, indeed, can a man properly be said to save anything if he only lays it up. You may as well throw your money into the sea, as bury it in the earth. And you may as well bury it in the earth as in your chest, or in the Bank of England. Not to use is effectually to throw it away. If, therefore, you would indeed "make yourselves friends with the mammon of unrighteousness," add the third rule to the two preceding. Having, first, gained all you can, and, secondly, saved all you can, then "give all you can."

2. In order to see the ground and reason of this, consider, when the Possessor of heaven and earth brought you into being and placed you in this world, he placed you here not as a proprietor but a steward. As such he entrusted you, for a season, with goods of various kinds; but the sole property of these still rests in him, nor can be alienated from him. As you yourself are not your own but his, such is, likewise, all that you enjoy. Such is your soul and your body, not your own, but God's. And so is your substance in particular. And he has told you, in the most clear and express terms, how you are to employ it for him, in such a manner that it may be all a holy sacrifice, acceptable through Christ Jesus. And this light, easy service, he has promised to reward with an eternal weight of glory.

3. The directions which God has given us touching the use of our worldly substance may be comprised in the following particulars. If you desire to be a faithful and a wise steward, out of that portion of your Lord's goods which he has for the present lodged in your hands (but with the right of resuming whenever it pleases him), first, provide things needful for yourself: food to eat, raiment to put on, whatever nature moderately requires for preserving the body in health and strength. Secondly, provide these for your wife, your children, your servants, or any others who pertain to your household. If when this is done there is a surplus left, then "do good to them that are of the household of faith." If there is a surplus still, "as you have opportunity, do good unto all men." In

so doing, you give all you can; nay, in a sound sense, all you have. For all that is laid out in this manner is really given to God. You "render unto God the things that are God's," not only by what you give to the poor but also by that which you expend in providing things needful for yourself and your household.

4. If, then, a doubt should at any time arise in your mind concerning what you are going to expend, either on yourself or any part of your family, you have an easy way to remove it. Calmly and seriously inquire, "(1) In expending this, am I acting according to my character? Am I acting here not as a proprietor, but as a steward of my Lord's goods? (2) Am I doing this in obedience to his Word? In what Scripture does he require me so to do? (3) Can I offer up this action, this expense, as a sacrifice to God through Jesus Christ? (4) Have I reason to believe that for this very work I shall have a reward at the resurrection of the just?" You will seldom need anything more to remove any doubt which arises on this head; but by this four-fold consideration you will receive clear light as to the way in which you should go.

5. If any doubt still remains, you may further examine yourself by prayer according to those heads of inquiry. Try whether you can say to the Searcher of hearts, your conscience not condemning you, "Lord, you see I am going to expend this sum on that food, apparel, furniture. And you know, I act here with a single eye as a steward of your goods, expending this portion of them thus in pursuance of the design you had in entrusting me with them. You know I do this in obedience to the Lord, as you command, and because you command it. Let this, I beseech you, be a holy sacrifice, acceptable through Jesus Christ! And give me a witness in myself that for this labour of love I shall have a recompense when you reward every man according to his works." Now if your conscience bear you witness in the Holy Spirit that this prayer is well-pleasing to God, then have you no reason to doubt but that expense is right and good, and such as will never make you ashamed.

6. You see then what it is to "make friends for yourselves with the mammon of unrighteousness," and by what means you may procure "that when you fail they may receive you into the everlasting habitations." You see the nature and extent of truly Christian prudence

SERMON 44

so far as it relates to the use of that great talent, money. Gain all you can, without hurting either yourself or your neighbour, in soul or body, by applying yourself with uninterrupted diligence, and with all the understanding which God has given you. Save all you can, by cutting off every expense which serves only to indulge foolish desire; to gratify either the desire of flesh, the desire of the eye, or the pride of life; waste nothing, living or dying, on sin or folly, whether for yourself or your children. And then, give all you can, or, in other words, give all you have to God. Do not stint yourself, like a Jew rather than a Christian, to this or that proportion. "Render unto God" not a tenth, not a third, not half, but all that is God's, be it more or less; by employing all on yourself, your household, the household of faith, and all mankind, in such a manner that you may give a good account of your stewardship when you can be no longer stewards; in such a manner as the oracles of God direct, both by general and particular precepts; in such a manner, that whatever you do may be "a sacrifice of a sweet-smelling savour to God," and that every act may be rewarded in that day when the Lord comes with all his saints.

7. Brethren, can we be either wise or faithful stewards unless we thus manage our Lord's goods? We cannot, as not only the oracles of God but our own conscience bears witness. Then why should we delay? Why should we confer any longer with flesh and blood, or men of the world? Our kingdom, our wisdom is not of this world: Heathen custom is nothing to us. We follow no men any farther than they are followers of Christ. Hear him. Yes, even today, while it is called today, hear and obey his voice! At this hour, and from this hour, do his will: fulfill his word in this and in all things! I entreat you, in the name of the Lord Jesus, act up to the dignity of your calling! No more sloth! Whatever your hand finds to do, do it with your might! No more waste! Cut off every expense which fashion, caprice, or flesh and blood demand! No more covetousness! But employ whatever God has entrusted you with, in doing good, all possible good, in every possible kind and degree to the household of faith, to all men! This is no small part of "the wisdom of the just." Give all you have, as well as all you are, a spiritual sacrifice to Him who did not withhold from you his Son, his only Son. Thus

"laying up in store for yourselves a good foundation against the time to come, that you may attain eternal life!"

For Readers

Questions

1. Does the advice given here rule out socialism as an economic and political option? Why or why not?
2. Is the pleasing simplicity of the rules laid out by Wesley an adequate guide for our gaining, saving, and giving money?
3. What plausible, if not convincing, suggestions does Wesley make about the kind of work open or not open to a Christian?
4. Is the rule about the ordering of our spending (self, family, church, all in need) a helpful one? Why or why not?
5. How would you handle a person with a fortune who asks for guidance on how to spend it?

Helpful Information

Wesley was deeply worried about the effects of riches within early Methodism; he becomes more and more troubled by it as he gets older. Ironically, becoming a serious Christian frequently led to improvement in one's financial situation because he or she worked hard, was radically honest in handling money, had developed skills in leadership and organization, and the like. So, Methodists became rich merely by being serious Christians. Sociologists have named this causal thesis Wesley's Law.

This sermon represents his last shot at trying to get his people to heed the challenge posed by an increase in riches. He rejects the popular nonsense that money is somehow intrinsically bad—it is the love of money that is the problem—so he naturally has to provide realistic advice that has a chance of being taken seriously.

There is surely a pleasing simplicity in the rules Wesley develops; certainly, they are easy to remember. Many who came to faith under his tutelage will have found them invaluable. He states boldly that on the first rule of making money he stands with the world of his day. The second two are much more demanding because they are beset with all sorts of traps that are far from easy to avoid. Thus, he provides timely advice on

SERMON 44

what principles should govern our decisions about work, and he works hard to provide reasons to motivate our use of money as an exercise in wise stewardship.

The long-haul history of Methodism shows that Wesley was right to be worried about future developments. However, he can at least claim that he gave us all fair warning in advance.